MASTERMINDS OF TERROR

MASTERMINDS OF TERROR

THE TRUTH BEHIND THE MOST DEVASTATING
TERRORIST ATTACK THE WORLD HAS EVER SEEN

Yosri Fouda and Nick Fielding

MAINSTREAM
PUBLISHING

EDINBURGH AND LONDON

First published in Great Britain in 2003 by
MAINSTREAM PUBLISHING (EDINBURGH) LTD
7 Albany Street
Edinburgh EH1 3UG

ISBN 1 84018 724 7

A catalogue record for this book is available from the British Library

Typeset in Garamond and Gill

Printed in Great Britain by
Mackays of Chatham plc

ACKNOWLEDGEMENT OF COPYRIGHT IN ILLUSTRATION SECTION:

Page 1 – Ramzi Binalshibh under arrest © Reuters/Zahid Hussein;
Khalid Shaikh Mohammed under arrest © Associated Press

Pages 2, 12, 13, 14, 15 – US Dept of Justice

Page 10 – Omar Sheikh outside a Karachi courthouse, courtesy of Getty Images

Pages 3–11 – images courtesy of Al-Jazeera

ALJAZEERA
CHANNEL

ACKNOWLEDGEMENTS

We have had help from many people in writing this book, some of whom will have to remain nameless, but many others whom we are only too pleased to name and thank. We have also been both supported and encouraged by our respective employers – Al-Jazeera Channel for Yosri Fouda and *The Sunday Times* for Nick Fielding – in embarking upon this project.

Yosri Fouda would particularly like to thank Al-Jazeera chairman Sheikh Hamad Bin Thamer Al Thani for his great help and support and give special thanks to vice chairman Mahmoud al-Sahlawi, director-general Mohammed Jasim al-Ali and head of marketing Ali Kamal, all of whom backed him while working on this story.

Nick Fielding would like to thank *Sunday Times* editor John Witherow for his support in writing this book. He is grateful for the encouragement offered by many colleagues and would particularly like to thank managing editor (news) Mark Skipworth for giving him the opportunity to report from Pakistan and Afghanistan in 2002. Special thanks also to Charles Hymas, Stephen Grey, Sean Ryan and Bob Tyrer.

The following people have all been of help in one way or another in the writing of the book and we offer them heartfelt thanks:

Nader el-Abd, Hussein Abdul-Ghani, Dr Zaki Badawi, Muhammad Belfas, Rudiger Bendlin, Rudi Dekkers, Richard Gammons, Hasnain Ghulam, M.J. Gohel, Dr Rohan Gunaratna, Rawan Hijazi, Karim Jammal, Abed al-Jubah, Rania Khoury, Nadeem Khuram, Arne Kruithof, Professor Dittmar Machule, Shah Mahmoud, Dr Rehman Malik, Alan Marmion,

Jehangir Masud, Hafez Mirazi, Kassab al-Otaibi, Nadia Rahman, Sadaf Razvi, Afzaul Shah, Muftah al-Suwaidan, Lili al-Taie, Ahmed Zaidan and Eric Zandvliet.

Not to mention Gary West at Metro Broadcast, Yosri's pizza delivery man, the crew of the MS *Caprice*, Nick Fielding's fixer Habib Ahmad in Kabul and many others.

Ailsa Bathgate at Mainstream has been a model of diplomacy and tact during the frantic editing process and thanks also to her colleagues Bill Campbell, Graeme Blaikie, Fiona Brownlee and Tina Hudson. Thanks also to our agent, Robert Kirby at PFD.

Not least we would like to thank our families and friends for putting up with us during the writing of this book. We hope, like us, they think it was worth it.

All omissions, errors, inconsistencies and other consequences of human frailties, we are happy to accept as the small change of this endeavour.

Yosri Fouda and
Nick Fielding
March 2003

CONTENTS

GLOSSARY

Al-Anfal: the spoils, Surah 8 of the Holy Koran
Ansar: supporters of the Prophet Mohammed
At-Taubah: Repentance, Surah 9 of the Holy Koran
Burqa: all-enveloping women's cloak
Dhabaha: to slaughter
Dar Harb: house of war
Dar Silm: house of peace
Djinn: a being or spirit in Muslim belief who could assume human or animal form and influence man by supernatural powers
Fajr: early morning
Fatwa: religious decree
Ghazwah: raid, battle
Hadith: the body of tradition about Mohammed and his followers
Hajj: pilgrimage
Hawala: informal banking system
Hijrah: migration
Imam: religious leader
Inshallah: God willing
Iftar: literally, breakfast, but in Iran and Afghanistan it also means the evening meal at the end of Ramadan
Jihad: holy war
Ka'aba: the House of Allah which Muslims believe was built by the Prophet Abraham in Mecca

Kaba'ir: major sins
Kunyah: Arabic pseudonyms, usually begins with 'Abu' or 'Ibn'
Laqab: title, family name
Madrassas: religious schools
Majlis al-Shura: consultative council
Muhajiroun: migrants (refers usually to early Muslims who followed the Prophet Mohammed from Mecca to Medina)
Mujahideen: holy warriors
Namaz: prayers
Pukhtunwali: a strict social code of the Pukhtuns in the tribal areas in Pakistan/Afghanistan
Sahour: pre-dawn meal during the fasting month of Ramadan
Salaam: greetings
Shuhadaa: martyrs
Shalwar kameez: traditional Pakistani two-piece costume
Shaytaan: Satan
Takbeer: the chanting of the words 'Allah-u-Akbar' (God is Great)
Ulema: religious scholars
Ummah: nation
Zakat: religious donations

INTRODUCTION

The attacks on the World Trade Center and the Pentagon on 11 September 2001 changed the world. Not since Pearl Harbor in 1941 had America suffered such a devastating attack on its own soil. Islamic groups had previously mounted attacks on American forces around the world, but this was something different.

For months after the attack, as American and Allied forces geared up for war in Afghanistan, intelligence and security organisations searched desperately for proof that Osama bin Laden's al-Qaeda organisation had planned and carried out the attacks. Each statement by bin Laden emerging from his fastness in Afghanistan was analysed to see if it provided any kind of irrefutable proof. The British government issued a document that in everything but name was the case for the prosecution. Even that lacked proof.

In the absence of a full claim of responsibility, arguments raged. Conspiracy theorists said the attacks had been organised by the American government itself to justify its attacks on Islam. Others blamed the Israelis. Sceptical governments demanded proof before considering taking action to freeze assets or arrest suspects.

Not until Yosri Fouda returned from his meeting with Khalid Shaikh Mohammed and Ramzi Binalshibh in Pakistan's southern port city of Karachi and the story broke in September 2002 did the world find out the identity of the real masterminds who had planned and carried out the most devastating act of terror the world had ever seen.

For 48 hours, Fouda lived with them, ate with them, prayed with them.

Khalid – the chairman of al-Qaeda's military committee – and his faithful coordinator, Ramzi Binalshibh, were proud of their 'finest hour'. Not only would they do it again, but also they called for a thousand similar operations.

Events following the interviews were just as dramatic. Within a few days of the story breaking, Ramzi Binalshibh was arrested in a dramatic two-hour gun battle in Karachi, the city where four months before he had been interviewed by Fouda. Six months later, in the early hours of 1 March 2003, al-Qaeda suffered an even more devastating blow when Khalid Shaikh Mohammed was also arrested in Rawalpindi, 15 miles from Islamabad, the capital of Pakistan. Now the two main planners of the attacks on Washington and New York were in American custody (see Afterword p. 181).

The interviews were the starting point for this book. They revealed new details about the planning of the attacks, the methods used by the hijackers, their training and planning. But they also stimulated the authors to research further into the background of all the principal players. Now, finally, we can learn what motivated 19 young men to die for their beliefs and in so doing take the lives of more than 3,000 innocent people. We can see how the al-Qaeda organisation was able to grow in the arid plains and forbidding mountains of Afghanistan and how its message has been taken up by thousands of recruits in neighbouring Pakistan and throughout the Islamic world.

The confessions of Khalid Shaikh Mohammed and Ramzi Binalshibh have finally answered the question of who planned the attacks on America. But America has not stood still. The 'war on terror' is still in full swing. Those who know and respect America will be deeply concerned about the impact this twenty-first-century war is having on that country.

Despite protestations to the contrary, the message from America is that Muslims are no longer wanted. Draconian, discriminatory laws have been introduced based on profiling, which require people entering the country from certain countries – mostly Arab – to be photographed and fingerprinted before they are allowed in. The demonisation of the enemy has unjustifiably developed into demonisation of individuals, their culture and sometimes their religion.

And despite hopes to the contrary in the immediate aftermath of the Washington and New York attacks, when President Bush appeared to sympathise with the view that America needed to curtail its open-ended support for Israel's policies in the Occupied Territories, the conflict there has gone from bad to worse.

The peace process is a dead letter. We are left to consider the fact that President Bush and his close associates are every bit as ideologically motivated as Osama bin Laden, Ayman al-Zawahiri and the rest. Somewhere, in the wreckage between these opposing forces, lie the principles and values of three great religions.

INTRODUCTION

We hope that this book will bring a greater level of understanding to the debate over the attacks on America. As journalists from two very different backgrounds, we have sought to understand and explain to each other what we have learned in the writing of this book. We hope that the insights we have developed will be appreciated and that others will see the benefits of such an approach.

PROLOGUE

Gun Battle in Karachi – The Arrest of Ramzi Binalshibh

'My name is Abdullah.'
Ramzi Binalshibh, answering his interrogators

On the morning of 11 September 2002 – exactly a year to the day since the al-Qaeda attacks on Washington and New York – anyone up in the early hours just before dawn around building 63C in the upmarket Defence Society area of Karachi might have caught a glimpse of a small group of men in paramilitary garb arriving in a couple of vehicles.

It was 3 a.m. and the group of about 20 armed men took up positions around the concrete apartment block and hid discreetly from public view. The block itself was typical: a shuttered ground floor of lock-up shops, a mezzanine floor above of offices and then three floors of apartments leading to a flat roof. Small balconies from the apartments overlooked the street below.

As the neighbourhood began to wake, parents leaving their homes around 7.30 a.m. to drop their children off at school found the area was beginning to take on the air of a siege.

By 9 a.m. the small contingent of intelligence officers and paramilitary rangers were still in their positions surrounding the four-storey residential building known officially as 63C, 15th Commercial Street, Defence Housing Authority, Phase 11 extension. Half an hour later, workers at the Karachi Electrical Supply Company situated directly opposite 63C, where employees worked on a 24-hour cycle, heard what sounded like a blast.

According to one agitated employee: 'It did not sound like firing, but rather like a bomb had gone off. We heard four such blasts and then within ten minutes saw two men, with eyes covered and hands tied behind their

15

backs being brought out of the building. Soon after that a *burqa*-clad woman with a little girl was also seen leaving the building. The woman was very calm and composed and was bare-footed. Then the firing began and continued intermittently until about 1 p.m.'

The dozen or so residents of the apartment block had moved in quietly about three months before – when neighbours had first noted curtains going up on the top-floor pair of apartments. The rental agreement had been signed on 14 June 2002 by one Noor Islam, who came originally from Bahawalpur, a rural part of the northern Punjab province.

One woman in the neighbourhood remembers seeing her new neighbours: 'I remember seeing four men who spent time playing cards and went for early morning prayers to the mosque just 200 yards from the apartment block.' Another eyewitness said he had noticed that the men he observed in the apartment often wore shorts and T-shirts while sitting out on the roof balcony. Sometimes they even stripped down to their bare torsos. They looked light-skinned to their neighbours and many speculated that the newcomers might be Chechens or of Central Asian stock.

Despite these odd glimpses, most people had neither seen nor heard their strange neighbours and thought the block was still vacant, with the exception of the mezzanine floor, which was being used as an office by the owner of the building. An employee of Shakil Airconditioning recalled seeing a satellite dish through one of the top-floor apartment windows. 'That was the first time I realised someone was living there,' he said. 'Later the dish was moved to the rooftop.'

The only people ever seen leaving the apartment were a woman and child who went to fetch groceries, itself unusual in an Islamic country where men often do most of the shopping.

'These people, they merge with the local population and they don't interact very much,' Brigadier Javed Iqbal Cheema, a senior interior ministry official, said later. 'They do not come out very frequently, so it becomes difficult to track them down. There hasn't been that much activity in these places. The women and children go out and get them the necessities.'

'I had been seeing them for the past one month,' said local religious leader Molvi Abdul Rehman. 'They did not mix with other people in the area.'

As the hot morning sun began to rise, bringing with it an intense humidity, the team decided to make its move, rushing up the stairs towards the apartment. They had watched as four or five men had left the apartment early in the morning to attend *fajr* (dawn) prayers at the mosque down the street. After seeing them return, they calculated that they would probably go back to sleep for an hour or two before getting up, making it a prime time to launch their mission.

On the stairs they met two men and tried to grab them. The men shouted out, raising the alarm in the apartments above, and as the officers dragged their captives down with them, shots rang out and several grenades were thrown into the stairwell behind them. The police returned fire and the siege had begun.

Neighbours now ran to their windows and quickly called the local police, who had not been informed about the raid, indicating that it was an intelligence-led operation, run by Pakistan's Inter-Services Intelligence Directorate (ISI). Now, as gunfire rang out and bullet holes began to pockmark the concrete surrounding the upper windows of the block, dozens of local police converged on the scene thinking there had been a bomb attack.

By the time the first reporters arrived on the scene around 10 a.m. hundreds of police and paramilitary rangers were in the surrounding streets and lanes – which they had cordoned off – and on nearby rooftops with a clear view of the building. Amidst chaotic scenes, at least two men from the building had moved up to the roof and taken positions on the northern and western corners, shielded by a low cement barrier. Police tried to fire teargas canisters onto the roof, but several missed and bounced back onto the policemen below.

Then, under a screen of smoke grenades, a group of rangers wearing body armour made their way to the pavement outside the shops on the ground floor, where they were protected by a three-foot overhang. Slowly and cautiously they made their way up the stairs.

A woman dressed in a red *shalwar kameez* and carrying what appeared to be an unconscious child was led out of the building. According to one senior official, she provided key information on the number of gunmen in the building.

Later, as more rangers poured up the stairs, a second woman with a child, clearly of Pakistani origin, was led out by two men in plain clothes. 'There are more inside. I don't know how many. I don't know,' she cried, speaking in the local language, Urdu.

During a lull in the firing, which was chaotic, police called on the gunmen to surrender. 'You can't get away,' someone was heard to shout. The defiant reply, '*Allah-u-Akbar!* (God is Great!)' could clearly be heard in the streets below.

Within a few minutes police led a well-built man out through the ground-floor doorway, his arms tightly bound behind him and a filthy shirt tied over his eyes. More gunfire from within was followed by further shouts of 'Allah-u-Akbar!' The captive had been forced out by teargas grenades fired through the now-shattered windows.

Around noon five rangers entered the building. According to witnesses they were muttering prayers to themselves. By this time the three remaining men were cornered in the windowless kitchen, using a rifle to fire at the officers. When asked to surrender they shouted back 'Bastard! Bastard!' in English. One of the militants ran out of the room and was shot dead by police.

Back inside the room, the rifle jammed and the two men began throwing anything they could – kitchen knives, forks and pans – at the officers. Realising what had happened, the police then fired tear gas into the tiny room and within seconds the two men walked out with their hands in the air.

The second man fell to his knees and, as he did so, the first made a grab for one of the rangers' guns. He was forcibly subdued, though he struggled fiercely, reciting verses from the Koran and shouting, 'You're going to hell! You're going to hell!' in Arabic.

A security man showed the prisoner at the window to the crowd below and flashed a sign that the battle inside was over. Down below in the streets the local police unleashed a fusillade of shots in celebration, emptying their magazines, despite calls for restraint from their officers. The prisoner, by this time down at street level and dressed in a blue shirt with his face covered and his arms tied behind his back, was pushed through the waiting crowd of police and journalists, shouting loudly in Arabic and trying to raise his hands in the air. It was none other than Ramzi Binalshibh, one of the two principal organisers of the attacks on America.

Almost immediately a row broke out between a rangers colonel and a senior policeman over who should have custody of the prisoners.

Talking to reporters on the spot, Inspector General of the Sindh Police, Syed Kamal Shah denied that the incident had any link with the anniversary of the 11 September attacks. 'This incident has nothing to do with the anniversary,' he said. 'We have arrested five terrorists after an encounter in which two others were killed.' The number of arrests was later upgraded to ten. He said the encounter took place after police gave those in the apartment a warning to surrender, but instead they had attacked the police. 'We warned them several times to surrender, but the firing from them continued and they also hurled grenades at the police.' Police later revealed that inside one of two apartments on the top floor they had found a message scrawled in blood on the kitchen wall, proclaiming in Arabic the recitation known as the first pillar or principle (*kalma*) of Islam: 'There is no God except Allah, Mohammed is his messenger.' In the streets nearby, chalked on the wall in Urdu, were the slogans: 'Long Live al-Qaeda' and 'Suicide attacks on America will continue'.

Two of those staying in the apartments were killed and at least six officers were wounded, two seriously, during the operation. Assistant sub-inspectors Omar Hayat and Baqar Shah and police constables Muhammad Zamir, Muhammad Yousuf and Sher Ali received injuries from bullets and grenade fragments. Two ISI officers, including a colonel in charge of the operation and a major, were also wounded. The two men who were killed were both Yemenis and named as Mohammad Khalid and Saleh Ibrahim, one of whom was shot on the roof and fell to his death. A senior police intelligence officer later said that the Yemenis were suspected of being involved in the murder of *Wall Street Journal* reporter Daniel Pearl six months earlier. 'We have very strong suspicions that one of them was the one who beheaded Pearl,' he said. 'We are rechecking this information from other intelligence agencies, but one of them looked like the person suspected of murdering Pearl.'

Their bodies were moved to the Jinna Postgraduate Medical Centre that evening for autopsy. At the mortuary the doors were locked and no one was allowed to enter. Police said the remaining ten prisoners were Arabs: eight Yemenis, one Saudi and one Egyptian.

They appear to have been involved in helping al-Qaeda militants fleeing from Afghanistan to escape back to the Gulf. A large number of documents were recovered, including travel documents – passports and identification papers. Also recovered was an instruction manual for their clients, outlining procedures and tactics to evade the prying eyes of police and the intelligence agencies while boarding aircraft or crossing borders. One source suggested that Jose Padilla, the US citizen referred to as the 'Dirty Bomber' who was arrested in Chicago on his return to the United States, was one of those who had passed through the apartment. Many of the Arabs who arrived in Karachi before boarding ships bound for the Gulf were posing as Pukhtuns from the wild border areas with Afghanistan. Their comparatively light colouring and good language proficiency in Pushto and Dari gained during their years of fighting in Afghanistan meant they could often travel on Pakistani documents.

Police also recovered a satellite telephone, several laptops and mobile phones, a few CDs, some books, a Russian AK-47 rifle, a pistol, two hand grenades and dozens of rounds of ammunition. They added that a Pakistani couple living in the building had been taken into protective custody. Their four-year-old daughter had fallen unconscious after breathing in the teargas.

Some reports suggest that American FBI agents watched the entire proceedings from a black four-wheel-drive vehicle parked nearby, although this was later denied by Pakistani officials.

Two days later, Pakistani president General Pervez Musharraf gave credit to the ISI for the arrests. 'It was a good operation,' he said. 'I'm told maybe there is an important person also involved.' At least nine more suspects were arrested in follow-up operations the next day from two locations in Karachi. One report stated that amongst those picked up were the wife and young daughter of Khalid Shaikh Mohammed, the other principal planner of the 11 September attacks, although he himself evaded capture.

The prisoners were initially taken to the fortified headquarters of the paramilitary rangers in central Karachi before being moved later to a well-guarded facility run by the ISI in a military area. During their interrogation in Pakistan, where they were held for three days, they were blindfolded and handcuffed. They were interrogated by two FBI men, while three Pakistanis observed from behind a one-way mirror. One, according to an army officer, was very tough and all he would say was 'My name is Abdullah' – literally 'servant of Allah'. Lieutenant General Moinuddin Haider later stated that this person was Ramzi Binalshibh.

On 16 September the captives were handed over to American security officials and taken to an unknown place outside of Pakistan, initially at least to a warship in the Indian Ocean. At the time of writing it is still not known where the captured prisoners are being held.

It has not been revealed what led the police to this nondescript building in Karachi. According to official comments by the Pakistani government, the lead came from two other raids conducted the evening before. In those raids, two Burmese men and several Yemenis were captured.

According to Major General Rashid Qureshi, press secretary to the president and director-general of Inter Services Public Relations: 'About two and a half months before the arrests, US intelligence passed on a list of the most dangerous and wanted terrorists connected to 11 September. They were looking for Ramzi Binalshibh because of his connections to Mohammed Atta, leader of the hijackers. The ISI started working on finding these people.

'Two days before the raid on the apartments, the ISI got hold of two foreigners in Karachi. We have learned to keep such things quiet. They told us that some Arabs had rented two apartments in Phase 11 of Defence Housing Authority. The building was placed under surveillance and we found that they were Arabs and they had rented a complete floor, comprising two adjacent apartments. The landlord was living in another adjacent flat and the ISI got hold of him and he gave them the layout and description of the apartments rented by the Arabs. He is still under protective custody.'

'The FBI was not involved,' said Qureshi. 'We thought initially that the other main organiser of 11 September, Khalid Shaikh Mohammed, was also captured, but he was not. All the people were identified after the raid.'

Qureshi confirmed that several computers had been seized. 'Pakistani and US intelligence went through the evidence in the computers together. I don't know what was in them, but it will certainly compromise their future operations and plans. All the cases cracked so far have been done by our ISI, except for Faisalabad, where Abu Zubaydah was caught on a US tip-off. But the operation itself was ISI.'

Qureshi was in optimistic mood after the arrests. 'Al-Qaeda are either hiding or on the run. Their back is breaking and we are getting constant leads, more and more with each arrest. It is snowballing. Even locals inspired by them are being caught.'

Lieutenant General Haider added: 'We had no names of the Arabs. Only descriptions. We did not even have Ramzi's photograph, only a newspaper photo of a biometric sketch drawn by an expert on the basis of a verbal description. The Americans gave us newspaper photographs of the sketch from which we think that it is Ramzi Binalshibh. We did everything. What can the Americans do here? They don't know the country or the language.'

The Pakistanis say that they did not even know that Binalshibh was in the apartment. 'If we had thought he was going to be there, we would have moved in at the beginning with more troops,' said one official.

But despite the Pakistani insistence that it was their own lucky break which led to the capture of Binalshibh, there is another, more intriguing possibility. Four days before his arrest, *The Sunday Times* published Yosri Fouda's interview with him and Khalid Shaikh Mohammed. The interview was recorded in April 2002 in Karachi. Until the interviews were published and Al-Jazeera Channel began running previews to Fouda's documentary, which was shown on 12 September 2002, US intelligence had little idea about the planning behind the 11 September attacks.

CHAPTER ONE

Invitation to the Unknown

'It is okay now, you can open your eyes. Recognised us yet?'
Khalid Shaikh Mohammed

Early one morning in the first week of April 2002, Yosri Fouda's mobile phone rang just as he got into his new office. He hadn't yet fully settled into Al-Jazeera's new London bureau on the Albert Embankment, but had quietly enjoyed the irony of the fact that directly across the River Thames he could clearly see the carefully screened windows and imposing buildings of Thames House, headquarters to Britain's domestic intelligence service, MI5.

On the line was a voice Fouda did not recognise. '*Salaam-u-alaikom*, brother Yosri. I am someone who means well,' a kind male voice struggled to explain in Arabic down a bad, distant-sounding line. Religious too, as most 'mainstream' Arabs would use the more common greeting, *Sabahel-Khair*, during the early morning hours rather than the Islamic greeting, *Salaam-u-alaikom.*

'I hope you are thinking of preparing something special for the first anniversary,' the distant voice enquired, and then quickly got down to business, 'because if you are, we can provide you with some exclusive stuff, *Sirri Lilghaya.*' It was an amusing comment. *Sirri Lilghaya* – Top Secret – was the name of Fouda's regular programme on Al-Jazeera and so the caller clearly knew what he wanted and who he was talking to. About 20 seconds elapsed before the unusual and un-named caller – whom Fouda later decided to call Abu Bakr – asked for a secure fax number and hung up.

Bewildered and unsure what to do next, Fouda looked at the silent mobile phone lying in front of him. Thoughts began racing through his mind. Who was this mystery caller? Is the fax machine on? Yes. Has it got enough paper?

Some more would not hurt. What about ink? Okay. The waiting had started, and the speculation too.

The caller had asked him if he was preparing anything for the first anniversary of the 11 September attacks. What was it that he was offering? How could he trust a person calling out of the blue like this? Checking out the credibility of Abu Bakr would later prove to be both a difficult and risky task, but Fouda made a few phone calls to contacts anyway to ask them if they knew what was happening. The insight of some of those who had previous experiences with al-Qaeda was not, however, very helpful.

As he waited for further contact from his mystery caller the same evening, at least Fouda was able to find it amusing when, by sheer coincidence, an interview producer with a famous international news network called him to ask for a favour. 'Would you happen to have a phone number for one of those al-Qaeda people?' she wondered. 'We need their reaction to some reports.' Unaware that she was actually serious, he suggested that it might be a good idea to try dialling 192 (the number for British Telecom directory inquiries).

The producer who called Fouda was sadly stereotypical of many of those in the Western media who were chronically ill-informed about the background to the 11 September attacks. As far as many of them were concerned, the whole thing was seamless – 11 September, bin Laden, Islam, Arabs, Afghanistan, Middle East terrorism: they all ran together.

Partly as a result of such ignorance, when global fame caught up with Al-Jazeera it did so for the wrong reasons. Many in the West, particularly in the US, who had little if any knowledge of the Middle East and/or Islam, were enraged when they heard after the attacks in Washington and New York that it was an 'Arab', a 'Muslim' TV channel called 'Al-something', which had sole access to the Taliban's Afghanistan. Very few were aware that CNN, months before, had been offered equal access, but had failed to see the story in Afghanistan that Al-Jazeera had spotted. And very few, in the run-up to the 'war on terrorism', resisted wondering, 'Can Arabs operate a camera, link it up to a satellite dish and beam a signal out? Can they really make good journalists?'

The pervasive prejudice really was that bad and only slowly did news reports begin to refer to 'Al-Jazeera', instead of 'an Arab TV station', or a 'Gulf-based TV station' or, even worse, 'bin Laden's TV station'.

The follow-up to that first intriguing phone call came four days later when the fax machine started buzzing and regurgitated a three-page message. It was from Abu Bakr, or someone close to him. The fax did not contain rhetoric or abuse, but was instead a general outline for a three-part documentary to mark the first anniversary of the 11 September attacks.

There was a certain arrogance about this. Didn't these people know that it is the programme makers who determine the content and structure of a programme, not its subjects? But here it was, as bold as you like. The fax proposed ideas, locations and personalities for the programmes. The proposed documentary should, according to the author of this outline, start with the photographs of the 19 'brothers' (the 11 September hijackers) accompanied by the voice of 'the Sheikh' (Osama bin Laden) reciting poetry:

> They swore by Allah that their *jihad* [holy war]
> Shall go on despite Khosrow [the Emperor of Persia] and Caesar:
> Our raids shall never end
> Until they leave our yards.

This, according to the proposal, should be followed by 'Bush's sound bite on the Crusade' – a reference to the infamous comment by US president George Bush in the days following 11 September: 'This is a new kind of, a new kind of evil and the American people are beginning to understand. This crusade, this war on terror is going to take a while.'[1]

This in turn should lead to a 'historical analysis of the conflict between Christians and Muslims'. The proposal named a number of prominent Islamic scholars who could take part in such a discussion. They included Dr Abdul-Adhim al-Deeb, Dr Abdul-Halim Oais and Dr Jamal Abdul-Hadi, none of whom had been approached by anyone to ask if they would want to take part and none of whom were known supporters of Osama bin Laden's al-Qaeda organisation.

Other names – including the Kuwaiti Dr Abdullah al-Nafeesi, Abdul Bari Atwan and Dr Mohammed Abbas – were recommended to talk about 'America's crimes against Red Indians, the CIA's crimes in Latin America, America's crimes in the black continent, America's crimes in Asia – Vietnam, Japan and North Korea – America's crimes in Iraq and America's crimes in Palestine and its unlimited support for Israel'.

It was also suggested that the programme should answer the following questions:

> ● What are the true unofficial statistics for the World Trade Center and the Pentagon victims? They remain unannounced, though preliminary estimates indicated the death of 25,000 people.
> ● Why have we not seen pictures of the victims' coffins in the news? Has bin Laden fulfilled his promise by sending more coffins(?)!!!!
> ● Why did America's free media hide the pictures of the graves and the wounded? And would the coming days reveal the truth behind the killed to break America's heart(?)!!!
> ● How do aviation experts evaluate the skill with which the aircraft were flown, especially the Pentagon attack – accurate and professional as it was? Is it credible that the executers had never before flown a

Boeing? Is it credible they only had some lessons on small twin-engine aircrafts and some lessons on simulators?

● What is the total damage to American companies in the aviation industry, travel sector, insurance companies, banking and financial institutions? And to what extent has this all affected the American economy, particularly in the long run?

● Do political analysts and military experts consider 9/11 a military action in terms of targets and timing in light of the repeated warnings that preceded it, and especially because the war had already been declared by bin Laden?

● How has America responded to the attacks? Will 9/11 be top of the agenda for the next presidential elections? Will it split America's national unity, especially in light of the carelessness and fragility of the security agencies, which failed accurately to predict such an operation or prevent it? The security agencies played down the warnings by their most formidable enemy, believing it would be enough to cancel scheduled military manoeuvres in Jordan and Egypt, pull some warships out of Bahrain and close down a few embassies, only for the catastrophe to hit them where they never expected.

● How does America's free press deal with the consequences of 9/11 in light of the blackout policy exercised by the US Administration in relation to progress in the War Against Terror? In other words, what is it that the world is not allowed to see or hear about 9/11?

● Why did so many political and military analysts and security experts initially fail to recognise al-Qaeda was indeed behind the operations of 11 September?

'These,' the document concluded, 'are but some ideas and suggestions for the first part of a documentary within your valuable programme, *Sirri Lilghaya.*' As for the second part, it was to focus on the lives of those who carried out what were referred to in the fax as 'the Tuesday Operations', in particular Mohammed el-Amir Atta, who led the attack on the North Tower of the World Trade Center; Marwan Yusif al-Shehhi, leader of the attack on the South Tower; Ziad Samir al-Jarrah, shot down over Pennsylvania, the fax claimed; and Hani Saleh Hanjour, leader of the attack on the Pentagon.

Ambitious as it was, the carefully typed outline clearly showed some rudimentary understanding of how the media works. It was simple, direct and well organised. And, it was tempting. 'If you are interested,' the confident author finally threw a carrot, 'we will provide you with addresses of people and locations which will help you bring about this investigation.'

At the time this fax arrived, more than seven months had elapsed since the devastating scenes in New York and Washington. Nobody had yet taken direct responsibility for the atrocities. The Bush administration had flatly accused bin Laden of involvement and the British government had produced what amounted to a prosecution brief naming him as the chief culprit. But real proof, the kind that could stand up in a court of law, was lacking. Not that this had prevented the US from making its move. Within a month of the attacks it had launched military action in Afghanistan and quickly deposed the Taliban government, bin Laden's host and protector.

And yes, bin Laden had spared no effort in praising the attacks and asking Allah to accept those who carried them out as martyrs. But he had not yet claimed responsibility. Even those who believed, or wished in their hearts, that it was indeed bin Laden's men who had been involved found it difficult to grasp the reality that their fellow human beings had planned, slept and then woken up to execute such an unprecedented and sophisticated act of terror.

People were desperate for answers and one result of this desperation was the proliferation of conspiracy theories that spread across the globe after what bin Laden later branded the New York and Washington *ghazwahs* (raids). Fouda could hardly cope with the volume of emails, faxes, phone calls and even SMS text messages that flooded into Al-Jazeera's offices offering explanations.

A French writer captured the mood of many in the Muslim world, as well as in the West, and secured himself a small fortune by claiming that the attacks had been organised by the American government itself. When interviewed, Thierry Meyssan vigorously defended his 'grand conspiracy' theory saying, 'First of all, I am not sure that the planes were hijacked by people. There is no evidence . . . to support this theory. Second, we know that the secret code for the White House was stolen and you need to have some people in George Bush's administration [to do that]. Third, when we examine the Pentagon attack we find it impossible to be done by a Boeing . . . the hole in the building [suggests] it was done by a cruise missile.'[2]

A bestseller, his book was translated into 28 languages, including Arabic. Meyssan was also invited to speak in some Arab countries.

Another theory, which was particularly popular in Saudi Arabia, stemmed from the fact that someone had spotted that in a clip from the American movie *The Long Kiss Goodnight* there is a scene in which an FBI agent sets out in detail to his colleagues a vision for a secret operation:

– 1993, World Trade Center bombing – remember? During the trial one of the bombers claimed that the CIA had advance knowledge. (*Laughing sarcastically.*) The diplomat who issued the terrorist visa was CIA. It is not unthinkable they paved the way for bombing purely to justify a budget increase.

– You telling me you gonna fake some terrorist thing just to get some money out of the Congress?

– Well, unfortunately, Mr Hennessey, I have no idea how to fake

killing 4,000 people. So, we're just gonna have to do it for real –
umm, and blame it on the Muslims naturally.

The fact that the movie was produced in Hollywood long before 11
September 2001 gave support to the arguments amongst conspiracy
theorists, including some Americans, that the whole idea of the attacks was
actually born inside America. 'Bin Laden could not have done this,' Edward
Spanaus of the *Electronic Intelligence Review* tells us. 'It was such a
sophisticated secretive operation that it had to be conducted from within the
US.' And the purpose? 'The purpose was very clear . . . to draw the US into
a general war in the Middle East, a clash of civilisations and a war against
Islam.'[3]

11 September was, therefore, in the conspiracy theorist Spanaus's opinion,
a pre-determined plan 'drawn intellectually by Zbigniew Brzezinski and
Samwell Huntington', promoted politically by 'some groups within the US,
perhaps assisted by people in Britain, some in Israel' and executed militarily
by 'a sort of rogue element within the US Army'.

It was also done, as the notable Egyptian scholar, Dr Zaghloul al-Naggar
put it: 'to stop the spread of Islam that has been sweeping the West in recent
years, to make it even more convenient for the Israelis to put the Palestinian
issue beyond recognition, to provide the US with a pretext to extend its
influence to Afghanistan and strengthen its position in the Far East without
risking a third world war with Russia and China, and to give oil merchants
and arms dealers the chance to become even richer.'[4]

Dr al-Naggar, who taught Islam in the US and the Gulf, also makes the
following point: 'The CIA once suggested to President JFK that 30 Cuban
migrants should be used to destroy two federal buildings in Los Angeles as a
pretext for a US invasion of Cuba. But he turned the offer down when they
estimated that between 1,000 and 1,500 people might be killed.'

Meyssan goes further back in history to the nineteenth century when the
Americans were on their way to invade Cuba. 'They destroyed some of their
own military boats, killed many of their own sailors and claimed they had
been attacked by Spain. Thus, they had a reason to launch a retaliatory war.'

While these theories proliferated across the Internet, it was still unclear
what role, if any, bin Laden would claim for the attacks. All that changed,
however, with this first written message received by Fouda. For the first time,
someone from within al-Qaeda itself was expressing concern about 'attempts
to strip the brothers of the credit'.

And yet it was all still very confusing, despite the arrival of this fax.
Nobody had heard from bin Laden for months, although his presence was
vividly felt in every newsroom around the world. But how could Fouda be
sure that the invitation implicit in the fax had actually come from him?

That evening, Fouda went home with the three anonymous pages in his pocket and a mountain of thoughts on his mind. It was very tempting to share this with someone, but very risky. It was time to relax and think it all through. But his thoughts were interrupted as the sound of his mobile broke the silence. There was no number registered on the phone. It could be Abu Bakr again. If he were calling from Pakistan, which was the best bet, it would have been around 2 a.m.

'Would you like to come to Islamabad?' the distant voice asked. 'We will make sure that you are, *Inshallah* (God willing), fine and that you get what you want.' So, things were beginning to move. Someone, somewhere had taken a decision. If he did not take the opportunity now, who knew if there would ever be another chance? 'Absolutely,' Fouda replied urgently, knowing full well that his anonymous caller would not stay on the line for longer than a few seconds. 'As soon as I can get a visa you will find me, Inshallah, at your end.' Abu Bakr then hung up without telling Fouda where exactly in Islamabad or when, if at all, someone would meet him.

Getting a journalist's visa to visit Pakistan was not particularly difficult, but the press section at the London Consulate always wants to know what you are working on. Fouda had the perfect reason for making a return visit to the country. His investigation into the detainees held in Guantanamo Bay, Cuba, by the Americans, *The Road to Camp X-Ray*, partly filmed a few months earlier in Pakistan, had been warmly received by Al-Jazeera's viewers and so it was only natural that he would want to return to make a follow-up. Locations this time round would have to include the tribal areas between Pakistan and Afghanistan, where already some 130 al-Qaeda fighters who had crossed from the Tora Bora mountains after extensive bombing by the US Air Force had been captured by Pakistan's Border Scouts and Army. To allay suspicions further, Fouda even requested an interview with the Pakistani interior minister, Moinuddin Haider, during his visit.

A two-visit media visa was issued with no fuss in London on 9 April 2002. Seven days later Fouda, putting aside his many concerns, was in the Gulf in Dubai, changing flights for Islamabad. He called his mother just to say he might see her in Egypt in a couple of weeks. He knew from long experience that she would not expect any more details. But more problematic was what to tell his boss.

Al-Jazeera's director general, Mohammed Jasim al-Ali, trusted Fouda when he told him that he was on his way to investigate a new angle for a second part of *The Road to Camp X-Ray*. Abu Jasim, as Fouda usually calls him, was quick to wish his colleague good luck. More than six weeks later, when things were a lot clearer, it would take him a little longer before he could manage an understanding smile.

Fouda arrived at the airport in Islamabad in the early hours of Wednesday, 17 April 2002. Al-Jazeera correspondent Ahmed Zaidan quickly picked him up from outside the main terminal building. Ahmed knew that the 'brothers' were up to something with his visiting colleague, but that was all he knew and he was professional enough not to ask. Having been based in Islamabad for a few years, Ahmed had a feeling from the way things had been set up that an important meeting was in the offing. He dropped Fouda at a modest hotel near the Al-Jazeera office and left, as neither of them had a clear idea about what was likely to happen next.

Fouda enjoyed a much-needed shower, ordered food up to his room, read for a while and quickly became bored with the three Pakistani TV channels on offer. It was hot, but at least the air conditioning had finally started working. It was noisy and the hours passed slowly. His patience was being stretched to the limit. Here he was in Islamabad, where he had come on the strength of a fax and a couple of conversations with someone he had never met. Doubts were beginning to set in. Waiting for something to transpire was bad enough, but waiting for the unknown was unbearable.

It was now 12 hours since he had arrived and nothing had happened. How long should he stay before admitting that this had all been a waste of time? Two days should be the limit – three at most – and then it would be time to leave. As if prompted by the thought, the phone began to ring. It had to be his contact. Who else knew where he was staying?

He picked up the receiver to hear the now much clearer voice of Abu Bakr. 'Hamdellah Alas-Salamah (thank God you have arrived safe),' he said, without giving a name. 'Take the night flight tomorrow to Karachi.' That was it. The phone clicked and only then did Fouda begin to take this journalistic fantasy a little bit more seriously. They knew he was there and that he had at least kept his part of the bargain. Now he was putting himself in their hands.

In an Iranian restaurant in Islamabad later that night, Fouda shared the most minimal of details with Ahmed. He would be the only one to know Fouda's whereabouts – at least as far as Fouda himself was allowed to know. Ahmed's advice was to stay at the Marriott Hotel in Karachi and follow any instructions exactly.

Fouda was unable to sleep that night. Why had he been called in the first place? Why bring someone all the way over from London when they could have spoken to Ahmed, who lives and works in their realm? And why not use one of those journalists who are commonly believed to be more sympathetic to the Islamist cause?

He could not think his way around these questions. From now on, it was all going to be about survival. Getting back home in one piece was his main concern. If he got a reasonable story on the back of the trip, that would only be a bonus. 'It's pointless and even foolish to go after a big story and not come back,' the former BBC war correspondent Martin Bell had once told a young and impressionable Fouda when he had worked alongside him in Bosnia for the BBC. And at the forefront of his mind was also the fate that had befallen Daniel Pearl, the *Wall Street Journal* reporter who had been kidnapped in Karachi at the end of January 2002 and literally slaughtered. His body had been found only a couple of weeks earlier, buried in the grounds of a Karachi nursery.

The following day Fouda made his way back out to the airport and joined a crowded flight south for the two-hour flight to Karachi. Once again his mind began to wander. Was there anyone on the flight who knew what he was doing? Was he being set up? He might just as well act as if he was under surveillance and try to be as quiet and natural as possible.

Why would bin Laden's people go to so much trouble to kidnap him? Daniel Pearl, after all, was not a Muslim, but a Jew, and, as far as his murderers were concerned, a Zionist whose father was a 'Zionist bastard'. Pearl had not been invited to meet his killers, but had been forcibly abducted. As far as his abductors were concerned, he had been asking too many questions and getting too close to important people within their network. These are not the kind of people who appreciated being tracked down. But if they wanted to see you, that was another matter: they would dog your movements until they got what they wanted.

As he found his way out of Quaid-e-Azam Airport in Karachi and into a taxi, Fouda began to believe that his would-be hosts could gain little or nothing from harming a fellow Muslim who was working for the only Arab TV channel which had been praised for its openness and willingness to criticise Arab regimes. Had he not just criticised the US administration for the bizarre way it was handling the 'illegal combatants' issue in Guantanamo Bay? And as Bush's war on terrorism was aimed primarily at politically assassinating, before physically eliminating, an uncompromising militant organisation, Fouda also managed to find comfort in the fact that they were probably now looking for sympathy rather than challenge.

Better to think positive. It was obvious that his contact, who was clearly close to the leadership of al-Qaeda, wanted to make sure that their interpretation of events received some kind of an airing. They must have known by then that even if some of their supporters around the world admired the mouse that dared step on the elephant's toes, many did not approve of the way in which it had been done. If they were hoping to emerge from a phase of operational activism to another of political existence, then they probably felt that they needed to justify themselves – politically as well as religiously. And to do that they were going to have to deal with journalists. Who would trust them if harm befell anyone who came to tell their story?

In the teeming city of Karachi, the taxi driver told Fouda that they were now a few minutes away from the Marriott. Once again, the phone rang. It was Abu Bakr and he was not keen on the hotel. 'Ask the driver to take you to the Regent Plaza instead.' The Marriott was too close to the US Consulate and there were too many foreigners staying there, Abu Bakr told him later. Within weeks the Marriott was the target for a huge car bomb which killed

14 people, including 11 French naval technicians working on a contract for the Pakistan Navy.

Fouda reflected on the fact that he was almost following in the footsteps of one of the men behind the 11 September attacks. He knew that seven months earlier Said Bahaji, who had lived with Mohammed Atta and Ramzi Binalshibh in a tiny flat in Hamburg, had also travelled to the same city. On 3 September Bahaji had shaved off his beard, told his wife he was off to Pakistan for a computer seminar and boarded Turkish Airlines Flight 1056 bound via Istanbul for Quaid-e-Azam International Airport in Karachi. Here, he made his way with two companions to the Embassy Hotel. He stayed for only one night, paid $30 and then vanished.

A similar hotel but in the noisy Faisal Street, the Regent Plaza, was undergoing renovation when an Arab-looking businessman produced his British passport and asked to pay in cash. Fouda would not be specific with the receptionist on how many days he would be staying as this 'would depend on my business deals'.

Half an hour later Room 322 was to be the venue for Fouda's first meeting with an al-Qaeda representative. A knock on the door brought Fouda running from the shower. When he opened the door he saw a tall, middle-aged man – probably an Arab, but dressed in the Pakistani costume of shalwar kameez.

The visitor quickly slipped into the room as soon as the door was open. He did not shake hands, did not kiss on the cheeks, but used a form of greeting that is common among Sudanese. He stretched his right arm to Fouda's left shoulder and sort of hugged him – right and left. But the voice that had lived in Fouda's ears for the previous two weeks had not sounded very Sudanese. It was hard to tell if switching between different Arabic dialects was a deliberate attempt to cover his origins or if it was the result of having dealt for a long time with other Arab nationals. From the way he looked and sounded, he could have passed for a Yemeni, a Sudanese, an Egyptian, a Saudi or even a Somali.

Though in the beginning Abu Bakr had restless eyes, there was an instant sense of trust between the two men, even after a few minutes when he asked Fouda if he could use his shower. In the circumstances, it was an unusual request. But Fouda had noticed that Abu Bakr really needed a shower. Fouda also asked Abu Bakr if he would like something to eat. 'Yes, please, if it is not too much trouble,' he immediately replied.

Twenty minutes later, Abu Bakr had finished his shower and asked Fouda to join him in evening prayers. Over a bowl of lentil soup and a couple of chicken sandwiches, Abu Bakr gave Fouda his first piece of news: Osama bin Laden was not dead as many commentators had speculated. 'Sheikh Abu Abdullah [bin Laden], God protect him, is an avid viewer of your channel,' he said.

'How does the Sheikh watch us now?' Fouda asked, hoping for a few more hints.

'Do not worry, brother Yosri. Sheikh Osama, God protect him, is alive and well. Whatever he misses he gets on tape.'

As politely as he could, Abu Bakr started to criticise Al-Jazeera, and Fouda had to listen. 'How come you interview those Zionists and you do not give the brothers who are in jihad for the *ummah* [nation] what they rightly deserve?' he asked. He did not like Fouda's attempt to avoid the question and sterile discussion by picking up the phone to order some tea.

'Do not forget that we have been strongly criticised for broadcasting your tapes and yet we do what we believe is right,' Fouda answered. 'By the way, who wrote that outline that was faxed to me?'

But Abu Bakr would not be specific. 'One of the brothers,' he said as he prepared himself for more questions.

'Why me?' Fouda asked, and his question was met by a confident smile on Abu Bakr's face.

'The brothers had been discussing this for some time,' he answered, 'and they thought that you are a professional journalist with integrity.'

He paused for a moment and then threw another surprise at Fouda: 'Sheikh Abu Abdullah, God protect him, told us to take Robert Fisk [a journalist for *The Independent*] to Oum-Abdullah [bin Laden's wife] and to take Yosri Fouda to the brothers.'

Tea arrived just as Fouda thought the man was beginning to open up. But Abu Bakr gulped down his tea and started to wrap up the first encounter. 'Do not worry, brother Yosri, you will, Inshallah, know everything tomorrow,' he said. Since 'tomorrow' was a Friday, Fouda wondered if he was going to see him in the mosque. But Abu Bakr did not think so. 'You better not move from the hotel,' he advised Fouda, with just a hint of menace.

'But what about Friday prayers?' Fouda asked.

'Allah will forgive you,' replied Abu Bakr, effectively issuing an instant *fatwa*.

It was past midnight when Abu Bakr made his excuses and left, leaving Fouda with more questions than answers. The man was impertinent. Who was he to think that he could offer divine dispensations? Who on earth has the authority to exempt a capable Muslim from performing the most important prayers in Islam? Certainly al-Qaeda makes it clear in its own literature that tough situations dictate desperate measures, but this casual comment from Abu Bakr was almost a discourtesy. Where do you draw the line? How applicable are the laws of Islam and who decides? And how much difference is there between this logic and the logic of President George W. Bush, who, in the name of fighting against the 'enemies of Western civilisation' was in danger of compromising its very essence – by intimidating journalists, introducing discriminatory laws and detaining people indefinitely without charge? How can we then believe either side? How can we tell if what we are being told is really the truth or if it is just a lie for the sake of the truth?

Fouda woke up that morning with a prayer that Friday, 19 April 2002 was going to be a turning point in his career, if not his life. He was still in the dark as to what was going to happen. He divided the whole morning between praying and listening to recitations of the Holy Koran on a Pakistani TV channel. Abu Bakr would not call him again and he would not leave his room. At exactly 5 p.m., he was to follow his new instructions.

He had been told to go out of the hotel's back door and hail a taxi – 'avoid hotel taxis' – to another address and wait there by the stairs on the second floor. Fouda followed the instructions precisely. After five minutes by the stairs a heavily bearded man with more of a Pakistani than an Arab face came up and after the usual greeting of 'Salaam-u-alaikom', said to him, in English: 'I have just given my mother-in-law a lift home. We can go now.'

The new guide drove Fouda to a busy square and parked the car to get a glass of mango juice. 'Do we have time for this?' Fouda asked as politely as he could.

'It is not that we do not have the time,' the bearded man answered, just as politely. 'These are the instructions, brother.'

Whose instructions? Who was Fouda going to meet? Who were those brothers Abu Bakr was talking about? Long Beard was not forthcoming.

Fouda was told to wait in the hot, sticky car with his mango juice while the man made three visits to a telephone box. As he sat there, he began to reflect on the interviews he had conducted with some of the relatives of the alleged hijackers. It had been heartbreaking to listen to some of them resort to desperate explanations as they attempted to defend themselves and their sons in the face of overwhelming hostility. 'Fanatics? Us? Fanatics? Come and take a look at our girls!' the weeping but dignified father of Ziad al-Jarrah, the alleged pilot of United Airlines Flight 93, had said to the media in the aftermath of the attack.

Nothing on earth would convince Mohammed Atta senior that his son was on board American Airlines Flight 11 on that morning of 11 September. 'He telephoned me the day after. It was in the morning and, as usual, he asked me about my health and whether I had given up smoking yet,' he told Fouda, though he was not sure where his son had called him from. 'I am absolutely sure that my son is either somewhere in America or has been liquidated by the Americans.'[5]

The lack of concrete facts and the absence of a responsibility claim more than eight months on allowed the conspiracy theories to grow, particularly amongst Arabs and Muslims. Many were already critical of American foreign policy, particularly over the question of Israel. Now they were disgusted by what they saw as US attempts to capitalise on the tragedy by striking against

Afghanistan, and opinion in the Arab world turned more resolutely anti-American. 'A thug takes his clothes off and walks down the street in front of women and nobody can stop him. This is America,' said Atta senior, father of the man accused of being the principal hijacker. The anger welled up inside him, consuming him, overlaid onto his confusion over his son's fate.

Fouda's driver finally came back from the telephone box with new orders. The next stage of the journey would be by rickshaw to a place that must remain a secret. It was all becoming rather silly, like a scene from a bad spy movie. The rickshaw man took him on a noisy, bumpy ride through dark alleys – hitting a dead end at one point.

It was quickly becoming apparent to a weary Fouda why Karachi had been chosen for his rendezvous. A city of 12 million people with no shortage of anti-American sentiment, it has a lot of 'safe' neighbourhoods inhabited not only by people who openly sympathise with Osama (they usually call him by his first name) but also by the diehards who have been to Kashmir, Afghanistan, Chechnya, the Philippines and other 'Islamic flash points'.

Eventually the journey came to an end. Fouda got out of the rickshaw, only to be picked up almost immediately by a waiting car. 'Lahore?' the driver shouted. That was Fouda's cue. Hassan, the driver, was an intelligent young Arab with a Palestinian dialect. 'I have a present for you,' he said as he drove at breakneck speed out of Karachi. It was a pirated CD-ROM of *The Road to Camp X-Ray*, the programme Fouda had made about the detainees held in Guantanamo Bay. 'It is now everywhere in Pakistan, thanks to our brothers who dubbed it into English.'

About five miles outside Karachi, Hassan stopped by a car that looked at first as if it had broken down. Yet another man appeared and they blindfolded an obedient Fouda: two balls of thick cotton were taped to his eyes and then covered by sunglasses. They were in business.

Now it was the new man's turn to drive Fouda. Unlike Hassan he was virtually silent. Fouda could sense they were moving back from a rural area into the city. Soon he was sure they were back somewhere in Karachi. There was something familiar about the smell and sound.

The car stopped and they got out. 'Can you help me carry this box inside?' the silent man suddenly asked in Arabic. Fouda felt the end of a box thrust into his hands, expecting it to be of considerable weight to justify the need to carry it between two men. But it was empty. Fouda was puzzled at first, but then realised what was going on. To the casual observer two men had got out of a car. If anyone had noticed one of them guiding the other up some stairs, it could have raised suspicions. The empty box allowed the scene to take on the ordinary appearance of two men carrying a heavy weight. It was very simple and yet very clever. These were highly trained people, professionals.

Fouda counted four floors as they ascended the staircase and before he heard a doorbell ringing. The door opened and he was immediately pulled inside. Two hands began to take his blindfold off. All kinds of thoughts went through his mind. Everything had followed in the wake of that first call in London and now he was here, in Karachi, in a strange building with people he did not know. It would be the moment when all was revealed.

'It is okay now, you can open your eyes,' an authoritative but friendly voice said. Fouda did so and instantly recognised, less than two feet away, Khalid Shaikh Mohammed, one of the most important figures in the al-Qaeda leadership and a known and wanted man. Even before 11 September, the FBI had put a $5 million price on his head. A 38 year old, he is an uncle of Ramzi Yousef, the Pakistani who is now serving life in an American prison for organising the first attack on the World Trade Center in 1993.

Khalid led Fouda into a near-empty flat. There was a room (room one) to the immediate left of the entrance door. It was half open and it was the kind of room where guests could be isolated from the rest of the flat. Then there was an archway leading to a wide central room (room two) with two windows to the left. It would be best used as a living room. Out of it there were three doors: one closed (room three) in front of you as you went in, one to the right that was the kitchen (room four) and one with a balcony and en-suite shower/toilet (room five) right next to the kitchen. As Fouda was shown into this last room, he noticed it had a carpet, two long padded mats stretching alongside two of the walls and a few cushions.

There, in room five, another shock awaited Fouda. Ramzi Binalshibh, a 30-year-old Yemeni accused by the FBI of involvement in the bombing of the USS *Cole* in October 2000 and top of the German authorities' most wanted list after 11 September, was sitting on the floor surrounded by three laptops and five mobile phones. He had been a flatmate of the key 11 September hijackers when they had shared a first-floor flat at 54 Marienstrasse, Hamburg, northern Germany, and was also a wanted man.

'Recognised us yet?' Khalid joked as Ramzi shook Fouda's hand warmly.

'You will when your door is knocked at by intelligence dogs,' Ramzi said with a half-sneer. In the Arab manner, Fouda began to address them by their first names, and that is how we shall refer to them now. It is how they are known among their own people.

'They say that you are terrorists.' Fouda surprised himself by throwing in this line so early as he took his place on the floor between them.

Calm and serene, Ramzi just offered an inviting smile. But it was Khalid who answered: 'They are right. That is what we do for a living.' Khalid had wasted no time in cutting to the quick.

An artificial cough by Ramzi interrupted a moment of early silence. 'If terrorism is to throw terror into the heart of your enemy and the enemy of Allah then we thank Him, the most Merciful, the most Compassionate, for enabling us to be terrorists,' continued Ramzi as he went off to the kitchen to make tea. 'It is in the Koran, brother Yosri.'

Meanwhile, Khalid started to outline the strict conditions for Fouda's interview, for this is what was now being offered. 'You will not talk about our means of communication, nor will you mention our real codenames,' he said. 'When – not if – they ask you what we now look like, you will say we look exactly the same as those photos they will show you.' Fouda was then asked to place his right hand on a copy of the Koran and solemnly swear to this.

Khalid struck Fouda as shrewd and blunt. Annoyed to find that Fouda had brought his mobile phone – a potential major breach of security – Khalid snatched it, switched it off, removing as he did so the SIM card and battery, and buried everything in the furthermost room (room one). But if Khalid was a man of action, Ramzi was a man of Allah. He was friendlier, more polite and certainly more knowledgeable in religion and ideology. Though eight years Khalid's and Fouda's junior, he led them both in prayer. This is allowed in Islam only if the younger knows by heart more of the Koran.

For prayers, the three men had all moved to the reception room. It, too, was empty except for a plastic rug, a couple of hard cushions and an old, noisy fridge. The prayers were important: apart from performing his religious duty, Fouda had been waiting for this moment for another reason. Ramzi used the brief form of prayers that a Muslim is allowed to perform when making a journey. 'So you are travelling?' Fouda asked.

'Yes. You did not expect us to show you where we live, did you?' Ramzi replied, sounding as if he had expected the question.

By now Fouda had got over the initial shock of arriving in the apartment and meeting the two men. It was time for him to show that he was not intimidated. 'I think it is my turn to make us all some tea,' he suggested as Khalid got busy once more with his mobile text messaging. He was as fast as a storm, sitting there in that corner, handling three mobiles at the same time. Ramzi, however, was so hospitable that he insisted on looking after his guest. As he stood up, Fouda followed him into the kitchen for a while and then strolled back to room five.

'Are these electrified?' Fouda shouted from inside the room. Khalid came quickly into the room to find Fouda curiously looking at the iron bars reaching from the floor to the ceiling just behind the balcony door. Still holding a couple of mobiles, he wandered away again as if nobody had spoken. A minute or two later and he came back showing more interest.

'Can I have a look at your British passport?' he suddenly asked. Surprised and a little concerned, Fouda handed it over. 'Nice one that,' Khalid said, leafing through it swiftly until he reached the Pakistani visa issued in London. He noted the serial number and handed it back.

Khalid, it seemed, was never off duty. A man who regularly used fake and forged passports, he had a 'professional' interest in noting the latest numbering system being used by the border controls.

Fouda was by now desperate for a cigarette, for obvious reasons. He looked at Ramzi as he placed the tea tray on the floor and asked hesitantly, 'I know I should not be doing this, but could I possibly step out for a smoke?'

Ramzi was unimpressed. He started to give Fouda a lesson in religion and morality but, surprisingly, Khalid interrupted him by saying: 'Take it easy on the guy. As long as he knows it is bad he will, Inshallah, give it up.'

It was truly a much-needed cigarette after four hours that felt more like forty. Approaching 10 p.m., Fouda had cut the ice, but was still looking for a proper way to get down to business. He understood by now that Ramzi was the author of the faxed outline suggested for the documentary. But he also understood that Khalid was in charge. He held the cards when it mattered.

Fouda summoned every thread of experience, looked Khalid in the eye and asked: 'Did you do it?' But Khalid didn't flinch.

'No filming today,' he declared, 'and you do not have to worry about a camera or a cameraman for tomorrow. We will provide everything.'

Ramzi added his own detail of the arrangements: 'You will be going straight from here to your flight whenever we are done.'

Then, with little fanfare, Khalid got down to business by making an announcement that hit Fouda like a heavyweight punch. 'I am the head of the al-Qaeda military committee,' he said, 'and Ramzi is the coordinator of the Holy Tuesday operation. And yes, we did it.'

NOTES

1. Quoted in *Philadelphia Enquirer*, 29 September 2001.
2. Exclusive interview with Thierry Meyssan, Paris, July 2002. See also Thierry Meyssan, *L'effroyable imposture: 11 Septembre 2001 (9/11: The Big Lie)* (Chatou, Carnot, 2002).
3. Exclusive interview with Edward Spanaus, Washington DC, July 2002. He has also repeated these claims in the *Electronic Intelligence Review*.
4. Exclusive interview with Dr Zaghloul al-Naggar, Cairo, July 2002.
5. Exclusive interview with Mohammed Atta senior, Cairo, July 2002.

CHAPTER TWO

Jihad in Pakistan

'We are going to organise a 500,000 mujahideen force to fight against
the Indians.'

Maulana Masood Azhar, founder of Jaish-e-Mohammed

When Akram Khan Durrani was sworn in as the new chief minister for
Pakistan's North West Frontier Province in November 2002, amongst his first
acts were the banning of the sale of alcohol and laws to end gambling and the
playing of music in all public vehicles. For a country that is, however
reluctantly, part of the US coalition against terrorism, this must have caused
a raised eyebrow or two in Washington.

But like Jam Mir Mohammad Yousaf, who holds the same post in the
neighbouring Baluchistan province to the south, Durrani clearly intends to
press much harder for the implementation of strict shariah laws, including a
ban on cable television and cinemas.

Pakistan's Islamic radicals fared substantially better in the November 2002
elections than many people expected, winning 20 per cent of the vote on a
ticket campaigning for an end to corruption, the establishment of Islamic
shariah law and the removal of American soldiers and law enforcement
officials from Pakistan.

In the areas bordering Afghanistan, religious parties, which explicitly
support the restoration of the Taliban – and implicitly approve of al-Qaeda
and Osama bin Laden – won large majorities. Very quickly they released
hundreds of radical gunmen picked up in the wake of 11 September or
imprisoned after returning defeated from fighting in Afghanistan.

Even before the elections, the government of Baluchistan issued a letter to
the public prosecutors in the four anti-terrorist courts in the province

withdrawing cases against over 100 activists of religious parties. This allowed many of them to be nominated for office without the threat of criminal charges hanging over them.

Within weeks this was followed by reports from Pakistan that suicide squads were being trained in the country to hit targets in Afghanistan. The Pakistani government denied the presence of such training camps, but privately some officials in the intelligence community and Interior Ministry supported the claims.

Respected Associated Press reporter Kathy Gannon interviewed the nephew of Maulvi Abdul Kabir, the Taliban's third in command, who said camps were located in Bajour and Mansehra, both remote towns in the North West Frontier where the central government's influence is limited.[1]

During two weeks of training, would-be bombers are told by Arab instructors that they are waging war on the Jews and 'will go straight to Heaven and their family will get $50,000', Gannon reported Kabir's nephew as telling her. And to illustrate that the stories are more than idle speculation, in November 2002 Afghani forces captured several men in Kabul, including an Iraqi, who had trained at a camp for suicide missions in Pakistan.

This new political force in Pakistan has complicated an already very complex situation, which sees the country torn between national support from the president and the army for American foreign policy in the war against terror, and the close affinity felt by many Pakistanis for their co-religionists – and often close kin – in neighbouring Afghanistan. Strong suspicions that elements within the ISI, the military-based intelligence service, continue to sympathise with the Taliban and al-Qaeda remnants will not go away.

It is often forgotten that Pakistan is one of only two countries in the world – the other is Israel – that was established on the basis of religion. Pakistan – founded out of the wreckage of post-Imperial India in 1947 as a refuge for Muslims – has no clear ethnic or even geographical unity, made up as it is of Punjabis, Sindhis, Kashmiris, Baluchis, Pukhtuns and numerous other smaller ethnic groups.

Even geographically it is fragmented. Part of the Punjab is in India, part in Pakistan. Kashmir is divided likewise. Baluchistan is divided between Pakistan and Iran. And most Pukhtuns rightly assert that the Durrand Line, drawn up under gunfire a century ago to divide British India from wild Afghanistan, cuts right through their traditional and historic heartland.

Peshawar, now the capital of Pakistan's North West Frontier, was once an Afghan town until captured by the British in the nineteenth century and held by a series of outlying hilltop forts. Even before the early 1980s, when the first of several million Afghan refugees began arriving to escape the fighting following the Russian invasion, Peshawar retained its character as a frontier city. It was easy to spot Afghan tribesmen in the old bazaar and huge numbers of Afghani nomads arrived each summer to trade and graze their herds.

During the war against the Russians, Peshawar became the centre of resistance to communism. Competing Afghan warlords mixed uneasily with British and American Special Forces advisers and Pakistani Army officials. Intelligence agencies of a dozen different nations operated out of clandestine buildings, dispersing gold and weapons, the lingua franca of the border tribes. In tribal towns such as Darra Adam Khel and Landi Kotal near the Khyber Pass, hundreds were employed in the manufacture of high-quality copies of Russian assault rifles, pistols and rocket launchers. Afghani and Arab *mujahideen* were taught by Western military personnel to fire sophisticated Stinger and Blowpipe missiles against Russian Hind helicopters and turned the unending mountain areas into a hell for Russian conscripts. Slowly at first, and then in their hundreds and thousands, Arab volunteers began to arrive, anxious to fight against the godless communists in Kabul.

Afghanistan was a proxy war, the final act of the Cold War, designed to bleed the Russians dry. After they retired, bloodied and broken in 1989, within months the Soviet Union collapsed in on itself. In the West the military strategists chalked it up as a famous victory. By making use of the renowned warrior qualities of the Afghan tribesmen – men who would march all day at high altitude in threadbare clothing and shoes made from car tyres, sustained by little more than dried fruit and the odd crust of bread – the West had brought down its oldest enemy.

As the advisers packed up and left for home, little thought was given in Washington or London to the legacy left behind or to the new social forces stirred up in the wake of the war. While the West congratulated itself, the young Arabs who had fought with gusto alongside the Afghans claimed the victory for Islam. They too had raised millions of dollars from governments and wealthy benefactors in the Gulf, had taken part in the fiercest battles and honed their religious beliefs in the heat of war. Was it not like the early days of the Prophet Mohammed?

For Arabs who for a generation had experienced a succession of defeats at the hands of Israel, it was also the first great victory in their lifetime, harking back to a time when their forebears, under the banner of Islam, had been a force in the world. It is not surprising that out of this morass would emerge a new kind of militant Islam, given form by the warrior traditions of Pukhtuns in Afghanistan and the austere version of Islam followed by many of the Arabs who had come from Saudi Arabia, Yemen and Egypt.

The influx of militant Arabs into the North West Frontier, and the money they brought with them through direct grants from Gulf States and the rapidly expanding network of Islamic charities, fuelled the growth of *madrassas* – religious schools that teach a narrow and often sectarian syllabus centred on the Koran. No reliable figures exist for the total number of madrassas in Pakistan, but it is clear that there has been a massive growth.

At the time of Partition in 1947 there were 137 registered madrassas in Pakistan. Since then this number has risen to around 10,000, with as many as 1.5 million pupils attending classes for at least short periods.[2] This figure excludes another 25,000 unregistered madrassas. Most are boys and young men aged between 5 and 18 years old. Ministry of Religious Affairs officials estimate that 10 to 15 per cent of the madrassas may have links with sectarian militancy or international terrorism, although figures are very unreliable.

During the war against the Soviet Union, the madrassas, particularly the Deobandi seminaries in the Pukhtun areas bordering Afghanistan, proved to be excellent recruiting grounds for mujahideen fighters.[3] It was from these same seminaries that the future leadership of the Taliban emerged in 1995–6, supported at that time by the Pakistani military. As Afghanistan descended into chaos under the competing claims of rival warlords, the Taliban appeared to be a strong power, capable of uniting the rival Pushto-speaking factions into a force that could dominate the country.

Two kinds of madrassas took part in the Afghan jihad. The first, such as the Jamaat-e-Islami's (JI) Rabita madrassa, produced literature, mobilised public opinion and recruited and trained volunteers.

The second kind were more independent and encouraged volunteers to travel to Afghanistan to fight. Many were linked to the Jamiat-e-Ulema Islam (JUI). Both networks were financed from abroad, with the ISI controlling access to funds. The target of their vitriol was not confined to the Soviet Union, but also included sectarian rivals within Pakistan. Weapons began appearing on the campuses of Pakistani colleges during the 1980s, particularly at Punjab University and the University of Karachi. Mutually antagonistic Sunni and Shia factions, financed by generous donations from Saudi and Iranian sources respectively, also sprang into existence.[4] Some religious activists blamed the US and the ISI, saying they encouraged the formation of sectarian Sunni madrassas to counteract the influence of the 1979 revolution in neighbouring Iran.

Undoubtedly the militants did receive educational support from the West. The University of Nebraska-Omaha, for example, received $51 million from the US government between 1984 and 1994 to produce special textbooks in Dari and Pushto, which extolled jihadi values and militant training. More than 13 million were distributed around Afghan refugee camps and Pakistani madrassas. They were only replaced by non-fundamentalist textbooks in Afghanistan in March 2002.[5]

The madrassas are effective fundraisers, accumulating more than $1 billion a year within Pakistan from donations alone and further income from lands, shops and other investments. Little, if any, of this fundraising is monitored by the central government. When the Musharraf government attempted to regulate madrassa finances in the wake of 11 September, Mufti Usman Yar Khan, leader of one of the largest schools in Karachi said:

> If a person who has donated even a rupee to the madrassa questions us, I will open up my books to him. But the government has done nothing at all to facilitate the functioning of madrassas, nothing to help us. Why should it now come in and question us?[6]

Khan was not strictly correct in suggesting the Pakistani government had not funded madrassas. In 1980 the government of General Zia ul-Haq identified 100 madrassas that were to receive religious donations (*zakat*), most of which were Deobandi, based in the North West Frontier and actively involved in supporting the Afghan jihad.[7]

While much of the funding came from the governments of Saudi Arabia, Iran, Iraq, Libya and Kuwait, even UK-based charities are involved in raising funds, with one report stating that as much as £5 million a year is raised through collection boxes in British mosques.[8] Much of this money is transferred using the informal *hawala* banking system, which relies on close personal ties. Money is made available in one country on the word of another person abroad. The principals meet regularly to settle their books. The advantage of this system is that it allows funds to be moved rapidly without leaving any paper trail. For this reason it has created a headache for banking regulators trying to stop the flow of funds to militant organisations.

Despite General Musharraf's stated intention of reining in the influence of the madrassas after he came to power in a military coup in October 1999, his efforts have been hamstrung by the regime's reliance on jihad volunteers to fight in Kashmir, where Pakistan and India have been involved in a dispute ever since the partition of India. The two countries have fought three wars over Kashmir and in 2002 came close to a nuclear showdown, with more than one million troops mobilised on both sides of the border. The army itself has been divided over the question of how far it should reduce the power of the Islamic militants.[9]

In reality the regime cannot afford to take on the militants: one estimate is that there are 700 militant madrassas in the Punjab alone and a further 120 in the North West Frontier. The weakness of central government was clearly illustrated in October 2001 when Sufi Mohammed, leader of the now-banned Tehrik Nifaz-e-Shariah, crossed the border into Afghanistan with up to 10,000 volunteers to fight alongside the Taliban against US forces. Many of these volunteers, some armed only with swords or ancient bolt-action rifles, were later killed at Kunduz in northern Afghanistan or suffered for months in the prisons of Afghani warlords who held them captive while extorting a ransom from their families. Sufi Mohammed was himself sued in the courts in Lahore for misleading his supporters and later arrested and sentenced to seven years in prison, possibly saving him from a worse fate at the hands of his erstwhile supporters.

The much-trumpeted closure of madrassas, which the government announced in January 2002, also proved to be temporary. Leaders were put under house arrest and the doors of madrassas were sealed. But most militants were arrested under three-month detention warrants and then released after giving courts assurances of good behaviour. Freezing bank accounts of militant organisations also had little impact as most had been cleared out weeks before. The accounts of Jaish-e-Mohammed (JEM), one of the most militant jihadi organisations, for example, contained only $15, while two accounts of the Harakut-ul-Mujahideen (HUM) contained little more than $50.[10]

As well as finance from Arab countries, thousands of Arabs have also joined the madrassas as students, many of them known militants who did not dare to return home after the war ended in Afghanistan for fear of being arrested. Estimates of the number of foreigners involved range up to 35,000, half of whom are Arabs, while the rest come from Central Asia, Bangladesh, Indonesia and even some, like the so-called 'American Taliban' John Walker Lindh, who are converts from Western countries. They are concentrated around the more extreme Deobandi or Ahle Hadith sects and have tended not to mix with local communities, preferring to live in their own enclaves. Some were expelled in March 2002 and others have drifted away under their own steam, but many remain. The arrest of al-Qaeda leader Abu Zubaydah in Faisalabad in the same month alerted many that their time in the country was coming to an end.

In November 2001, the government also announced a new curriculum for 'model' madrassas, which involved the introduction of tuition in English, maths, social studies and elementary science, as well as computer science, economics, political science, and law for older students. Only limited progress has been made, however, with most madrassas making it clear that they will not countenance the introduction of secular or atheistic views. According to the International Crisis Group:

> It appears that the clergy's defiance will prevail. Instead of taking strong action and laying down a clear legal framework, the Musharraf government is dithering. Its policy is incoherent and it has displayed a lack of will to introduce any law that might antagonise the clergy.[11]

The huge growth in the number of madrassa students has fuelled the expansion of the so-called jihadi organisations. Most important of these is the now-outlawed Markaz ad Dawa wal Irshad organisation and its armed wing, Lashkar-e-Toiba (LET) – Army of the Righteous – whose members have fought in both Afghanistan and in Kashmir.[12] Its guerrillas were responsible, for example, for the attack on the Indian parliament on 13 December 2001, which came close to killing senior members of the government and provoking a nuclear war between India and Pakistan.

Markaz was formed in 1989, directly under the influence of two academics, one of whom, Palestinian-born Sheikh Abdullah Azzam, was Osama bin Laden's mentor and inspirer. Bin Laden himself was a major financial contributor to the organisation and Markaz is in many ways a Pakistani version of al-Qaeda. Until 1992, when he was banned from travelling and staying in Pakistan, bin Laden regularly attended rallies at its 190-acre campus at Muridke, 45 kilometres from Lahore. Bin Laden reportedly gave 10 million Pakistani rupees to finance a huge mosque and guest house within the compound.

Both Ramzi Yousef, who helped plan the first attack on the World Trade Center in 1993, and Mir Aimal Kansi, who was executed in America in November 2002 after being convicted of killing two CIA officers outside the organisation's Langley headquarters, also in 1993, stayed at the guest house while on the run.

LET volunteers go to great lengths to disguise their real names, and, like many fundamentalist organisations, they use *kunyahs*, the Arabic pseudonyms adopted from the names of the Companions of the Prophet and later Islamic heroes. Bin Laden himself is referred to by members of the organisation as 'Sheikh Abu Abdullah'. LET volunteers neither shave nor cut their hair and they are taught to kill ritualistically, by beheading or slitting of the throat. About 80 per cent of its members are thought to originate from outside Pakistan.

Like al-Qaeda, Markaz is opposed to democracy and is critical of the presence of US troops on Saudi soil. It sees Hindus and Jews as the opponents of Pakistan. It describes Kashmir as the gateway to India and foresees the creation of three Muslim homelands: a united Pakistan and Kashmir, another for the Muslims of Northern India and another in the south. It was closely associated with the original signatories to the formation of the International Islamic Front for Jihad Against Jews and Crusaders, formed by bin Laden in 1998. Following 11 September its funds in the United States have been frozen, as have those of charities such as the al-Rashid Trust which funded it. In the UK it was outlawed under the Terrorism Act 2000.

Despite the ban on its activities, Markaz held its annual rally at Patoki, outside Lahore from 1–3 November 2002. Nearly 100,000 people attended, to hear speakers accuse the United States of imposing a war on the Muslims of the world. The organisation also held a jihad conference attended by members of dozens of jihadi groups.

According to the Pakistani newspaper *The News*:

> The Lashkar [LET] operates six private military training camps in Pakistan and Azad Kashmir where several thousands of cadre are given both military and religious education . . . With more than 2,200 unit offices across the country and over two dozen launching

camps along the Line of Control, the Lashkar boasts of the biggest jihadi network in Pakistan . . . The followers of Lashkar come from all walks of life, from the defence and nuclear establishment, to industrial labourers.[13]

Another organisation on the periphery of the International Islamic Front for Jihad Against Jews and Crusaders was the Pakistan-based organisation, the Harkat-ul-Mujahideen, also designated by the US State Department as a Foreign Terrorist Organisation. According to the US State Department, it 'continues to be active in Pakistan without discouragement by the government of Pakistan'. Members of the group were associated with the hijacking in December 1999 of an Air India flight that resulted in the release from an Indian jail of former HUM leader Maulana Masood Azhar and the British-born militant Omar Sheikh.[14] HUM has several thousand supporters in Pakistan and Kashmir, including a number of Afghan and Arab veterans, and until the Taliban was defeated it ran training camps in eastern Afghanistan. A Kashmiri group calling itself al-Faran, which kidnapped and executed five tourists in 1995, is thought to be a cover name for HUM.

Even before he was captured by India in 1994, Azhar had very close connections with al-Qaeda and with the Taliban leader Mullah Omar, and is known to have played a role in helping Somali militants attack US Marines in 1993 in an incident later portrayed in the Hollywood movie *Black Hawk Down*. He was also involved in the training of militants in Yemen. When he was released from Indian custody in exchange for 154 hijacked Indian hostages in December 1999, Azhar decided to make a clean break with HUM and align himself clearly with Osama bin Laden.[15] Amidst bitterness from some of his former comrades, in February 2000 he went to the Binori mosque in Karachi and announced the formation of Jaish-e-Mohammed to fight primarily against India and the United States. The Binori Town complex of this Deobandi seminary is a centre for those who support the Taliban. For months afterwards members of the new organisation and the HUM feuded with each other over money, property and influence.

The choice of the Binori mosque to announce the formation of JEM was significant. It is one of the largest in Pakistan and promotes a hard-line form of Deobandi Sunni Islam, which is particularly anti-Shia. Since its formation in 1951, the mosque has been in the forefront of the anti-Shia movement in Pakistan and is a base for the sectarian Sipah-e-Sahaba organisation.[16] In January 2001 *The Times* in London reported that over 300 Muslim clerics had gathered at the mosque and declared that bin Laden was a great Muslim warrior whose protection was a religious duty for all Muslims.[17] It trains up to 3,500 students at a time in its madrassa, many of them from Afghanistan and the Federally Administered Tribal Areas (FATA) along the border of Pakistan. Hundreds more students have been recruited from Africa, the Philippines and Malaysia.

JEM quickly made its mark, planting bombs in Indian Kashmir, which killed dozens of people, and claiming responsibility for the outrageous attacks on the Jammu and Kashmir Legislative Assembly on 1 October 2001, on the Indian parliament on 13 December 2001, as well as an attack on Indian Army barracks in Srinagar on Christmas Day 2000. The suicide bomber for this latter attack, Asif Sadiq, also known as Mohammed Bilal, was recruited from Birmingham, England, in 1994. He has been eulogised by the JEM as a holy warrior who attained martyrdom in the cause of Islam. Commenting on the attacks, JEM leader Maulana Masood Azhar said that Bilal was fortunate to die in the cause of Islam during the holy month of Ramadan.

As the remnants of al-Qaeda have made their way into Pakistan, the indigenous jihadi organisations have become increasingly involved in following its political and military agenda. While American troops scoured the remote border areas of Afghanistan, the al-Qaeda militants have cooperated with local militants in organising attacks in Pakistan. 'Recent attacks carried out principally by Pakistanis show what officials call visible signs of al-Qaeda involvement: detailed planning, Western targets, and in the two recent attacks, suicide bombing,' noted the *Washington Post*.[18]

The list of murderous incidents aimed at Westerners in Pakistan is now substantial. It includes an attack on a Protestant congregation in the city of Bahawalpur in the Punjab in October 2001 in which 18 people died; a grenade attack on a church in Islamabad's diplomatic quarter in March 2002, which killed five people including the wife and daughter of an American diplomat; a suicide attack on a Navy bus in Karachi in May 2002 which killed 14 people, including 11 French technicians upgrading a Pakistan Navy submarine; several assassination attempts against President Musharraf; a car bomb outside the US Consulate in Karachi in June 2002 which killed 12 people, mostly innocent bystanders; an attack on a missionary school at Murree, outside Islamabad, on 5 August 2002, which killed six people; a grenade attack on a missionary hospital in Taxila, 12 miles from Islamabad, on 9 August which killed four people, including three nurses; and an attack on the Karachi offices of the honorary consul of Macedonia in November 2002.

In the last mentioned attack, the bodies of two men and a woman were found in the rubble of the building, which had been destroyed by a powerful bomb. The victims' hands and feet were bound and they had had their throats cut. The weapon used was still in the body of one of the victims. Police also found slogans written in Urdu on a wall inside the building: 'al-Qaeda Pakistan – Result of Adultery'. Below was a couplet titled 'Message for Infidels'. It read, 'Loyalty will be returned in loyalty, Oppression in Oppression, We are men like you. We will do what you will do.'

This attack may have been in response to an incident that occurred in Macedonia in March 2002. Police opened fire on a vehicle that had tried to crash through a roadblock. They killed seven Pakistanis who were armed with grenades, assault rifles and ammunition. Macedonian officials said the men were involved in planning attacks on embassies in the country.

Pakistani militants, acting in close concert with al-Qaeda, have carried out almost all these attacks. The attacks against Christians, for example, appear to have been the work of JEM. Two men from the organisation were arrested in Karachi in August 2002 in the process of planning yet another attack. They were in possession of maps and plans showing places of worship and foreign establishments. Police said the maps showed exit and entry points for Christian sites in Karachi.

Following the attempt to kill President Musharraf in September 2002, a dozen suspects were arrested. All were members of a group calling itself al-Almi. Seven of those arrested were wanted in relation to the US Consulate blast and for a previous attempt to kill Musharraf on 26 April 2001. According to intelligence sources, al-Almi is yet another manifestation of the HUM, whose fighters were mostly trained at camps in Afghanistan. One of the seven arrested, known as Sharib, was believed to have personally driven a vehicle packed with explosives in the unsuccessful April attack on Musharraf.

Just as worrying to US authorities is the whole question of Pakistan's nuclear arsenal. When the government of Pakistan authorised the army to conduct a series of atomic tests in 1998, the world found out that a new nuclear power had come into existence. India had developed a nuclear weapon in 1974 and today the two rivals face each other armed with nuclear missiles. In 2002 they came very close to a nuclear duel over the continuing infiltration of guerrillas from Pakistan into Indian Kashmir, much of it coordinated by the ISI.

Of particular concern is the clear sympathy felt by sections of the nuclear sector in Pakistan for bin Laden and for jihad. In October 2001, two senior Pakistani nuclear scientists were taken into custody at America's behest after reports surfaced that they had crossed into Afghanistan where they had been in touch with Osama bin Laden.

Sultan Bashiruddin Mahmood and Chaudhry Abdul Majeed had both worked for the Pakistan Atomic Energy Commission and had helped Pakistan become a nuclear power. Mahmood had retired in 1999, strongly opposing moves for the country to sign up the Comprehensive Test Ban Treaty. He dedicated himself full time to creating a welfare agency called Ummah Tameer-e-Nau (TeN) – Reconstruction of the Muslim Nation – which delivered aid to Afghanistan and another organisation called the Holy Koran Foundation. Funding came partly from the now-outlawed al-Rashid Trust.

Mahmood, who said he had gone to Afghanistan to deliver blankets and humanitarian aid, was questioned over his close relationship with the Taliban leader, Mullah Omar, and with bin Laden, whom he met on at least one occasion. The Tameer-e-Nau organisation had an office in Kabul and appeared to have been very active in the country. According to a 21-page document given to Bloomberg News, Mahmood had brought together a group of consultants to prepare 'feasibility reports, project planning and implementation in nuclear and non-nuclear fields'.

He told his friend Faratullah Baber in Pakistan that he had gone to Afghanistan after the start of the American bombing to expand the activities of TeN. He said he had been very impressed by the accuracy of the American bombing. 'In the hills above the flour mill in Kandahar which TeN had built, they had a small antenna which they used to keep in contact with the office in Kabul. Mahmood said that the bombers had knocked it over, without damaging the main installation.'[19]

By Western norms, Mahmood has an unusual attitude towards science, based almost entirely on the Koran. He believes that physical forces and metaphysical forces are somehow linked. He believes in *djinns* – a being or spirit in Muslim belief that can assume human or animal form – and says that the correct science could make use of their energy for humans. He also wrote in his book *Cosmology and Human Destiny* about the ways in which sunspots can affect life on earth. Heavy sunspot activity, he argued, had coincided with the French Revolution, the American Declaration of Independence, the Russian Revolution and both world wars. According to his calculations, the year 2002 was likely to be a year of maximum sunspot activity. This in turn would lead to upheaval, particularly on the Indian subcontinent, with the possibility of nuclear exchanges.[20]

Mahmood was strongly suspected of having offered Osama the expertise to build some kind of 'dirty' bomb – made up of a conventional core of explosives, around which would be packed radioactive material. The explosion would not be nuclear, but deadly radioactive dust and debris could be spread over a wide area, rendering it uninhabitable for a considerable length of time.

After several weeks in custody, Mahmood was released following a suspected heart attack. He was arrested again and then released to house arrest, where he remains. Despite claims by bin Laden that he had acquired some kind of atomic weapon, no evidence has been found to date to substantiate his claim. But, in January 2003, British intelligence agencies confirmed to the BBC that al-Qaeda had succeeded in making a crude 'dirty bomb'.

In the aftermath of 11 September, the creeping Talibanisation of Pakistan has thrown the country into chaos. While the war against the Russians was going well, no one – particularly in the West – cared about the radicalism of Arabs and Afghans fighting jihad. They were positively encouraged. The Taliban was strongly supported by the Pakistan military.

In May 2000, General Musharraf spoke for the first time of his reasons for continuing to support the Taliban. Considering the demographic and geographic pattern of ethnic Pukhtuns, who make up 40 per cent of Afghanistan's population of 20 million, and are the second largest ethnic group in Pakistan after Punjabis, it was, he said, in Pakistan's national interests to continue supporting them.

It would also give Pakistan 'Islamic depth' by making Afghanistan a gateway to the external trade of the Central Asian republics. The Taliban had brought peace to the country and disarmed the warring factions, he said, although his speeches were strongly criticised by the former King Zahir Shah in Rome and by the Northern Alliance, the main opposition to the Taliban, which is largely made up of Tajiks and other non-Pukhtun ethnic groups.

This policy only changed in the aftermath of 11 September. Within 48 hours Musharraf withdrew military advisers from Afghanistan, ordered the ISI to close down its operations there and offered his full cooperation to the Americans. But by then the Islamic jihadists had become a force in the land.

A fire at a Pakistani government building in Islamabad on 15 January 2002 illustrated that there were still supporters of the jihadists in central government. The fire broke out on the building's sixteenth floor in the middle of the night, in a section of the Interior Ministry that kept records of gun licences, as well as sensitive files on militant Islamic organisations. Another fire in two army offices in Rawalpindi on 10 October 2001 destroyed records of the training and budget departments. The fires appear to have been designed to destroy information that some Pakistani officials did not want the United States to see.

Developments since 11 September have created an uncomfortable situation for the Pakistani authorities. Under American pressure they have been forced to send troops into the tribal areas for the first time in many years. Normally these areas in western Pakistan along the border with Afghanistan are strictly off-limits to the military. The Pukhtuns jealously guard their autonomy – in reality it is a form of independence, with separate legal and administrative systems to the rest of Pakistan – and have not taken kindly to troops arriving in large numbers, sometimes accompanied by Alliance Special Forces troops.

There were dozens of armed incidents in these areas in 2002. In one incident ten Pakistani soldiers were killed when they tried to arrest a group of suspected al-Qaeda guerrillas who had taken refuge in a Pukhtun village. The local law, known as *Pukhtunwali*, imposes strict duties of protection of guests on all Pukhtuns. When Arab fighters arrived from over the border in Afghanistan fleeing from the US attacks, no Pukhtun clan could, therefore, possibly refuse to offer support without severe consequences.

Many of the fighters relocated to Kashmir, where it is hard for outsiders to travel without protection from the army. Others moved on quickly to the cities of the Punjab and Sindh in the hope of getting out of the country to a safer haven. In the meantime, they have built up a strong network of supporters, based around the mosques, who have tried to hide them until they can be moved. Pakistan has acted strongly to try and break these networks, handing over almost 500 arrested militants to the Americans, but they are still very strong and continue to prove embarrassing for General Musharraf and the army leadership.

NOTES

1. Kathy Gannon, 'Al-Qaida Suicide Teams Train in Pakistan', Associated Press, 12 December 2002.
2. International Crisis Group, 'Pakistan: Madrassas, Extremism and the Military', *Asia Report* No. 36, July 2002, p. 2.
3. Deoband, like Bareili, which gives its name to the other Sunni branch of madrassas, is a town in Uttar Pradesh (now in India) where these sects emerged in opposition to the British Raj in the nineteenth century. In outlook they are similar to the Saudi Arabia Wahhabis.
4. Ali is the central figure at the origin of the Shia/Sunni split, which occurred in the decades immediately following the death of the Prophet in 632. Sunnis regard Mohammed's cousin, Ali, as the fourth and last of the 'rightly guided caliphs' (successors to Mohammed as leader of the Muslims), following on from Abu Bakr 632–4, Umar 634–44 and Uthman 644–56. Shias feel that Ali should have been the first caliph and the caliphate should pass down only to direct descendants of Mohammed via Ali and his wife Fatima (who was Mohammed's daughter).
5. Joe Stephens and David B. Ottaway, 'The ABCs of Jihad in Afghanistan', *The Washington Post*, 23 March 2002.
6. Mufti Usman Yar Khan interviewed by Tehmina Ahmed, *Newsline* (Karachi), January 2002.
7. Quoted in ICG *Asia Report*, No. 36, p. 15.
8. Shrabani Basu, 'Kashmir's hidden war chest in Britain', *The Telegraph* (Calcutta), 10 June 2002, p. 1.
9. Lt Gen. Imtiaz Shaheen, who was Corps Commander, 11 Corps, at Peshawar, strongly criticised the army's support for the terrorist activities of the Taliban and bin Laden at a conference of Corps Commanders in March 2001. A month later he was transferred to Rawalpindi. See *Far East Economic Review*, 26 April 2001.
10. ICG, *Asia Report*, No. 36, p. 22.
11. *Ibid.*, p. 27.
12. In an effort to avoid the consequences of a legal ban on its activities, Markaz ad Dawa wal Irshad changed its name to Jamaat Ud Dawa and stated it had broken all links with its armed wing, Lashkar-e-Toiba. Its leader, Professor Hafiz Mohammad Saeed, was arrested twice, but released in November 2002.
13. *The News*, 22 April 2001.
14. Omar Saeed Sheikh is a British-educated Muslim who kidnapped five Westerners

in India in an attempt to bargain them for the freedom of Azhar. See below, Chapter Three.

15. 'Asia Overview', *Patterns of Global Terrorism, 2000*, US Department of State, April 2001.

16. The Sipah-e-Sahaba (Soldiers of the Prophet's Companions) is an extremist Sunni organisation that has been at the centre of a vicious feud with Shias in Karachi, resulting in hundreds of deaths. JEM leader Maulana Masood Azhar is also a senior member of the organisation.

17. *The Times*, 17 January 2001.

18. 'Al-Qaeda tied to attacks in Pakistan Cities', *Washington Post*, 30 May 2002.

19. Interview with Faratullah Baber in Pakistan, February 2002.

20. Sultan Bashiruddin Mahmood, *Cosmology and Human Destiny: Impact of Sunspots on Earthly Events – Our Past and Future* (Islamabad, Holy Koran Foundation, 1998).

CHAPTER THREE

Omar Sheikh – The Deadly Apprentice

'They initially planned a "stick 'em up and grab 'em approach".
I thought that charm was a better idea.'

Omar Sheikh

Just inside London's North Circular Road at Snaresbrook, where the outer reaches of the East End give way at last to the genteel villages of Epping Forest, is a fee-paying school of 1,100 pupils that counts among its former students the England cricket captain Nasser Hussain and the Manchester United midfielder Quinton Fortune.

The Forest School, founded in 1834, is proud of its sporting traditions. It also does well in exam league tables and exudes a quiet respectability. Many of its pupils come from the families of successful Asian entrepreneurs in the area.

One boy who was expected to do particularly well when he left to study at the London School of Economics (LSE) ten years ago was Ahmed Omar Saeed Sheikh – better known as Omar Sheikh. He was not too good at orthodox sports – he preferred arm wrestling in pubs – but he was bright enough to have earned A-grade passes at A-level in maths and economics.

All who have met him speak of his charm, his humour, his good looks. His former tutor in economics, George Paynter, remembers: 'He was pleasant and communicative, had a jolly good brain and was a willing and capable student.'

A decade later, 28-year-old Sheikh was on trial for his life in a top-security Pakistani prison, imprisoned with three other men in a cage, accused of involvement in the kidnapping and particularly cruel murder of the American journalist Daniel Pearl.

The high, spacious courtroom was divided in two: one part for the four prisoners in their metal cage, the other for court officials. Defending lawyers had their thumbprints checked by a computer. No journalists or members of the public were allowed in. Outside, up to 200 armed police stood guard.

Sheikh came to court each day wearing white shalwar kameez, his glasses and trimmed beard giving him a studious look. He tried both to charm and to intimidate those around him. He regularly objected to the court proceedings, saying they were based on English law and that he wanted to be tried under Islamic shariah law. 'I don't accept this English court. I should be tried under shariah law,' he shouted at the judge, Arshad Noor Khan.

At the same time he exhibited the charm that had enabled him effortlessly to entrap at least half a dozen Westerners, in Pearl's case leading to murder. 'He is a nice man. He makes no complaints. He is very well behaved,' said Amanullah Niazi, a senior official at Karachi Central Prison.

Sheikh pleaded not guilty to the Pearl charges, but shouted out to reporters during one of his court appearances that he was behind other crimes, including the bombing of the Kashmir parliament in October 2001; the attack on the Indian parliament in December 2001, which almost resulted in war between India and Pakistan; the kidnapping of Indian businessmen for ransom; and the attack on the American Cultural Center in Calcutta in January 2001.

Both the Americans and the British would like to interrogate Sheikh, who is wanted in the United States for his kidnapping in 1994 of an American citizen, as well as for conspiracy to commit hostage taking in relation to Pearl.

But the real story is unlikely ever to be told in court. For Sheikh is no ordinary terrorist, but a man who has connections that reach high into Pakistan's military and intelligence elite and into the innermost circles of Osama bin Laden and the al-Qaeda organisation and the planners of the 11 September attacks on America.

His use of charm, intelligence and brutality to achieve his ideological ends draws an obvious comparison with Carlos the Jackal – the glamorous Venezuelan-born terrorist Ilich Ramirez Sanchez, who played cat-and-mouse with Western governments in the 1970s when Sheikh was a small boy at an east London primary school.

Most people in Britain had never heard of Sheikh until after the attacks on the World Trade Center and the Pentagon. His name had been published in the British press, but no one had closely followed the kidnappings for which he was arrested in India in 1994. He had never been tried for those crimes and the only reports were about his arrest. For the next five years he had been forgotten, not even noticed when he was freed in exchange for 154 passengers on a hijacked Indian Air jet in December 1999.

The first inkling that Sheikh had not given up his life as a committed mujahid came in August 2001 when it emerged in India that the British authorities were asking for legal assistance to try to find a man called Omar Sheikh for questioning. Police in Britain were known to be worried about him, saying in private that, although almost unknown to the Western public, this Londoner was considered to be a potential leader of the Islamic fundamentalist movement.

It was the start of what was to become a tumultuous year for this clever young man who, uniquely among the leading members of al-Qaeda and its closest supporters, was brought up to be an English gentleman.

In 1968, a young Pakistani businessman called Saeed Ahmed Sheikh and his wife Qaissia left the village of Dhoka Mandi near Lahore and travelled to Britain, where they settled in Wanstead, one of east London's more leafy suburbs. Five years later, on 23 December 1973, their son Omar was born at nearby Whipps Cross hospital. Later they had another son, Awais, and a daughter, Hajira.

After attending Nightingale Primary School in Wanstead, Omar transferred to the £8,000-a-year Forest School, a ten-minute bus ride away, where he studied until he was thirteen. In 1987, his father sold up his business in London and decided to move the family back to Pakistan. Some say it was because he thought his children would have a more moral upbringing.

The family semi in Wanstead was rented out and Omar Sheikh went to live with his grandparents on Ravi Road in Lahore. He was sent to Aitchison College, a prestigious school favoured by Pakistan's elite, but he left after only two years. 'He was a violent person, into boxing,' says Syed Ali Dayan Hasan, who studied with him. Hasan says Sheikh was expelled for beating up fellow pupils, but Sheikh has claimed it was because he failed his higher secondary exam.

In Pakistan, Sheikh's father and three relatives had invested about £250,000 in a business, Crystal Chemical Factory Ltd. But the company failed and Sheikh's father decided to return to Britain in December 1989. Back in east London, he started Perfect Fashion, an import–export business that still exists today in a grimy Commercial Road shopfront in London's East End garment district.

By December 1990 Sheikh had been called back from Pakistan and was once again at Forest School, studying for his A-levels and applying for admission to the LSE, where he was accepted to read applied mathematics, statistical theory, economics and social psychology. Having matured into a powerfully built young man, he relaxed through arm wrestling, a sport that thrives in a network of pubs. He even attended the 'world championships' in Geneva in 1992 as part of the 17-strong British team.

'He was a very nice guy, well mannered and educated,' recalls David Shead, head referee of the European Arm Wrestling Federation. 'He liked a joke and always had a bit of nerve. Sheikh never won any titles, but competed for a year or two.'

Shead remembers Sheikh turning up for an arm-wrestling match with a fierce former convict known simply as Mr X. 'Mr X always wore dark glasses and on the day Omar showed up for the match, he too was wearing the same kind of glasses. He was trying to psych him out, to get an edge and to have a laugh at the other guy's expense,' says Shead.

But he was also apparently a caring young man. In 1992 a man waiting for a train at Leytonstone tube station in east London lost his balance and fell onto the tracks. The 18-year-old Sheikh jumped down onto the tracks to save him, despite the danger from a train pulling into the station. He received a commendation from London Underground for his selfless act of bravery.

What was it that drove this congenial figure towards terrorism? The first clue came in October 2001 when Sheikh's confessional diary was discovered among forgotten legal papers in a courthouse near Delhi. The 35-page diary, written in neat longhand in prison after he was shot in an attempted kidnapping in India in 1994, explains in a matter-of-fact manner how he turned his back on his comfortable middle-class existence in Britain at the age of 20 to join a Pakistan-based organisation that supported bin Laden and dedicated himself to a jihad against the 'corrupt' West.

Showing a complete lack of conscience, Sheikh sets out in black and white how he kidnapped gullible Western backpackers in India by offering to take them to a fanciful feudal village that he had inherited from an uncle. 'It seems amazing that the story was greeted with such credible enthusiasm. But the newly arrived traveller to India yearns to hear extraordinary stories which will increase his insight into this strange and colourful culture.'[1]

Later, a confession written by Sheikh or possibly dictated to him by Indian interrogators after his 1994 arrest also emerged. Drier than his diary, it nonetheless filled in many of the gaps.[2]

'During my initial period in the LSE I became a member of the Islamic Society,' Sheikh wrote. 'In November 1992, "Bosnia Week" was observed and various documentary films on Bosnia were shown. One such film, *The Death of a Nation*,[3] shook my heart. The reason being Bosnian Muslims were shown being butchered by the Serbs.'

It was the start of Sheikh's political involvement and radicalisation. He helped organise a student conference on Bosnia and began fundraising. At the end of February 1993, despite his studies, Sheikh accompanied his father on a business trip to Pakistan, taking with him propaganda videos on the war in Bosnia, and made contact with Islamic militants.

On his return he decided to join a 'convoy of mercy' to Bosnia in the Easter holidays. This expedition, said Sheikh, was run by a Pakistani businessman living in Finchley, north London. The six-vehicle convoy took relief material to Bosnia, although Sheikh said it was also organising clandestine support for the Muslim fighters. When he got to Split, near the border between Croatia and Bosnia, he was unable to go on 'due to indisposition and fatigue'. While recuperating he met Abdur Rauf, a Pakistani veteran of the fighting in Afghanistan who had arrived to join the Muslim militia.

Rauf belonged to the Harakut-ul-Ansar (later to become the Harakut-ul-Mujahideen (HUM)), an Islamic guerrilla group. Sensing a potential recruit, Rauf advised Sheikh not to waste his time as an aid worker in Bosnia but to train as a fighter in Pakistan. According to the interrogation document, Rauf suggested that Maulvi Ismail, *Imam* (religious leader) of the Clifton mosque in north London, who had connections to radical Muslims in Pakistan, could help Sheikh to get his father's permission to take up jihad.

Five months later, Sheikh arrived in Lahore 'with zeal and intention to undergo arms training and joining the mujahideen'. He was directed to Miranshah on the Afghan border. 'I saw approximately 20 youths waiting to undergo arms training in Afghanistan. Miranshah is a place where arms/ammunition are easily available and smuggling of arms is also open,' Sheikh told his Indian interrogators.

From here he crossed into Afghanistan to the Khalid bin Waleed training camp where he joined the *Istakbalia* – a 40-day introductory training course.[4] 'The training schedule included morning *namaz* [prayers] in the mosque followed by physical exercise till 0800 hours. After breakfast we were imparted classes in the handling of small and medium firearms, Kalashnikov and Seminov, till lunch, followed by a rest of two hours and then namaz . . . Other exercises included night security duties and firing practice. For the latter we used to get six cartridges each.'[5]

After two weeks, ill health forced Sheikh back to the Lahore home of his uncle, Tariq Sheikh, who 'tried to persuade me to quit arms training and go back to the UK. But I remained adamant and resumed training after a hiatus of ten days'.

He soon joined a special course from September to December 1993. The instructors, Sheikh says in the interrogation document, were from the Pakistan Army's Special Services Group and taught surveillance techniques, disguise, interrogation, secret writing and codes, first aid, making attacks and night ambushes. 'This special training was sort of a city warfare training. Apart from the above-mentioned, weapons training in assault rifle, rocket launcher etc., was also imparted by the same instructors.'

At the end of the course, senior HUM leaders visited the training camp. One of them, Maulana Masood Azhar – who would later visit Sheikh's father during a trip to Britain – asked Sheikh to come to India with him on an important mission. Azhar had been asked by Osama bin Laden to attempt to heal a rift between rival factions of the organisation in Kashmir and he needed to visit Indian territory to carry out his mission. He had done something similar for Osama in 1993 when he had visited Somalia, again in an attempt to bring rival factions together. It was a dangerous undertaking, but Sheikh gave his agreement in principle.

His dual British and Pakistani nationality was a problem, however, as it would make it difficult for him to get an Indian visa. So he returned to Britain in January 1994, starting martial arts classes in Crawley, West Sussex, for a group of Muslims and trying to interest his old friends and classmates in joining the jihad in Afghanistan.

He renewed his British passport and dropped his dual nationality. Finally in March 1994 he got an Indian visa and the following month left for Afghanistan. Azhar had gone on ahead, travelling to New Delhi via Bangladesh on a forged Portuguese passport with the intention of reaching Indian Kashmir to unify two factions fighting the Indian military. But the trip had gone wrong: he had been captured and was now in prison.

Before Sheikh left Britain, Maulana Abdullah of the HUM called him by telephone and told him that he was planning to host a conference of renowned Muslim scholars and leaders of Pakistan to urge Amnesty International to campaign for the release of Azhar. Soon after, probably in June 1994, he was asked by the HUM leadership to spring Azhar from prison.

He was told that several British backpackers had been kidnapped in Kashmir with a view to them being exchanged for Azhar, 'but due to weak planning they had to be released unconditionally'. Sheikh arrived in Pakistan and quickly made his way to the training camps run by HUM close to the eastern Afghan city of Jalalabad where he attended a refresher course and became an instructor on another course for new recruits. After the course was completed, for a while he was given the jokey name 'Britannia Jindabad'. This literally means 'Long Live Britannia', but was clearly an ironic joke in this case.

Sheikh and his new-found comrades struggled to think of a way they could capture Westerners and hold them in exchange for Azhar. One far-fetched idea suggested to Sheikh was that he should join a cruise ship in America and make friends with passengers whom he could later kidnap: 'I smiled at this suggestion because it appeared to be a very funny idea to me.'

Instead they decided to organise a kidnapping in India, either of foreigners or leading members of the BJP, the ruling Hindu nationalist party. Its supporters had been behind the destruction of the beautiful sixteenth-century Babri Masjid mosque in 1992, which had inflamed Muslim opinion across the world. The Hindu nationalists claimed it had been built on a site which was sacred to them and which predated the mosque by several thousand years.

Sheikh was willing to take part in the mission and booked himself a flight in July 1994 via the Gulf. After arriving in Delhi, he checked in to the Holiday Inn with some of the £600 and 20,000 Indian rupees he had been allocated for his mission. There, with several accomplices, he set about his plan.

Sheikh appears to have been something of an ingénue. Instructed to spend his first night in India in a good hotel, he had chosen one of the most expensive in the Indian capital. 'I registered under my own name and gave my passport number,' he wrote. 'The bill was an astounding $210 a night. I did not know I had picked the most expensive hotel in town.'

He quickly met up with an accomplice, Sultan, who explained more about their kidnap mission. 'I asked them what they had in terms of weapons and he said that he had an AK-47 and a couple of pistols. He said that Farooq [another accomplice] had a couple of pistols and some grenades also . . . Later on I learnt that they had come from Kashmir.'

Sheikh continued his narrative: 'Over the next month, every place I visited I analysed from various points of view as a "future conqueror", as I fondly imagined myself to be, as a social scientist, a traveller, noting down the intricacies of a new country and as an introspector. I went to mosques and madrassas and talked about ideas pertaining to jihad.'

Sheikh's somewhat intellectual approach to his task angered his superior, Shah Sahib, the leader of the cell in India: 'He said all my travelling and talking around had probably gotten us exposed already. He said if I didn't pull my socks up he'd send me back. He said until we'd started our mission I ought simply to have stayed in a room and relaxed.'

The gang initially planned what Sheikh described as a 'stick 'em up and grab 'em approach', where they would seize hostages at gunpoint. But under his influence their approach changed. Sheikh preferred to use his middle-class charm to entrap tourists. Shah Sahib told him: 'Your responsibility is the foreigners . . . I'm pursuing the other channels also but the people concerned won't know about you and you won't know about them. Remember, American first priority, then British and French.'

'I sat around cafés, slowly sipping or eating something and gradually developed a knack for opening up conversation,' Sheikh wrote. His first 'catch' was an Israeli, whom he thought would be an ideal hostage. But his arrival at the safe house in Nizamuddin near Delhi late that same night did not bring the reaction he was hoping for. Shah Sahib was furious.

'Shah Sahib gazed at me incredulously, peered out of the window and saw the 6 ft 3 in. hulking Israeli standing there alarmed at seeing so many bearded men sleeping in one room. "You fool," hissed Shah Sahib, "you'll get us all killed. Take him back to his hotel at once and come back in the morning."'

Sheikh returned the confused Israeli to Delhi. The following day he began once again to scour tourist venues for likely victims. Meanwhile, the group had located a safe house in the town of Saharanpur, 200 kilometres east of Delhi. Sheikh was still not convinced that he could talk anyone into coming to the remote house and thought he may have to use strong-arm tactics after all.

This time he refined his technique, pretending to be an 'Indian-blooded British national' and using the story that his uncle had left him a village. One person who had a lucky escape was Briton Trevor Matthews. Matthews later wrote:

> I was one of the first 'Britishers' to strike up a rapport with Mohammed Omar Sheikh soon after my arrival in Delhi in September 1994. I met him in a café in Paharganj and he was a welcome guide to the Old Town on my first afternoon on the subcontinent. Coming from the Essex/London border as I did, Sheikh, or Rohit Sharma as he introduced himself, was charming and intelligent company and invited me to his uncle's village, an offer I was thrilled to accept. However he did not show up at the YMCA two days later as promised so I took it as the kind of encounter that often happens 'on the road'. I went ahead and booked houseboat accommodation and a bus ticket to Kashmir for the following day. Sheikh showed up as I was about to leave and apologised for not being around the previous day. He looked crestfallen when I told him my plans.[6]

Over games of chess, Sheikh was, however, successful in persuading another Briton, Rhys Partridge, to visit his 'uncle's village'. In a van hired by the gang a gun was pulled on the unsuspecting tourist and he was chained up and locked into a room in the safe house. Two further Britons, Myles Croston and Paul Ridout, made the same fateful journey a few weeks later.

'At Saharanpur the door was opened by Siddique. He saw that I was accompanied by two guests and so he immediately called the others to attention, telling them the Maharaja was here. There were Sultan, Salahuddin and Maulana Sahib. The same drama as before happened, except that this time there was an AK-47 in the picture, brandished by Sultan.'

Sheikh was sent out again, this time to find an American. It was 25 October 1994. At a café in Delhi he met Bela Joseph Nuss, an American about to leave India. 'He was a lonely sort of fellow who found in me someone he could talk to,' wrote Sheikh. He invited Nuss to dinner at an Indian family's house, but en route picked up two of his co-conspirators. Nuss got nervous, but before he could do anything Shah Sahib pulled out a pistol with a silencer. They taped his mouth and put a burqa, the all-enveloping women's cloak, over his head to stop any questions at checkpoints.

Nuss was taken to a house in Ghaziabad, separate from the three Britons, and Sheikh prepared letters to be sent to the British and American embassies, the BBC, Voice of America radio station and the Indian prime minister's office, demanding the release of Azhar and five other HUM terrorists held by India. He then went out and bought a Polaroid camera to take pictures of the four prisoners.

'Then I returned to Shah Sahib's. It was going to be a waiting game, said the Big Man [Shah Sahib]. I was forbidden from leaving the house, so I settled myself down to catch up with my Arabic.'

When there was no response to their demands, they decided to send out a further batch of letters. Incredibly, Sheikh decided to hand-deliver a new set of letters to the BBC and the *Hindustan Times* – where he had to make a rapid exit as the public relations manager began to open the letter in his presence.

Two days later, however, the plot fell apart. They decided to visit the house in Ghaziabad where Nuss was being held because he had stopped eating. In a lane nearby two armed policemen challenged them. 'I thought it was a routine patrol and asked what the matter was,' wrote Sheikh. 'The policeman swore at me and tried to drag me to one side by the collar, at which I got furious and started hitting him. The next thing I felt a stinging blow on my back and I looked around to see the other swinging his rifle at me – the comrades had disappeared. I turned towards him and BANG! I felt the anger being drawn out with the blood. I thought it was the end. It was the end . . . of one era and the beginning of another.'

For Sheikh it was the beginning of five years in prison in India without trial. He did not know that shortly before his arrival in Ghaziabad the police had accidentally discovered the hideout while combing the neighbourhood in connection with another case. In the scuffle Sheikh was shot in the shoulder while Shah Sahib and Siddique escaped. After freeing Nuss, the police rushed to the Saharanpur hideout to rescue Croston, Partridge and Ridout. They met with a fusillade of shots in which two policemen and one of the kidnappers were killed.

Omar Sheikh was taken to Ghaziabad hospital for treatment, where he punched a deputy superintendent of police and threatened to track down and kill the constable who had slapped him. He was incarcerated at Meerut Jail, but after he kicked the jail superintendent in November 1998 he was moved to the high-security Tihar Jail in New Delhi, the Uttar Pradesh State Police having categorised him as 'dreaded'.

The 400-acre Tihar Jail is the largest in South Asia and holds 11,000 prisoners in 10 by 8 foot cells. It was here that Sheihk wrote his 35-page account in longhand. He also wrote pen sketches of his associates and a 'rundown' of the events that had led to his arrival in India as a jihadi.

Nowhere in his diary is there even a hint of remorse. The only sign of that came from an interview carried out by an Indian television journalist, Zubair Ahmed, shortly after Sheikh was first arrested. He was seen in a private hospital under heavy armed guard. Ahmed recalls:

> The authorities clearly had no idea who he was. With police permission we filmed an interview at his hospital bed. Sheikh looked

extremely worried and he told me he would give anything to return to life in Britain. Over and over, he repeated he had made a mistake . . . I asked him if he was released, would he go back and tell people in Britain that we Indian Muslims were free to build mosques, say our prayers and work in government offices? He said he would. He appeared repentant, but clearly not enough.[7]

HUM, the organisation of which Sheikh was now a fully fledged member, did not forget about its captured comrades. Once again it decided on a strategy of kidnap. Six Western tourists were captured in the southern Kashmiri hill resort of Pahalgam on 4 July 1995. Two Americans, John Childs and Donald Hutchings, two Britons, Keith Mangan and Paul Wells, a German, Dirk Hasert, and a Norwegian, Hans Christian Ostro, were held by a group called al-Faran, simply a *nom de guerre* for a secret group within HUM. Its members had been trained in Afghanistan by al-Qaeda.

Until this point the Kashmiri fighters had not killed foreigners, but their new alliance with al-Qaeda, which was beginning to emerge as a force in Afghanistan, changed their strategy. Childs managed to escape and gave important information to US investigators. But despite international pressure on the Pakistan government at the time, the remaining prisoners were not freed. Ostro's severed head was found on a mountain path in August 1995 with a note demanding the release within two days of fifteen jailed Islamists, including Omar Sheikh and Azhar. The remaining hostages were probably killed in December 1995 when the group realised their demands were not going to be met. Their bodies have never been recovered.

With part of its senior leadership now in Indian prisons, the HUM grew closer to al-Qaeda, particularly after Osama bin Laden moved his headquarters from Sudan to Afghanistan in May 1996. It continued its operations against India in Kashmir, but began to build links with the Abu Sayyaf group and Moro Islamic Liberation Front in the Philippines and groups in Myanmar (Burma). It also provided weapons training to Chechen fighters in the Caucasus. Despite these actions, HUM remained a legal organisation in the UK until the Terrorism Act passed into law in 2000. Its supporters continued to raise money and even operate a printing press in Britain despite the new laws.

Sheikh's release was to prove as dramatic as his capture. After five years held without trial, he was freed in December 1999 along with Maulana Masood Azhar after militants hijacked an Indian Airlines airbus with hundreds of passengers on board. Flight IC-814 took off from Kathmandu in Nepal just before 5 p.m. on 24 December 1999. The five hijackers, led by Azhar's brother, Ibrahim Azhar, demanded to go to Lahore in Pakistan, which refused landing permission. Instead, it landed at Amritsar in north-west India at 7 p.m. but was denied refuelling and took off again, this time landing at an air force base in Dubai in the Gulf at 1.30 a.m. on Christmas Day.

The hijackers were now demanding the release of 35 prisoners and $200 million in cash. After negotiations with the authorities, some of the passengers were released. The body of Indian national Rupin Katyal, who had been killed ritualistically by having his throat cut while he sat in his seat, was also off-loaded. The same method was later used by the 11 September hijackers and also by the killers of *Wall Street Journal* reporter Daniel Pearl.

The aircraft took off again and landed at Kandahar in southern Afghanistan at 6.30 a.m. where it remained until 31 December. A tense stand-off ensued during which time the Indian authorities agreed to negotiate. In exchange for releasing the remaining 154 passengers the Indian authorities agreed to release Omar Sheikh, Maulana Masood Azhar – ironically, the man Sheikh had originally come to India to free – and Mustaq Ahmed Zargar, another Islamic fundamentalist. The freed passengers returned to Delhi on 1 January 2000 on two special flights.

The captain of IC-814 later told investigators that the hijackers had powerful communications equipment – possibly smuggled on board by sympathisers once the plane had landed in Taliban-controlled Kandahar – and received instructions from an unknown source. They also seemed to have upgraded their weapons, arriving on board armed only with knives, but later brandishing automatic weapons and explosives.

After flying to Kandahar on the same aircraft as the Indian foreign minister Jaswant Singh, who was handling the negotiations with the hijackers, Sheikh, Azhar and Zargar were released into the custody of the Taliban authorities who quickly spirited them away. Taliban militiamen stood guard around the hijacked aircraft armed with Stinger missiles to deter any attempt to storm the plane.

Sheikh later told his Pakistani interrogators, after he had been arrested in connection with the murder of Daniel Pearl, that Osama bin Laden had hosted an *Iftar* party for all three men in Kabul to celebrate the end of the Muslim holy month of Ramadan. 'When he was being interrogated, these were the utterances and admissions made by him, as recorded by the police officers,' said trial prosecutor Raja Qureshi.[8]

Azhar and Sheikh returned to Pakistan where no attempt was made to arrest them, suggesting that the ISI had a role in springing them from prison. Shortly afterwards, Azhar announced the formation of Jaish-e-Mohammed at the Binori mosque in Karachi. Some reports say that Omar Sheikh was appointed deputy leader. Azhar kept up his relations with al-Qaeda and became *Amir* (supreme leader) of the Taliban in Jammu and Kashmir.

Only weeks after Azhar was freed, he was able to make vitriolic speeches to large crowds throughout Pakistan calling for a jihad against the US, Israel and India. The authorities made no attempt to arrest him. Sheikh appears to have fallen out with Azhar at this point, reportedly because he disagreed with Azhar's support for the sectarian, anti-Shia, Sipah-e-Sahaba organisation. Instead, he moved closer to al-Qaeda and reported to Abu Zubaydah, chief of external operations.[9] As far as British and US investigators were concerned he had disappeared, although it is now clear that he began living within the Sheikh family circle in Lahore in the Punjab and that he married and had a child. He appears to have kept little back from his family about his activities and it is inconceivable that the Pakistani authorities did not know where he was.

His apparent disappearance did not stop US investigators from investigating his crimes and in June 2001 a Grand Jury meeting in secret in Washington DC indicted Sheikh for the kidnap of Bela Nuss in Delhi, charging him with hostage taking and conspiracy. In March 2002 he was also charged by a Grand Jury in New Jersey with conspiracy to commit hostage taking, resulting in the death of Daniel Pearl.

In announcing the charges, US Attorney General John Ashcroft said:

> With today's indictments, we begin the process of securing justice for Daniel Pearl and Bela Nuss, solace for their families and vindication for the values they and all civilised people share. The department's investigation of this case is an ongoing one. And we will not rest until we do everything possible to complete an understanding of the entirety of individuals, charging – bringing to justice – the entirety of the individuals involved.[10]

There was no similar indictment in the United Kingdom, which has been conspicuously silent during the whole Omar Sheikh saga. He is even reported to have returned to the UK after being freed by India to visit his family. The failure to deal effectively with Sheikh, who transformed himself from a student activist to a kidnapper and gunman and was promoted into the upper reaches of al-Qaeda on the strength of his intellect, has had far-reaching consequences for the many victims who died or were seriously traumatised by his activities.

When the first reports were broadcast about the kidnapping of Daniel Pearl in January 2002, those who had closely followed Sheikh's career quickly saw his hand in the affair. Confirmation came within a few days when three people arrested over the case, including a cousin of Sheikh, confessed he had provided them with photographs of Pearl to email to news organisations. Sheikh had had a meeting with Pearl in a Rawalpindi hotel and it was from there that the reporter's kidnap in Karachi was set up.

Journalist Asif Faruqi, who worked with Pearl, said the two men had gone to a meeting on 11 January where Pearl told Sheikh that he was working on a story about the 'Shoe Bomber', Richard Reid. Sheikh, who was using the name Bashir, invited Pearl to Karachi where he said he would be introduced to a mullah who knew Reid.

Sheikh followed up the meeting with emails to Pearl drawing him further into the plot. Soon Pearl left for Karachi and on 26 January he disappeared after going to meet a contact. Shortly after his kidnap, the conspirators sent an email from 'kidnapperguy@hotmail.com' declaring that 'The National Movement for the Restoration of Pakistani Sovereignty' had kidnapped him and was holding him in 'very inhuman [*sic*] circumstances', similar to the way that 'Pakistanis and nationals of other sovereign countries were kept in Cuba by the American Army'.[11]

The email also stated that, 'If the Americans keep our countrymen in better conditions we will better the conditions of Mr Pearl and all the other Americans we capture' and demanded that all Pakistani prisoners should be returned to Pakistan and that Afghanistan's Taliban ambassador to Pakistan, Mulla Zaeef [*sic*], who had been captured by the Americans, should be returned. It also demanded that the US government provide F-16 fighter planes to Pakistan or return the money Pakistan had paid for the planes with interest. This referred to a deal that was cancelled when the Pakistan military seized power in October 1999.

Attached to the email were four photographs of Pearl in captivity, one of which showed him in shackles with a gun pointed at his head. A fifth attachment contained a message written in Urdu that restated the same demands.

A second message arrived on 30 January, entitled 'Daniel News' and from the email address 'strangepeoples@hotmail.com'. Besides repeating the demands in the first email, it threatened that Pearl would be executed within 24 hours unless the demands were met. It also warned other American journalists to get out of Pakistan within three days.

There were three attachments to the email: two photographs of Pearl, including one depicting him with a gun pointed at his head; and a restatement of the demands in Urdu.

According to both his Pakistani trial and the US indictment, Sheikh wrote the emails and also passed on pictures of Pearl in captivity to his accomplices. It is now thought that by the time the second email was sent, Pearl was already dead.

Sheikh had left his home in Lahore with his wife and newborn baby four days before the Pearl kidnapping and was now on the run. But he would not stay hidden for long. The Pakistani police were determined to find him and arrested every male member of his immediate and extended family, including his 80-year-old grandfather, to put pressure on the fugitive to surrender.

His uncle, Rauf Ahmed Sheikh, a Pakistan district court judge, told the Daniel Pearl murder trial, held in camera (i.e. the press were denied access) in a high-security prison in Hyderabad,[12] that both he and Sheikh's father, Saeed, were with him when he gave himself up to police on 5 February. In a statement to the court Omar Sheikh claimed he was secretly held for a week so that police would have time to manufacture evidence against him. What is clear is that when he first appeared in court Sheikh shouted out that he had turned himself in to the home secretary of the Punjab, retired Brigadier Ejaz Shah. This contradicted another version of the arrest date given on a visit to America on 12 February by President Musharraf, who announced that police in Lahore had captured him that day.

Brigadier Shah, who had served in the ISI, used to direct the activities of two Islamic terrorist groups fighting in Kashmir. He reportedly passed on the news of Sheikh's surrender to General Mohammad Aziz Khan, chairman of the Joint Chiefs of Staff committee and former head of the ISI section dealing with India and Afghanistan. Khan knew Sheikh personally.

It would appear that the ISI had its own reasons for holding Sheikh for a week before announcing to the world that he was in custody. One thing it would have wanted to do was to make sure that its protégé did not give more away than was absolutely necessary about his relationship with Pakistan's intelligence services. This 'missing week' sheds new light on unsubstantiated Indian reports that Lieutenant General Mahmud Ahmed, director-general of the ISI, had been forced into retirement by the FBI shortly after 11 September, when investigators uncovered credible links between him and Sheikh.

According to these reports, an FBI team established that in early September 2001, Ahmed had instructed Sheikh to transfer $100,000 to Mohammed Atta, leader of the hijackers who crashed into the World Trade Center.

There is a further angle that implicates the ISI. It had strong reasons for tailing Pearl: he was normally based in India, which to the ISI would have been prima facie evidence that he was reporting back to Indian intelligence. When the ISI discovered Pearl was trying to find out who was financing Jaish-e-Mohammed, it was the final straw, according to a source in Karachi. 'He was beginning to get too close to understanding the links between the ISI and the jihadis,' alleged the source. 'Sheikh was their [the ISI's] man and he was brought in to deal with Pearl. The ISI knew everything.'

The Karachi police, who deeply distrust the ISI, leaked details of their interrogation of Sheikh, in which he talked about his ISI connections, to the local press. As a result, ISI operatives broke into the newsroom of *The News*, Pakistan's largest English-language newspaper, in February 2002 in an apparent attempt to prevent publication of a leak in which Sheikh was reported to have said that the ISI helped him to finance, plan and execute the attack on the Indian parliament in December 2001.

The editor of the paper was Shaheen Sehbai, the first local journalist Pearl had contacted when he arrived in Pakistan. Failing to prevent publication of Sheikh's confession, the ISI demanded an apology from Sehbai, who fled to America fearing for his life.

M.J. Gohel of the Asia-Pacific Foundation, a security and terrorism policy assessment group that has been researching Pearl's murder, said: 'Sheikh is a vital key that can open all the doors to the al-Qaeda network, to the links between the Pakistani military intelligence establishment and the terror groups, and can destroy General Musharraf's credibility with Washington. He is a vital piece in the jigsaw and for that reason it is highly unlikely the US will ever be allowed to interrogate him.'

The full story of the kidnapping of Pearl will probably never come to light. What is clear is that Sheikh has for long been very close to the elements within ISI and that it regarded him as an asset. The whole affair has been a setback and embarrassment to Musharraf and has destabilised the country. Small wonder that Musharraf is said to have told Wendy Chamberlain, the American ambassador, that he would rather 'hang Sheikh myself than have him extradited'.[13]

Another intriguing possibility is that Pearl was kidnapped because he was getting close to Khalid Shaikh Mohammed, the main organiser of 11 September and head of al-Qaeda's military committee. Robert Baer, a former CIA case officer in the agency's directorate of operations, says that he spoke to Pearl about Khalid. Baer says that Pearl called him on the day of the 11 September attacks and he gave the journalist all his information on Khalid. The two men, according to Baer, then began working together.[14]

'I was working with Pearl. We had a joint project. Mohammed was the story he was working on, not Richard Reid.'[15] Pearl's paper, the *Wall Street Journal*, strongly denied Baer's claims, but other CIA officers have confirmed it. It had previously been believed that Pearl had gone to Karachi to meet Sheikh Mubarek Ali Gilani, head of the Jamaat-ul-Fuqra (Party of the Poor), which has thousands of supporters around the world, including in the United States. He had been told that Gilani had information on Reid. However, Gilani lives in Lahore, and it does not make sense that he should travel to Karachi, hundreds of miles to the south, to see him.

The trial of Omar Sheikh was an extraordinary affair. He had apparently made a complete confession of his role in the Pearl kidnapping and to several other attacks to the Karachi police once he had been handed over from ISI custody.[16] He later shouted out the same confession from the dock in the courthouse in Lahore. However, he then retracted his confession, forcing Judge Noor Khan to abandon the case and hand it over to another judge while he gave evidence in the new trial about what Sheikh had said from the witness box.

The new judge selected to try Sheikh and three accomplices was Judge Syed Ali Ashraf Shah, sitting in the Anti-Terrorism Court within the precincts of Hyderabad Jail. Under Pakistani law, the recording of the evidence in the case should have lasted no more than a week without adjournment. In fact, the trial dragged on from 5 April until 15 July 2002.

A driver testified that on the day Pearl was kidnapped, the journalist and Sheikh travelled in his taxi and a hotel clerk from the Akbar International Hotel in Rawalpindi identified Sheikh as having met Pearl in Room 411 on 11 January. No evidence was produced linking Sheikh to the murder itself, although an FBI agent from the Computer Analysis Response Team, Ronald Joseph, presented a 50-page report describing the Dell Latitude laptop used by the kidnappers, the emails they sent and the routing they took.

The investigation of the murder continued while the case took place and just before it finished, police arrested several men who led them to the spot where Pearl's dismembered body had been buried. This was on 16 May. Police did not officially identify it using DNA samples until the trial was over, although they knew very quickly that it was the reporter.

The body, cut into ten pieces, was found buried on a plot of land of the Gulzare Nursery in the Gulshan-e-Maymar area of Karachi. There was an improvised shed on the site where it is likely Pearl was held until his murder. The land belonged to the al-Rashid Trust, a charity that, as previously mentioned, has been added to the US watchlist of terrorist organisations because of its financial support for both the Taliban and al-Qaeda. Formed in 1999, it is also closely linked with Jaish-e-Mohammed, the militant Islamist organisation led by Maulana Masood Azhar who regularly writes for its magazine *Zarb-I-Momin* (Force of the True Believer). It raises money in Pakistan and amongst the Pakistani diaspora, particularly in Britain.

One of those taken into custody by police in connection with the discovery of the body was Fazal Karim. Significantly, he said that the group that carried out the ritual murder of Pearl included three men whose fathers were Yemeni and whose mothers came from Baluchistan in south-west Pakistan.[17] This ties in with reports that two of the men killed by police when Ramzi Binalshibh was arrested in September 2002 were of Yemeni descent. The police described one of these men as the killer of Pearl.

In February 2003, *Time* magazine reported that Fazal Karim had named Khalid Shaikh Mohammed as the person who had slit the journalist's throat. The two officials who interrogated Karim told *Time* that when he was asked to identify the three unknown Arabs who had taken part in the killing he pointed to a picture of Khalid and said, 'He was the one who wielded the knife.'[18]

On 21 February, before the trial started, news emerged that a video was circulating on the Internet showing the gruesome killing of Pearl and Sheikh's defence lawyers requested that it be played to the court.[19] At the end of the short video a series of demands are printed, including calls for the release of al-Qaeda prisoners from Camp X-Ray in Cuba, US withdrawal from Afghanistan and a demand for America to supply Pakistan with F-16 jets.

The Arabic verb for slaughter – *dhabaha* – which is used in the Arabic subtitles to the video, is the same one used by the Twin Towers hijackers in a five-page note found in Mohammed Atta's luggage, describing how to kill with a knife any of the passengers who resisted.

Pearl is shown in the video with a black cut-out superimposed around his head to hide the background. Also superimposed onto the background are pictures that appear to be Palestinian women and children killed during the Intifada. It is clear that the video has been edited as, in addition to the extra images, it also carries an Arabic translation of everything Pearl says.

On the video Pearl's words are clearly spoken under duress and appear to have been reordered. He is seen talking about his parents and the fact that the family made trips to Israel, where a street in one town is named after his great-grandfather. He also says that as a result of his own situation he can understand the predicament of al-Qaeda members held at Camp X-Ray in Cuba. Later he says that Americans will not be able to travel easily abroad unless their government changes its policies on the Middle East and Afghanistan.

'We can't be secure, we can't walk around free as long as our government's policies are continuing and we allow them to continue,' he says. His statements are immediately followed by gruesome scenes of decapitation that Rai Bashir, counsel for Sheikh's co-defendants, falsely claimed were faked.

Throughout the trial, Sheikh and his co-defendants shouted insults at witnesses and made obscene gestures at the prosecutors. Rai Bashir also accused the lead prosecutor of blasphemy, an allegation that is tantamount to putting a price on someone's head in Pakistan. Sheikh himself issued a statement during the trial, following the US bombing of a wedding party in Afghanistan:

> Following the barbaric bombardment of a wedding ceremony in Afghanistan in which a number of innocent women and children were killed, and the demolition of houses by Israeli troops in Palestine, which again claimed a number of innocent lives, the Americans should have realised by now that whatever happened on 11 September, not only did they deserve that, but also there is more to come.

As well as condoning the attacks on America, he said that all the evidence presented against him had been fabricated. 'The entire case is a tissue of lies. All the witnesses are police officers, police spies or police touts and agents despite their outward calling.'[20]

There was little surprise when Judge Shah announced the guilty verdicts on 15 July. Police had prepared for a violent backlash in Hyderabad with 500 police and paramilitary rangers patrolling the jail, with a further 2,000 security staff patrolling the city's streets. Sheikh was sentenced to death by hanging and his three co-defendants were sentenced to life imprisonment. None of the defendants, all wearing beards and traditional clothing, showed any reaction to the sentences. The judge said that Sheikh had 'engineered the entire plan of creating a sense of fear nationally and internationally' and was the 'principal offender' who had instructed the co-accused in what to do. Outside, the streets remained calm.

The prisoners' later reaction to the sentences was predictable. Defence lawyer Rai Bashir read out a statement from Sheikh outside the court:

> We will see who dies first – me or the authorities who arranged the death sentence for me. I have been saying before, this entire trial is just a waste of time . . . It is a decisive war between Islam and infidels and everyone is individually proving on which side he is.

His father, Saeed Sheikh, said that the case against his son had been a horrible ordeal and that it highlighted US hypocrisy: 'The jihadis used to be the apple of their eye,' he said, 'now they are rotten apples.'

Threats continued to be made against people involved in the case long after it had finished. On 16 October 2002 nine police officers involved in the investigation were injured by four parcel bombs mailed to their offices. One of the injured officers lost his hand. Jamil Yusuf, who was the last person Pearl interviewed before his abduction, also reported that he had received letters threatening his wife and children. And Raja Qureshi, who prosecuted Sheikh, resigned his post in November 2002, following a series of threats. He is under constant police guard.[21]

At the time of writing Sheikh and his co-defendants have appealed against their sentences. The appeals are unlikely to be heard until after the trial of three other men arrested in connection with the discovery of Pearl's body.

The story of Omar Sheikh clearly illustrates the close connections between the Pakistani jihadis and al-Qaeda. Sheikh's intelligence, his familiarity with Western ways and his willingness to do almost anything to further the cause of jihad, marked him out as someone who was likely to rise to the top. Clearly unimpressed by the fratricidal tendencies within the Pakistani groups, he made a conscious decision to work with al-Qaeda. He had connections with Abu Zubaydah and – through the kidnap of Daniel Pearl – with both Ramzi Binalshibh and Khalid Shaikh Mohammed, three of the organisation's most senior figures. In the background are the more shadowy connections he kept up with the ISI. The privately educated east London schoolboy had come a long way indeed.

NOTES

1. Authors' copy of Omar Sheikh's diary, first published by the *Indian Express*, is quoted extensively in this chapter.

2. 'Ahmad Omar Saeed Sheikh – A trained militant of Harkat-ul-Ansar and a British

National of Pakistani Origin', undated Indian police interrogation report, quoted extensively in this chapter.

3. *Yugoslavia: Death of a Nation,* (1995). Documentary in four parts. Production: Brian Lapping Associates; Coproduction: BBC (UK), Canal+ (France), Discovery Channel (USA), ORF (Austria), VPRO (The Netherlands), RTBF (Belgium), SVT2 (Sweden), NRK (Norway), Danmarks Radio (Denmark) ABC (Australia); Executive producer: Brian Lapping; Narrated by Robin Ellis; Directors: Angus McQueen and Paul Mitchell. This film features a lot of documentary footage and interviews with most of the leading figures in the Bosnian conflict. The directors' central theme is that the Serbs, rather than the Slovenes, Croats or Muslims, were the principal secessionists.

4. Khalid bin Waleed was the fiercest military commander in the history of Islam. He lived during the time of Mohammed.

5. While he was at the Khalid bin Waleed camp, Sheikh met Aukie Collins, an American convert to Islam who had become a jihadi fighter. Sheikh asked Collins if he would come with him to Kashmir to kidnap some Westerners, but Collins refused. See Aukie Collins, *My Jihad* (Guilford, CN, Lyons Press, 2002).

6. Letter to Nick Fielding, dated 18 October 2001.

7. Quoted in M. J. Gohel, *Profile of Sheikh Omar,* Asia-Pacific Foundation, UK, February 2002.

8. Quoted in *Los Angeles Times,* 16 July 2002.

9. The arrest of Zubaydah in March 2002, during a raid by FBI officers in Faisalabad has not been publicly linked to Sheikh's arrest a few weeks earlier, but it is worth considering that there could have been a connection.

10. Transcript of News conference, Dept of Justice Conference Center, USA, 14 March 2002.

11. US District Court, District of Columbia, Indictment of Ahmad Omar Saeed Sheikh.

12. The trial started off in Karachi but was moved to Hyderabad Central Prison as a result of security fears.

13. Wendy Chamberlain has an interesting past, having worked as a CIA officer in Afghanistan in the 1980s. Previously she had been US ambassador in Laos and when she was nominated as ambassador to Pakistan, she was strongly opposed by America's Lao community on the grounds that she had failed to protect ethnic minorities.

'The freedom-loving people in Pakistan, Afghanistan and South Asia need to be informed and aware that Wendy Chamberlain has a deplorable track record of utter and total appeasement,' said Philip Smith, director of the Lao Veterans of America. 'She has never met a military general or dictatorship that she did not like.' See *Washington Times,* 28 June 2001. She was also director of counter-terrorism affairs in the National Security Council from 1980 to '91.

14. For more information on Baer's claims about Khalid Shaikh Mohammed, see Robert Baer, *See No Evil: The True Story of a Ground Soldier in the CIA's War on Terrorism* (London, Arrow Books, 2002), p. 404.

15. UPI, 20 September 2002.

16. 'One day, the lead investigator . . . visited his cell. They discussed the Koran, and the investigator said, "Show me in the Koran where it says you can lie."

"'Give me half an hour," said Sheikh. He said his prayers and made his ablutions, and then he told them nearly everything.

'He'd learned that Danny had been killed, he said, when he called "Siddiqui" from Lahore, 5 February, and ordered, "Shift the patient to the doctor" – a pre-arranged code for Danny to be released.

"'Siddiqui" replied, "Dad has expired. We have done the scan and completed the X-rays and post-mortem" – meaning that Danny had been videotaped and buried. As he understood it, Sheikh said, Danny had been shot while trying to escape. Where the videotape was or what was on it, he said he didn't know.' Robert Sam Anson, *Vanity Fair*, July 2002, p. 53.

17. Some reports also link the killers to Ramzi Yousef, the militant who planned the first attack on the World Trade Center in 1993. Yousef, who is the nephew of 11 September mastermind Khalid Shaikh Mohammed, is serving a life sentence in the USA. See 'Police: Yemenis said to kill Pearl', Associated Press, 18 August 2002.

18. *Time* magazine, 3 February 2003.

19. Yosri Fouda was given a copy of this tape by Khalid Shaikh Mohammed when he interviewed him and Ramzi Binalshibh in April 2002. The tape is entitled 'The Slaughter of the spy journalist Daniel Pearl the Jew at the hands of the National Movement for the Restoration of Pakistan's Sovereignty'. This was the group that originally claimed to have abducted Pearl.

20. Associated Press, 5 July 2002.

21. 'Former Pearl Prosecutor Remains Key', *Wall Street Journal*, 21 November 2002.

CHAPTER FOUR

Living With the Enemy

'No one who could not get on with me in my life should visit me after my death, kiss my face or say farewell to me.'

Mohammed Atta, in his final will

A familiar face stared at Fouda from across the left shoulder of the immigration officer at Hamburg International Airport. It belonged to Ramzi Binalshibh, clearly identifiable by those distinct eyes and lips, and was on a 'most wanted' poster next to two photos of his former Marienstrasse flatmate, Said Bahaji. 'Any information on them?' the German officer asked in English as he leafed through Fouda's British passport, full of exotic visas, and owned by someone who was clearly an Arab.

'I could ask you the same,' Fouda replied with a smile as he avoided the question. He could scarcely tell the unsuspecting officer that just a week previously he had been talking with Ramzi in Karachi. He took back his passport and stepped for the first time into the streets of Hamburg, trying to see them through the eyes of the 11 September coordinator.

Seven years previously, on 22 September 1995, a scruffy 23-year-old Yemeni man arrived by ship in Hamburg with one piece of luggage. Five days later, to support his claim for political asylum in Pinneberg under the name of Ramzi Mohammed Abdullah Omar, he told his case officer that he had been illegally detained and tortured for two weeks after student riots in Sudan where he said he had been born, in the capital Khartoum, in 1973. In fact, Ramzi was born in San'a, the capital of Yemen, in 1972.

But from then on, Ramzi Binalshibh would be known amongst Hamburg's Muslim community as Omar. On his first Friday there, he went to the Turkish mosque to pray. As the faithful congregated outside the mosque after the prayers, he approached a white-bearded, kind-looking, 50-year-old man to ask directions to the al-Muhajereen mosque. 'He said that he was looking for "the minister of immigrants",' Muhammad Belfas remembers, 'I told him I did not know anyone by that title in our community, but gave him directions anyway.' Later that day, some people pointed at Belfas himself and told 'Omar' laughingly: 'That is our "minister of immigrants".'[1]

His name sounds Moroccan, but Muhammad bin Nasser Belfas is an Indonesian of Yemeni descent. His roots are in the Hadramaut in south-eastern Yemen where, incidentally, both Osama bin Laden and Binalshibh also have their roots. Born in Sawahbesar, Jakarta, on 21 February 1946, he travelled at the age of 12 to the Hadramaut, Yemen, and then on to Cairo, Egypt. In 1972, he went to Germany and, like many before him, found himself a job in the 'black economy', where he worked for 13 years.

In 1985, Belfas was arrested and held in detention prior to deportation. Very much to his own surprise, he was not only pardoned and given leave-to-remain status, but also, in 1991, was granted a work permit. And just before the end of 2000 he was finally issued with a German passport, number 12971335303. By this time he was a well-known figure in Hamburg. Since 1979 he had led regular classes on Islam for German converts or those who were curious about the religion and through his activities hundreds had embraced the faith.

'Many of the brothers who live and work here usually come to my flat – Arabs, Indonesians, Germans, Turks. They sometimes bring friends and we all drink tea and talk about life, Islam and common interests,' says Belfas – defensively. 'I am very well known. They come from everywhere and off they go again. Some come back, and some do not.'

It was not surprising that Ramzi would quickly be drawn towards Belfas. When he told the older man that he had no transport to get to the meetings, and that he was awaiting the outcome of his asylum request, Belfas agreed to allow him to share his rented flat in Zimmerstrasse for a few months until the decision came through.

Belfas has been working for Deutsche Post Service for the last 11 years. He often does night shifts and, therefore, did not know exactly what Ramzi used to do during the day while he was asleep. 'Come the night and he would come back just as I would be leaving for work,' he says, 'but I think he was at that stage looking for a place to study.'

In San'a, Yemen, Ramzi's eldest brother, Ahmed Binalshibh, confirmed that Ramzi went to Germany to study economics and political science. Ramzi was only 16 when his father died in 1988 in Hadramaut. The fourth among six brothers, he was close to his mother and 'always did his best to help her in his upbringing'. Just before he left for Germany, he worked for a private commercial bank and took several courses in English. 'He was a simple, easy-going person, admired by all members of the family, relatives and neighbours. He was very keen on visiting his relatives and friends. Polite and sociable, his most loved hobbies were football and reading,' said his brother.[2]

This would also be Belfas's recollection of Ramzi. 'Very polite, very kind, but also very bright and knowledgeable in religious matters,' he said as he tried to restrain his emotions, 'and very shy too. It was difficult to get him to interact during our meetings.'

During his stay in Zimmerstrasse, Ramzi got to know another Indonesian who also lived with Belfas. This was Agus Budiman, who was arrested in the USA ten weeks after 11 September on suspicion of assisting Binalshibh. 'Agus and I were good friends,' said Belfas. 'Our relationship really spans over some time. But he is not the terrorist type. Nothing like that.'

Having graduated from university in Hamburg, Budiman went to America where he stayed with a younger sibling in Maryland. In October 2000, he invited Belfas over. 'I thought this was a great idea, so I went and stayed there for three weeks, visiting Maryland, Virginia and Washington,' Belfas explained. 'Fortunately, I did not visit New York. Thank God. If I had, I am sure the accusations against me would have been worse.'

During his short visit, Belfas applied for a driving licence. There was at least one lie in his application. 'I simply had one made as a memento that I had stayed in America,' he said. 'I showed them my German driving licence, then I paid $12. So, what is false? Indeed, the address used was Agus's old address in Virginia, but that was the only falsehood.'

With these kinds of details in his background, it was not surprising that Belfas was arrested and questioned once again. This time it was serious. At 2.30 p.m. on Thursday, 13 September 2001, two days after the attacks in New York and Washington, officials from the Bundeskriminalamt (BKA) – Germany's equivalent of the FBI – stormed his flat.

'There were many of them, so many that the main road was closed,' said Belfas, unable to repress a cynical smile. 'They had no search warrant, but they stayed from 2.30 p.m. to 2.30 a.m. the following day.'

At the time, Arab friends of his were visiting. They had all been discussing the 'unbelievable events' of two days earlier. All were then handcuffed and pushed into the bathroom as the security police went through each and every small detail in the flat. 'Who knows what they were looking for? They took away many of my belongings: cassettes, videos, my jacket, pants, belt, books, passport and other items. Also a compact disc belonging to Agus Budiman.'

After three days in custody at police headquarters in Hamburg he was closely cross-examined on what he knew about several men. 'They showed me a number of photographs of the suspected World Trade Center terrorists.' He recognised a number of them from Hamburg, including Mohammed Atta, Said Bahaji and, of course, Ramzi Binalshibh. But Belfas, who has yet to get his belongings back, was more concerned about his own safety and his lifestyle. 'My neighbours, mostly elderly people, became frightened. My friends at the post office also became suspicious,' he said. 'How are you supposed to explain if you are named in the media as the head of Osama bin Laden's network in Hamburg?'

So soon after the attacks, the German authorities were only just beginning to realise the significance of Hamburg in the planning and execution of the most devastating act of terror the world has ever seen.

But all this was in the future. Nearly four months after his arrival, Binalshibh was officially informed on 17 January 1996 that his request for political asylum had been rejected and that he would be deported from Germany. He appealed against the decision. Awaiting a final verdict, the authorities relocated him to the container estate of Kummerfeld community for asylum seekers. For nearly two years he was on Germany's list of those who were to receive social support, but he hardly ever picked up his allowances.

Little is known about how 'Herr Omar' spent the rest of the year 1996, except that he was frequently seen in various mosques and that he was struggling to learn German. He earned a few Deutschmarks from different companies looking for cheap labour. One such company, which he briefly worked for in early 1997, was in Ellerhoop, situated north-west of Hamburg. He earned 12 marks per hour on a building site. 'But he was too slow and of slight build,' said manager Volker Offen. 'He was unable to carry paving stones. I kicked him out after ten days.'[3]

According to Belfas, Ramzi then moved to the eastern part of Germany. During the search for evidence, investigators came across some strange facts. This mysterious man had numerous registered addresses and was using five different names. One of his former landlords, the Algerian 'H', who once registered him in Hamburg, claimed he knew him only briefly. 'I met him in a coffee shop and registered him with me because he was nice and Arab,' he said.

Though it is not clear whether the man who was later to coordinate the 11 September attacks was already a member of al-Qaeda before arriving in Germany, certain dates, locations, names and 'coincidences' raise some interesting questions. Just a few months prior to Binalshibh's arrival in Hamburg, Mohammed Atta – who had been living and studying there for the previous three years under the name of Mohammed el-Amir – went to Mecca, Saudi Arabia, for pilgrimage, an unusual practice among single Egyptians in their 20s. And just a few months after his arrival, the German-Moroccan Said Bahaji, who is presently a wanted fugitive, commenced his studies at the Technische Universitat Hamburg-Harburg (TUHH) – the same university where Atta was studying.

Add two more months and the Lebanese Ziad al-Jarrah would be arriving in Germany, on 3 April 1996. Eight days after that Atta would be signing, at the age of just 27, his last will and testament in a mosque frequented by radicals in Hamburg. Then add 17 more days and Marwan al-Shehhi would be arriving in the country from Dubai. This was a cell in the forming. The young men would be scattered in various parts of Germany, slowly gravitating towards Hamburg, until 32 months later it was time to bring them all together on the first-floor flat at 54 Marienstrasse. It would prove to be the most devastating terror cell the world has ever known.

From the beginning, Atta was in charge of the cell. Born in Kafr el-Sheikh in the heart of Egypt's Nile Delta on 1 September 1968, Mohammed el-Amir Awad el-Sajid Atta moved soon after with his parents and two sisters to a rough suburb of Giza, Greater Cairo, called al-Omraniya – just a few minutes walk from the pyramids. A lower middle-class outspoken lawyer, his father brought him up the classic Muslim way. The tiny child would be allowed to play with his friends in the densely populated neighbourhood, but would have to go to the mosque and excel in his studies. And all that he did.

'God bless the soul of King Faisal [of Saudi Arabia in the 1960s and early '70s] who told off Henry Kissinger [former US secretary of state] in 1973,' Atta senior says enthusiastically. 'When Kissinger tried to twist his arm by suggesting that there were voices in America calling for the forceful occupation of the Gulf oil fields, he was man enough to tell him that it would make no difference to us going back to eating dates and drinking milk.'[4]

Long years of hopes and frustrations were passed from an opinionated father to an obedient son. Mohammed Atta was five when, as his father saw it, Egypt and the rest of the Arab world managed to restore some dignity during the 1973 war with Israel, nine when Egyptian president Anwar Sadat 'shamefully' flew to Jerusalem to address the Knesset, thirteen when gunmen from the Islamic Jihad Organisation[5] assassinated the 'traitor' Sadat during a military review.

It was at school that the young Atta truly found himself. At the age of 18 he finished his crucial high school studies in impressive style. His grades in science were so high that he was spoiled for choice about where his family should send him to college. In the end it was decided he should study to become a town planner at the faculty of engineering. In October 1986 he joined Cairo University, the same university where Yosri Fouda had graduated a few weeks earlier and had been appointed as a lecturer in TV journalism.

Atta's photos from college days show a happy town-planning student. Teachers and fellow students remember a dedicated, funny, impressively intelligent Mohammed, who was so short and tiny the university guards used to turn him back every morning until he produced his identity card.

During his study at Egypt's most prestigious university, Atta also took some advanced English-language courses at the American University in Cairo. Once again he excelled at his studies.

As Atta was his parents' only son he was exempted from wasting three years with national service in the Egyptian Army upon graduation in 1990. Instead, he threw himself into a crowded market of newly graduated students in search of a job. At the same time, he studied German at the Goethe Institute in Cairo.

In the eyes of a religious, patriotic, sensitive young man there was little satisfaction to be found in being Egyptian or an Arab at this time. Iraq had invaded Kuwait. The Americans had encircled Iraq. The Palestinians had recognised Israel. And the burdens of life in Egypt had become even tougher. In search of himself, he decided to leave.

Under the name of Mohammed el-Amir (in English, the prince), Mohammed Atta (in English, the gift) set foot in Hamburg for the first time on 24 July 1992. He was lucky enough to be invited to join a cultural exchange programme between Egypt and Germany, through which he went to live with a German family. Though on a non-residential visa, he took the opportunity to look for a post-graduate course in architecture.

When the Fachhochschule in Hamburg turned down his application, he appealed. While he was searching in other directions, his application was finally accepted, but only after he had already found a town-planning course at the TUHH.

The 23rd of November 1992 was a significant day in the life of Mohammed Atta. It was the day he began to study at the Technical University in Harburg, a quiet suburb of Hamburg. Now he knew he could stay legally in Germany and dream of a bright future. From day one he never failed to impress. 'My first impression was that of an intelligent young man who was a little bit reserved, but, nevertheless, had very interesting and interested eyes – very interested in everything we could offer him,' said his professor, Dittmar Machule. 'What was unusual about him though, was his religiousness. He prayed – very seriously. It was a lifestyle to him. I had no problem with this as I am familiar with Islam and the Arab world, but the students found it a bit difficult to understand.'[6]

His German hosts too found it a bit difficult to understand when, eight months later, it was Ramadan. A dedicated Muslim, Atta faithfully observed the holy month, fasting from dawn to dusk and refraining from all that could spoil his fasting. The teacher couple with whom he was still living felt awkward every time Mohammed covered his eyes in front of television and every time he stayed up late in the kitchen preparing his pre-dawn meal, *sahour*. Eventually, he had to move out.

Atta soon found a cheap room in student accommodation, Am Centrumshaus, and quickly found his place in the many mosques of Hamburg. Nader el-Abd, a young Egyptian who owns and runs a small building company in Hamburg, was once praying in the al-Muhajereen mosque when his Palestinian friend, Mohammed Ali, approached him.

'There is one very good Egyptian young man I would like to introduce you to,' he whispered as Mohammed el-Amir (Atta) was still praying in the far corner of the mosque. They waited until he finished. When Ali introduced them they instantly liked one another.

'At the time I had just got married to a German girl,' el-Abd, whose name has been recently taken off the FBI Watch List, remembers. 'She kept asking me about Islam but I could not answer many of her questions. I needed help.'[7]

Believing Atta to be a kind, polite, intelligent, knowledgeable man, he visited him the following day in the student house and explained the matter. 'He was very welcoming and very brave. He did not hesitate when I invited him to our flat a couple of days later.'

In her white headscarf and long, modest dress, Nader's wife, Safeyya, is an embodied version of a Muslim's picture of the Virgin Mary. Serene and calm, she made Atta some tea and sat in front of him. 'He was very polite,' she said, 'he answered my questions in a neutral way. I did not feel that he wanted to convince me. When he told me from his knowledge, I listened, I discussed and I tried to understand.'[8]

Safeyya felt at ease with the young man and started to open up. 'I told him about some bad dreams that I had been having at the time and asked if he thought they had anything to do with my coming closer to Islam,' she vividly remembered. 'Then he explained that those nightmares were only the ill-deeds of the *Shaytaan* (Satan), and advised me to recite these prayers before I go to sleep: *A'ouzo bellahi minash Shaytaani rajeem, Besmellahi rahmaani raheem* (I seek refuge in Allah from Satan, the cursed, in the name of Allah, the Beneficent, the Merciful).'

A few days later, Safeyya converted to Islam and, together with her Egyptian husband, became a regular participant in Belfas's religious meetings, which Atta was now attending. There, Atta himself got acquainted with many Arabs and Muslims. 'He was polite, respectable and very quiet,' says the host of the meetings, Muhammad Belfas. 'He never interfered in other people's business and hardly talked until he was invited to. But he was not comfortable with mixed company of men and women.'

Another Egyptian, Ayman Negm, who is also married to a German convert, looked at his wife as he remembered a funny Mohammed el-Amir. 'We used to tell each other funny lines from Egyptian comedy plays,' he says, 'and I know that he always dreamt of marrying a good Muslim and settling in Egypt. Some of our Turkish friends offered to find him a bride in their community, but he wanted to finish his studies and go back to his country first.'[9]

A German classmate of his remembers Atta as short, slight, with short black hair and a firm, quiet look – classical, almost Greek features. 'He used to wear flannel trousers and a pullover,' said fellow student Martin E., 'and was very reserved and tight-lipped. Mohammed el-Amir always made me feel that he was not going to talk about his private life. His behaviour towards women was brusque – he felt uncomfortable. He never shook hands with them and always looked away.'[10]

Though he did not have to pay tuition fees, Atta had to find some money to pay for his insurance, transportation and other living costs. On 1 December 1992 he found a part-time job as a graphic designer with a company called Plankontor. Working 19 hours a week, he secured himself 1,700 marks a month during the five years he worked at the firm. He was admired and trusted by his boss and workmates. He had his own key to the office and was also in charge of the telephone calls. His former colleagues remember his kindness and care during the time they had bad backs or other work-related illnesses. Usually he would recommend natural remedies.

Meanwhile, as he had continued to perform well during his studies at the university, Atta soon acquired his teachers' trust, so much so that Professor Dittmar Machule started to recommend him to speak in specialised seminars. At a seminar on 'Planning and Construction in Developing Countries', an eloquent Atta spoke enthusiastically of the necessity to preserve the Islamic architectural identity. He made it clear that he despised the Americanisation of Egypt's culture and heritage, and called for an end to high-rise buildings in favour of more traditional-style, neighbourhood-friendly ones.

'He was a perfectionist – indeed, indeed. He wanted to do everything the perfect way,' says Professor Machule. 'He would sit there quietly listening and observing, looking as if he was not there, and suddenly would come up with a sharp, intelligent question or remark. He was very special – unusual.'

In 1994, Atta applied for a scholarship at the Carl Duisberg Society for Development Aid Policy. He wrote in his application:

> I was born and grew up myself in a developing country. I have seen many sides of the problems. During my education in the field of architecture and town planning in Cairo, I have studied thoroughly the many aspects of the planning of development policies. I am part of the so-called 'new generation' which has been debating the subject of development in a critical, but hopeful manner. Without really knowing how this should happen, we were trying to do something for our country. Since I am now in Germany, I am trying, consciously or subconsciously, to find out as an outsider, how the so-called 'new world' perceives us and how it relates itself to our 'Third World'.

Later that year, Atta went on a study trip to Istanbul, Turkey, and then to Aleppo, Syria, where he collected his data on the old quarter of Kharej Baben Nasr. This was to be the subject of his Masters thesis which, for reasons that will become clear, took him more than five years to complete. It is interesting to consider why such a dedicated Egyptian should choose to study a Syrian town rather than one in his own country, where he could have found hundreds of potential areas of research. Possibly it was due to the influence of his professor who had been on several expeditions to ancient excavations in Syria.

Ironically, it may also have stemmed from his Egyptian nationalism. Syria has always proven to be Egypt's best regional ally. Whenever they merged throughout history, they proved to be an invincible partnership. Saladin al-Ayyubi, the great leader of the Muslims against Richard I and the Third Crusade, had first of all united the two countries under a single banner to bring an end to hundreds of years of Christian occupation and influence in the Holy Land. Israel today clearly understands this issue and exploits its position between the two countries. Long after Nasser's short-lived United Arab Republic (1958–61), there remains a very strong bond between Egyptians and Syrians.

As he was busy studying the aroma of history in the narrow alleys of Kharej Baben Nasr in Aleppo, the ever-serious Mohammed Atta fell in love with a beautiful Syrian town planner. He tried to talk her into changing her appearance and attitude. They went out, but only as far as her traditions allowed her and his religiousness allowed him. In the end, he rejected her. She would not wear a headscarf and she was too provocative in the way she dressed, none of which was acceptable to him.

Atta left Aleppo with a lot of data for his thesis and a broken heart. A mainstream 27-year-old Egyptian man would naturally think that the future was still wide open. But it seems that Atta thought otherwise. For a committed Muslim, marriage is extremely important. The Prophet Mohammed commands that a capable Muslim should marry. Although marriage is not a pillar in Islam, unlike pilgrimage for example, a Muslim is advised to marry before he or she makes the sacred journey.

When he arrived back in Hamburg, however, Atta decided not to follow this recommendation. A few months later, in 1995, he made up his mind and went to Mecca and Medina, Saudi Arabia, to visit the most sacred places in Islam. It is a holy journey of self-purification after which a true Muslim feels as if he or she has been born anew.

Was this the time and place that Mohammed Atta was approached for the first time by someone from al-Qaeda? Though we do not have specific information, it might well turn out some day to be true. From then on, there would just be too many coincidences.

'Once he came back with a beard – for the first time in four years I saw Mohammed with a beard,' remembers Professor Machule. 'I do not know whether he said he was on *Hajj* (pilgrimage), but we joked about it. I told him: "Nice to see you, Hajji", and he smiled back. I did not read too much into it as I know a thing or two about Islam.'

On 1 August 1995, Atta embarked on a three-month study mission in his native Egypt. This was a good opportunity for him to spend some time with his family and to try and imagine himself back in Cairo forever. As he struggled to catch a bus every morning from al-Ahram Street past Cairo University through Central Cairo, changing buses at al-Tahrir Square (if he managed) and then going all the way to the Islamic and Coptic quarters of Old Cairo on a 75-minute journey of torture, he must have remembered the nice walk in the fresh air from his quiet neighbourhood to his beautiful university in Hamburg.

It would also be fair to assume that someone with Atta's mentality and education, especially having lived for more than four years in Germany, would be frustrated by the chaotic lifestyle and the bureaucratic management in Egypt. He would likely be further appalled by growing corruption in Egypt's relatively new 'open-economy policy',[11] which had created millionaires out of illiterates and which left college-educated Ph.D. holders with an average salary of $65 a month – if they were able to find a job.

When he flew out of Cairo at the end of October, Atta must have felt, deep inside, some sense of appreciation for some aspects of Western culture. But psychologically speaking, the contrast between his homeland and the efficient Germans may have helped turn the black smoke inside him even blacker. Even if we assume that, by that time, he had not yet been recruited by al-Qaeda, Mohammed Atta was clearly there for the taking. It also remains to be established whether, upon his arrival back in Hamburg on 31 October 1995, Atta was aware of the fact that Ramzi Binalshibh had already been there for the previous five weeks – living with Muhammad Belfas.

On 11 April the following year, Atta was not even 28 when he went to the al-Kuds mosque in Steindamm, Hamburg – this time not to pray, but to sign his death will.

Occupying the second floor in a mid-terrace block, the obscure mosque is mainly frequented by Islamic fundamentalists from North Africa, but also from other parts of the Muslim world. The worshippers do not give a warm welcome to outsiders. Filming inside was a definite 'No', and even filming outside was still risky. When Fouda's cameraman came too close, he was threatened with a beating. Fouda himself was told by two Algerian vigilantes hovering outside the door that 'Journalists are the brothers of Satan – all journalists.' Insisting that, being a Muslim, he had the right to pray, they could not stop him entering the mosque.

Inside, it looked like a typical small mosque in any European city, but it felt a bit different. There was a touch of tension in the air and defensiveness in the eyes of the faithful. 'People here have been put under a lot of pressure after what happened,' said a more moderate man who approached Fouda with an apology. 'Atta and the rest might have done it – we do not know for sure yet, but what have we all done?'

It is now widely believed that 'Atta and the rest' were all recruited in this mosque and that they took advantage of the sacred place to use it as a communication hub, although proof is hard to come by. We know that 'Atta and the rest' all prayed there and that they reportedly established a 'working group' and were planning to distribute an information leaflet. But Atta did not integrate. Nor would we have expected someone like him to. He was not keen on contributing to the leaflet, was often late to meetings and apparently did not hold much respect for the leader of the group.

Though it was a printed-out form devised by the mosque, Atta's death will remains a significant development in his thinking. These are some of the most important points that he signed up to:

- Those who will bury my body should be good Muslims, for that compliments Allah and His forgiveness;
- Those who will wash my body should close my eyes and pray that I will go to Heaven. They should wrap my body in new cloth;
- No one should cry for me, scream, rip off their cloths or hit their faces, for these are silly gestures;
- No one who could not get on with me in my life should visit me after my death, kiss my face or say farewell to me;
- No pregnant women or disbelievers should walk in my funeral or ever visit my grave;
- No woman should ask forgiveness for me;
- I am not responsible for animal sacrifices before my body, for that is against the teachings of Islam;
- Those who will wash my body should wear gloves so that they do not touch my genitals;
- My death cloths should be made up of three pieces of white material, but not of silk or any other expensive material;
- The funeral should take place quietly, for Allah values peace during such an occasion;
- At the entombment, I should be buried by good Muslims, and they should lay me on my right side with my face towards Mecca;
- People should stay for one hour by my grave so that I can enjoy their company. After that, an animal should be sacrificed and the meat should be distributed to the poor and needy;
- There is the tradition to commemorate the dead after 40 days or every year. I do not want that, for it is not in accordance with Islamic rituals;
- No one should write sayings or talismans for me, for that is all superstition. It is better to use the time to pray to Allah that He might forgive me;
- My financial capital that I left behind should be divided according

to the Islamic Shari'a [religious rules] – a third of it should go to the poor and needy. My books should be given to the possession of a mosque. The executors of my will should be leaders of the Sunnis;

● Should the ceremony not comply with the Islamic faith, the affected persons should be held responsible;

● Those that I leave behind should only fear Allah and not allow life to deceive them. They should pray to Allah and be good believers.

On the last page of this document, two people put their signatures next to Atta's as witnesses. One is Abdelghani Mzoudi, 29, an electronics student who lived with a friend in Fischbek, Hamburg. The BKA could not find enough evidence against him to charge him with any offence. But the other, 28-year-old electrical engineering student Munir al-Motassadeq, was convicted in February 2003, having been charged with more than 3,000 counts of accessory to murder and membership of a terrorist organisation. German prosecutors alleged that he played an important backroom role as the plot unfolded, in particular by funnelling money to the hijackers while they were attending flight school in the United States.

Al-Motassadeq's father, Ibrahim, in Morocco learned of his son's arrest accidentally through Al-Jazeera Channel. 'They said that he was preparing to run away,' he said when interviewed. 'This is a lie. It was me who arranged for him to come back to his own country. I paid for his study and living costs, and I paid for his ticket because he could not afford it. And they say he financed bin Laden?!'[12]

He had just arrived from Morocco to support his son when Fouda met him in an Islamic bookshop near the al-Kuds mosque. A few weeks later, the al-Tawheed bookshop itself was raided by German investigators in a campaign that resulted in the arrest of six men suspected of belonging to an extremist Islamic group.

A raid on al-Motassadeq's flat on 2 December 2001 turned up the business card of a diplomat from the embassy of Saudi Arabia in Berlin. The BKA's Joerg Klose told the court that the defendant also made 'repeated' calls to Saudi Arabia from Hamburg and that German intelligence had traced the calls to 'Islamic radicals' in the kingdom.

Now living with his Russian Muslim daughter-in-law and her six-month-old son, al-Motassadeq's father is tired of talking to lawyers. 'The lawyer told me that they are under a lot of pressure,' he said. 'When I asked him what pressure, he said it was outside pressure.'

Lawyers for al-Motassadeq asked the Hamburg court to throw out the charges because the US government has refused to allow Ramzi Binalshibh, now in secret American detention, to testify about their client. The presiding judge said he would delay ruling on the motion until the end of the trial, when all other witnesses have testified. It made no difference and al-Motassadeq was sentenced to 15 years in prison.

Back in Hamburg in 1996, one by one, the team was assembling. Eight days before Atta signed his death will, Ziad Samir al-Jarrah was saying goodbye to his family in Marj, in the Bekaa Valley, Lebanon, before flying out to Germany. On 3 April, he arrived in Greifswald where he stayed in Makarenkostrasse. Already fluent in English and French, he mastered German in a preparatory three-month course. The handsome young man full of *joie de vivre* was no stranger to the Western lifestyle. He drank alcohol, went to nightclubs and quickly found himself a Turkish girlfriend.

Born on 11 May 1975, al-Jarrah (in English, the surgeon) comes from a middle-class Sunni Muslim family. But it is a family with an interesting background. Ziad's great uncle, Assem Omar al-Jarrah, was registered with the then East German Ministry of State Security (MfS) as an 'unofficial member' under the codename of 'Karsten Berg' (Reg. No. XV/1309/85). The Lebanese, who registered himself (also at the University of Greifswald) as a pharmaceutical student in 1983, was, according to the files, recruited in 1985 by members of the MfS district administration in Neubrandenburg as an agent of the XV Section, responsible for foreign espionage. Three years later, Ziad's great uncle worked as an IMB (in touch with the enemy) agent for Section II (Counter Espionage) of the district administration Rostock.[13]

Another family member, Refet al-Jarrah, is registered in a database of the Central Evaluation and Information Group of MfS as a suspected terrorist with secret service connections. There is no further information about him.

But there is more about his uncle Assem. A note in a file confirmed that he worked for the Libyan secret service, while a handwritten card of Section XXII (Counter Terrorism) indicated that he had contacts with agents involved in an operation codenamed 'The Dealer'. The aim of the operation was to collect as much information as possible about the activities of one of the most notorious terrorists of the 1970s and '80s: Sabri Khalil al-Banna, alias 'Abu Nidal'. With this family background it is hard to imagine that Ziad's choice of Greifswald was accidental, though it is unclear whether he was or was not aware of his family's unusual connections with the East German intelligence services.

Having finished his German language course in 1996, Ziad set his mind on studying biochemistry, but failed to gain a place on the course. The flamboyant playboy also became so religious that he asked his Turkish girlfriend, Aysel S., to wear a headscarf and to cover her hands. The BKA investigators believe that his change of mind was the result of his contact with a man who still lives today in Makarenkostrasse.

His name is Abdul Rahman al-M., a Yemeni who acts as the imam of a small Muslim community in Greifswald. He told investigators that he knew Muhammad Belfas of Hamburg, and that the latter had helped furnish the prayer room of the local Muslim community. But as far as the investigators were concerned, Abdul Rahman seemed suspicious. He travelled a lot and had large amounts of money at his disposal from unknown origins. He also had contacts with the Aachen al-Aqsa Union, classified by the German authorities as being close to the Palestinian Islamic group, Hamas. The full nature of his relationship with al-Jarrah is still to be uncovered.

Whether al-Jarrah's great uncle Assem Omar al-Jarrah noticed the transformation of his nephew into an Islamic fundamentalist is a question that seems to have been overtaken by more pressing matters, as, in July 2002 he packed up the furniture from his Greifswald flat and flew back to Lebanon. His current whereabouts are unknown.

In al-Marj in the Bekaa Valley in Lebanon where he lives, another of al-Jarrah's uncles, Jamal, confirmed that, back in 1996, his nephew was thinking of marrying his girlfriend. He was, however, dismissive of suggestions that al-Jarrah had become a fanatic. 'There was no indication of this sort,' he said, 'he lived there very normally just like any other good student – studying, going out with his girlfriend. Nothing at all that would suggest that he belonged to any ideological or political group.'[14]

By the time he qualified to study medicine in Greifswald on 11 June 1997, al-Jarrah had already decided to change at least two things about himself: the course of his study and where he would be studying. Just over three months later, on 30 September 1997, he began a course in aeronautical engineering at the Fachhochschule, Hamburg – right opposite the al-Kuds mosque.

Twenty-five days after al-Jarrah's arrival in Greifswald, the son of a preacher from the United Arab Emirates was on his way to Germany, having secured a generous military scholarship. Born on 9 May 1978, Marwan Yusif al-Shehhi arrived in Bonn on 28 April 1996 where he enrolled in an intensive German-language preparatory course at the Goethe Institute. Coming from an oil-rich Gulf state, al-Shehhi was not short of money: he received about 4,000 Deutschmarks a month from the HSBC Middle East Bank in Dubai and an extra 10,000 Deutschmarks once a year.

A few months later, on 5 February 1997, Zakariya Essaber arrived in Germany from Morocco. He enrolled at the Fachhochschule in Anhatt, Kothen on a preparatory course. He then made his way to Hamburg where, on 1 October 1998, he started a medical engineering course at Hamburg's Fachhochschule – the same college Ziad al-Jarrah had joined a year earlier.

Marwan al-Shehhi had also changed his preparatory course in Bonn, in January 1998, for another one in Hamburg. He would later join the TUHH to study naval construction – the same university where Mohammed Atta and Said Bahaji were studying. He hardly ever attended his classes.

Over the course of a few months, all the principal members of the Hamburg cell had slotted into place. They had arrived singly from different parts of the Middle East and had for the most part kept out of the well-known haunts of Hamburg students. They had done nothing to alert the authorities in Germany to their presence or intentions.

Someone somewhere had already made many decisions about the fate of these men and others besides. They would prepare for their mission in the heart of Europe, learn the ways of the enemy, study his methods, the better to defeat him. Atta, Binalshibh, al-Jarrah, al-Shehhi, Bahaji, Essaber – they were all now in position, waiting for further instructions. Something brought them all together – something other than just a mosque or a university. As we will find out later, the year 1998 was to be a critical year in bin Laden's war on America.

NOTES

1. Exclusive interview with Muhammad Belfas, Hamburg, June 2002.

2. *Al-Majalla*, issue 1173, 10 August 2002, p. 12.

3. *Der Spiegel*, issue no. 41, 10 October 2001, p. 35.

4. Interview with Mohammed Atta senior, *op. cit.*

5. Later led by Ayman al-Zawahiri, bin Laden's deputy in al-Qaeda.

6. Exclusive interview with Professor Dittmar Machule, Hamburg, June 2002.

7. Exclusive interview with Nader el-Abd, Hamburg, June 2002.

8. Exclusive interview with Safeyya el-Abd, Hamburg, June 2002.

9. Exclusive interview with Ayman Negm, Hamburg, June 2002.

10. *Der Spiegel*, issue no. 48, 26 November 2001, p. 48.

11. Introduced for the first time in the mid-1970s by assassinated President Sadat.

12. Exclusive interview with Ibrahim al-Motassadeq, Hamburg, June 2002.

13. *Der Spiegel*, issue no. 41, 8 October 2001, p. 34.

14. Exclusive interview with Jamal al-Jarrah, Beirut, July 2002.

CHAPTER FIVE

Khalid Shaikh Mohammed – Family Business

'They say we are terrorists? They are right – of course we are.'
Khalid Shaikh Mohammed

Before the 11 September attacks, few people, even amongst the intelligence community, had ever heard of Khalid Shaikh Mohammed. The scattering of books on al-Qaeda or the Islamic fundamentalist movement published before September 2001 hardly mentioned him.

True, he had been indicted for his role in a 1995 Philippines-based plot to crash US airliners into the sea, but no one had ever questioned him over this – or for his alleged role in the first attack on the World Trade Center in 1993. He was little more than a name. But while the limited intelligence that was being gathered on al-Qaeda concentrated on Osama bin Laden and his deputy, Ayman al-Zawahiri, Khalid never stopped thinking of and planning for the 'spectacular' that he would one day pull off.

The only known photograph of him is a strange passport picture of a long-faced man staring out from under a Gulf Arab headdress, his thick beard and glasses obscuring most of his features. It glowers at you from the FBI 'Most Wanted' website,[1] along with an electronically enhanced version of the same picture showing Khalid wearing a shirt and collar and cleanly shaven.

The details on the FBI website are sketchy and contradictory: he was born on 14 April 1965 or 1 March 1965. His place of birth is Kuwait or Pakistan. He is olive or light skinned. He wears a full beard, a trimmed beard or a shaven face and is also known to wear glasses to hide his brown eyes. He is thought to be short at around 1.65m (5 ft 4 in.) and weighs about 60kg (132 lb).

The birthplace of Kuwait is correct, although Khalid is not an Arab. His father,

Shaikh Mohammed Ali Dustin al-Balushi, had migrated from Baluchistan in south-west Pakistan, a wild area of barren deserts and mountains that has always been lawless. The borders of Iran and Afghanistan nearby make it an ideal location for smugglers and robbers alike. The Pakistani heroin trade makes full use of the inhospitable terrain to smuggle opium grown in Afghanistan over the border into Iran for processing and sale onwards into Europe.

The Gulf had proved a magnet for thousands of young men from all over the Middle East and from southern Pakistan. The clannish Baluchis in particular had long-standing historic ties with the people of Oman, where they formed the backbone of the Sultan's army for many years. Hard-working and with an aptitude for engineering, they quickly spread along the Gulf Coast as the oil boom of the 1960s and '70s got underway.

In Kuwait, Khalid's father rose to become the first imam at the Emirate's al-Ahmadi mosque. He had been granted Kuwaiti nationality, but was stripped of his citizenship after a dispute with a leading Kuwaiti family. Like many Baluchis, he was a deeply religious man and clearly instilled in his children a strong desire to take part in the Islamic jihad. One of Khalid's brother's, Abid, was killed in 1989 during the final phase of the war against the Soviets in Afghanistan, while another, Zahid, became a senior figure in al-Qaeda with close connections to Osama bin Laden.

It was natural that Khalid's father should look for a fellow Baluchi to marry one of his daughters. The man chosen was Mohammed Abdul Karim and the young couple settled in a working-class suburb of Kuwait City where he worked as an engineer for Kuwait Airlines. In April 1968 they had a son, Abdul Karim Basit.

Khalid was just four years older than his new nephew. The two young boys spent much of their youth together, just as their later lives were to be inextricably interlinked in the cause of jihad. The younger boy would achieve fame under the alias Ramzi Yousef and international notoriety as the man who planned the first attack on the World Trade Center in 1993 and later nearly succeeded in blowing up a dozen US airliners over the Pacific. Previously it had always been thought that these attacks were exclusively the work of Yousef, but as more is learned about the relationship between these two men, the hand of Khalid can be seen behind Ramzi Yousef's every move.

Like his father-in-law, Yousef's father was also very religious. During Yousef's childhood, his father became first a Baluchi nationalist and then a follower of the austere Saudi form of Wahhabi Islam, intolerant of Shi'ism and any deviation from the true path as he saw it. Like many orthodox Sunni Muslims, he saw little to celebrate when in 1979 the Shi'ite Ayatollah Khomeini came to power in neighbouring Iran. During the futile war between Iraq and Iran that lasted for nearly a decade and cost hundreds of thousands of lives on both sides, Yousef's father strongly supported Iraq.

The two young men, Khalid and Yousef, were living in tumultuous times in a volatile region. Almost as soon as the Shah was forced into exile from Iran, the Soviet Union invaded Afghanistan, starting a conflict that dragged on for ten terrible years. Khalid and Yousef absorbed it all as they grew into young men, well aware that Baluchistan was one of the bases used by Afghan mujahideen in their hit-and-run raids on the Russians.

They never lost contact with the friends they made while growing up in Kuwait. It was there that Khalid and Yousef first met Abdul Hakim Murad, whose father worked as an engineer for the Kuwait Petroleum Company. In 1995, Murad was arrested in the Philippines where he had been working on the plot to hijack airliners with Khalid and Yousef. Murad had attended four US flight schools in preparation for the hijacks. Eyad Ismoil, who drove a bomb-laden vehicle into the basement of the World Trade Center in 1993 – an attack planned and executed by Khalid and Yousef – was another childhood friend from the nearby town of Fuhaheel in Kuwait.[2]

Khalid and Yousef went their separate ways in the 1980s. Yousef travelled back to Baluchistan in October 1986, aged 18. But by the end of November he was on his way to Britain to study, first at a higher education college in Oxford, before signing up for a higher national diploma in computer-aided electrical engineering in Swansea, south Wales. The course included micro-electronics – a skill he would later put to use as an expert bomb-maker.

Khalid had left Kuwait earlier. His first passport was issued at the Pakistani Embassy in Kuwait City on 6 December 1982. The next two years are a blank, but in the spring of 1984 he crossed the Atlantic to enrol on a two-year course at the Baptist Chowan College in Murfreesboro, north-eastern North Carolina. The college did not require an English proficiency certificate at that time and Khalid's aim was simply to improve his English. After just one semester he transferred to the nearby North Carolina Agricultural and Technical University in Greensboro to study for a mechanical engineering degree. Most students at the college were black and Khalid graduated in 1986 as one of about 30 Muslim students that year.

One of his former professors, David Klett, recalls teaching him a course on thermodynamics. 'We cover . . . the fundamentals of jet engines and propulsion and chemical reactions, combustion reaction . . . and those things would have been necessary for them to at least consider when they planned the World Trade Center attack with airplanes,' Klett told CNN, with the benefit of hindsight. 'I may have helped give him some background that would help him accomplish the World Trade Center catastrophe.'[3]

A former classmate, Sammy Zitawi, said that Khalid was always helpful and smiling and that he had no idea his religious fellow student was harbouring anti-American views. 'I mean, everyone was praising the US for helping out the Muslims in Afghanistan, so why would anybody have anything against the US back then?'

But despite Khalid's good humour and interest in acting, it was his religious beliefs that eventually won out. After graduation, he decided not to return to Kuwait, but headed for Peshawar in northern Pakistan, close to the border with Afghanistan and then the main organising centre for thousands of Arab and Afghani mujahideen fighting against the Soviet forces. In Peshawar he became secretary to one of the most ferocious and uncompromising of the Afghan warlords, Abdul Rab Rasool Sayyaf, a former Kabul University professor of theology who had spent several years in prison in the 1970s for his adherence to a Wahhabi-influenced form of Islam.

Sayyaf, a Pukhtun, had established an organisation called Ittihad-i-Islami (Islamic Union) after studying at Cairo's al-Azhar University and then living for several years in Saudi Arabia. He spoke excellent Arabic, preaching a strict, Salafist form of Islam. In particular he was deeply opposed to Sufism and Shi'ism, two forms of Islam that he considered to be heretical. His religious beliefs took precedence over any tribal loyalties, as he demonstrated when the predominantly Pukhtun Taliban came to power in 1996. Sayyaf opposed them and began to fight alongside the Tajik leader Ahmed Shah Massoud. Together the two men made the Panjshir Valley an impregnable fortress that the Taliban were never able to breach.

Because he spoke fluent Arabic, Sayyaf was an attractive contact for wealthy Saudis who wanted to fund the jihad against the Soviets, although he was never very popular with his fellow Afghanis who loathed his fundamentalist brand of Islam. The Ittihad-i-Islami therefore became a predominantly Arab organisation and a powerful force within the mujahideen.

It was as early as 1980 that Sayyaf met with Osama bin Laden. According to Peter Bergen: 'Within weeks of the Soviet invasion, bin Laden, then 22, voted with his feet and wallet, heading to Pakistan to meet with the Afghan leaders Burhanuddin Rabbani and Abdul Rasool Sayyaf, whom he had previously encountered during Hajj gatherings.'[4]

Sayyaf received millions of dollars thanks to his connections with bin Laden. In return, many years later, in 1996, it was apparently Sayyaf who invited bin Laden to move to Afghanistan after he was expelled from Sudan.

A generous donation from bin Laden in 1980 enabled Sayyaf to open the University of Dawal al-Jihad in the tribal areas outside Peshawar, which has been described as a training school for terrorists. Devout young men from all over the Islamic world came to study at the Dawal, including many from the Philippines.

Amongst them was Abdurajak Janjalani, who would subsequently be killed by Filipino government troops in December 1998. Janjalani met Sayyaf, who was highly respected amongst the mujahideen and when he returned to the Sulu-Basilan islands, Janjalani named his newly formed group Abu Sayyaf in his honour, dropping the name 'Rasool' since the latter was similar to the name of a rival group.

This organisation has since become a major terrorist force and ally of al-Qaeda in the southern Philippines and is responsible for many atrocities, including the indiscriminate use of bombs in public places, kidnaps and murders. The Abu Sayyaf group and the Philippines are also very closely connected to both Khalid Shaikh Mohammed and his nephew Ramzi Yousef.

This was the milieu into which the young Khalid immersed himself in late 1986. He already had close connections in Peshawar through his brother, Zahid al-Shaikh.[5]

According to police documents from Pakistan's Federal Investigation Agency, Zahid had first worked for a non-governmental organisation funded by the Kuwaiti government before moving on to Mercy International Relief, a Saudi-funded charity closely connected to bin Laden.[6] By the mid-1990s he was the regional manager and the Pakistani magazine, *The Herald*, reported that Zahid also ran the Islamic Coordination Council, established by bin Laden's mentor, Abdullah Azzam, which coordinated the activities of 20 charities in the city whose objectives were to fund the jihad and provide welfare services to the families of mujahideen.[7] Zahid was clearly an important figure in the city. When Pakistani President Farooq Ahmad Khan Leghari attended the opening ceremony at a Mercy International-funded orphanage in February 1993, Zahid made a speech of welcome to the president.[8]

Within a couple of years, Ramzi Yousef had joined Khalid and his other relatives in Peshawar. His first visit was in July 1988, during his summer vacation while he was still studying at college in Wales. In the autumn he returned to Britain to complete his studies, but was spotted again in 1989 at the Sadda training camp located in the Khumram Agency near Parachinar on the Pakistan–Afghanistan border. The camp was under the control of Abdul Rab Rasool Sayyaf[9] and Yousef instructed new recruits about explosives and bomb-making.

At this time neither Khalid nor Ramzi Yousef were members of al-Qaeda. The organisation only really came into its own once bin Laden moved to Afghanistan in 1996. The two young men were both motivated by their Islamic background and hatred for Israel and felt at home with Sayyaf's brand of fundamentalist Islam and sectarian hatred for Shi'ites. As Pakistanis who had been brought up in the Gulf, they could mix easily with the Arabs, conversing with them in their own tongue, while at the same time feeling comfortable in their own country.

While the Americans and other Western governments provided logistical support for the Arab jihad, Khalid and Ramzi Yousef had already begun to see beyond the end of the war and to nurture a deep hatred for the United States. American support for Israel negated everything they did in Afghanistan and once the Russians had been dealt with it would be the turn of the USA.

In the camps scattered along the border with Afghanistan, by now full of thousands of volunteers from across the Muslim world, these were the sentiments that were taking hold. Bin Laden was known and respected, but he had not yet achieved hegemony over the jihadis. Only later would the most dedicated fighters turn towards him and build their new organisation.

Not all of them did. Abdul Rab Rasool Sayyaf continued to rise among the mujahideen leadership. When the remnants of the communist government collapsed in 1992 he was appointed to the powerful interior ministry under his old friend, and new president, Burhanuddin Rabbani. Soon he was involved in vicious sectarian fighting against the Hazara minority – Shi'ites who lived in central Afghanistan and in the districts around Kabul. Whole areas of the capital were devastated and thousands were killed as rockets rained down on defenceless communities. When the Taliban took power in 1996, he fled into the hills to fight alongside the Northern Alliance and became deputy prime minister in Rabbani's government-in-exile.

Today he disavows any involvement with al-Qaeda and its founder, bin Laden: 'I knew him, but not deeply. When I saw him, he was a simple man. I think the media made him a huge man. He was not at that level. He's a stupid man and he's created problems for Afghanistan.'[10]

Nonetheless questions remain about Sayyaf. Despite his close relationship with Ahmed Shah Massoud, who became leader of the Northern Alliance and was assassinated in 2001, the Karzai administration in Afghanistan, installed after the fall of the Taliban, is wary of him, believing that he had close contacts with Pakistan's intelligence service, the ISI. At the *loya jirga* (gathering of elders) that decided on the composition of the Afghani government in 2002, Sayyaf was prominent in opposing the involvement of women in government and instrumental in getting the title 'Islamic' added to the new state's name. He was not given a portfolio by the new administration.

By the beginning of the 1990s Khalid and Ramzi Yousef had decided that they would dedicate their lives to jihad. The two men made a very powerful combination: the older man, the religiously motivated chief strategist; the younger, a man who could charm, use his wits and achieve the impossible. In addition they had a wide circle of close friends and relatives, including several of Ramzi Yousef's younger brothers, Abu Suleman, Abdul Rehman and Abdul Rahim, who were all involved in jihadi activities. It was rapidly becoming a family affair. Now they had to decide which path of jihad to follow.

The war in Afghanistan had been won. Bin Laden himself had already left, intending to settle with his four wives and seventeen children in Saudi Arabia. He had returned a hero, but quickly fell out with the Saudi Royal family when his naive offer to use his own mujahideen to repel Iraq's invasion of Kuwait and defend the Kingdom fell on deaf ears.

In the autumn of 1991, after an attempt to bring weapons into Saudi

Arabia from Yemen had been discovered, bin Laden left for sanctuary in Sudan, where he was welcomed with open arms. He was more determined than ever not to give up jihad and it was the Egyptians – in particular, Ayman al-Zawahiri and Mohammed Atef – who had become close to him in Afghanistan that persuaded him to create – and more importantly, finance – a new organisation.

As the American and Allied troops arrived in Saudi Arabia to fight the Gulf War and Afghanistan descended into factional warfare, the revamped al-Qaeda organisation began to take shape. It was no longer simply an instrument for organising the struggle in Afghanistan. In future the battlefield would be wherever Islam came into conflict with the West.

Khalid and Ramzi Yousef were marginal figures at this time. Neither of them had played an important role in the fighting in Afghanistan and as Baluchis they were not party to the innermost secrets of the Afghan Arabs. But their upbringing in the Gulf, the good contacts they had, particularly through Khalid's brother Zahid, and their knowledge of Arabic language and culture drew them into the debates taking place amongst the mujahideen along the Afghan border. Should they stay where they were or travel to Sudan to join bin Laden?

For the Arab jihadis, there was little real choice. Many had spent years in the border areas of Afghanistan, had learned the local languages and married local women. For years they had lived on wages paid by the Arab governments and the CIA. When Soviet forces withdrew, they had nowhere to go. In their own countries they faced imprisonment, while in Afghanistan they could take part in a bold new jihad, aimed at the enemies of Islam – once the fratricidal bloodletting of the Afghan factions had come to an end.

Abdul Rab Rasool Sayyaf, for example, was now busily engaged in a murderous sectarian campaign against his own fellow Afghans. While Khalid and Ramzi Yousef had no affection for the Shi'ite Hazaras, after the noble struggle against the godless communists this must have been a terrible anti-climax. The talk amongst the Arab jihadis who had stayed behind in Peshawar was now all about how they were to take their struggle on.

In the summer of 1991, Ramzi Yousef made the first of several trips to the Philippines in the company of Abdurajak Janjalani, who had received funds from bin Laden to establish his Abu Sayyaf organisation. Yousef and several companions travelled to Basilan Island and began training Janjalani's raw recruits in bomb-making.

Yousef had been asked to undertake the trip by Mohammed Jamal Khalifa. Khalifa, a close aide to bin Laden (he was married to one of bin Laden's sisters) had originally been sent to the Philippines in 1988 to encourage Muslim separatists not to make peace with the government and to continue their armed struggle. Janjalani's new Abu Sayyaf organisation was the result, but it was very short of skills and experience.

With hindsight, Ramzi Yousef's decision to travel to the Philippines at this time indicates that he had made a decision; he would pass on his skills and work for the day when he could make a reputation for himself. Back in Pakistan after three months, Yousef returned to Dawal al-Jihad to teach explosives courses before leaving for the United States at the end of August 1992.

It has never been ascertained who made the decision to launch a massive car bomb attack on the World Trade Center in New York, but the probability is that it was Khalid and not Yousef, even though he was the main planner and organiser in the US. Both men were now part of a well-trained network of guerrilla fighters. Khalid's job as secretary to Sayyaf would have brought him into contact with emissaries from rich Arabs in the Gulf.[11] Many of them were willing to support an attack on America, whose troops, following the Gulf War, were now based in the holy land of Arabia itself – something that radical Muslims considered to be an affront to their religion.

Yousef arrived at JFK in New York on 1 September and requested political asylum, claiming he had been persecuted by Iraqi soldiers during the Iraqi invasion of Kuwait. During his six-month stay in the United States Yousef always kept in touch with someone back in Pakistan. The likelihood is that it was Khalid. Intelligence sources say this contact, who was close to bin Laden, tried to obtain nuclear material so that the bomb detonated beneath the World Trade Center would be a radioactive 'dirty bomb'.[12] In the end, this attempt failed, but it did not stop Ramzi Yousef making the bomb and organising the attack.

His aim, it is now clear, was to explode the bomb under one of the towers and thus topple it into the second tower. The huge 1,200-lb bomb was slowly assembled, made from urea nitrate and nitro-glycerine. Added to this were three tanks of compressed hydrogen. Investigators said it was the largest improvised explosive device ever assembled in America.

When the truck carrying the bomb parked in the basement exploded just past midday on 26 February 1993 it killed six people, injured over a thousand others and caused huge structural damage to the World Trade Center complex. It could have been much worse, but nonetheless the shockwaves were felt across America. Islamic terrorism had arrived.

Yousef left New York within hours, flying first to Karachi and then on to Quetta in Baluchistan where he stayed with his two younger brothers and his young wife and child and began working for an Islamic charity as a cover. Under American pressure raids were quickly mounted on the Quetta house and later on the house in Peshawar that belonged to his uncle Zahid-al Sheikh. By the time the authorities arrived, however, both men had fled, leaving behind a trail of paperwork that tied them very closely to bin Laden.

During the search of Zahid's house, a copy of the application form for a passport in the name of Abdul Basit – Ramzi Yousef's real name – was recovered. According to an internal Pakistani police report: 'The photographs of Zahid al-Shaikh with General Zia ul-Haq, Mian Nawaz Sharif [later to become prime minister] and Mr Ijaz ul-Haq [Zia's son] were also recovered from his residence-cum-office, which indicated the level of his intimacy with the top brass of national politics.'[13]

Ramzi Yousef's career as a terrorist had started dramatically. His first operation had been a huge success, demonstrating that America could be hit with impunity in the heart of its most important financial district. From this point on, Yousef was under the protection of bin Laden, although he appears to have planned many of his operations either alone or with his uncle Khalid. Like his father, Yousef may have joined the sectarian Sipah-e-Sahaba organisation for a while at this time. Its primary objective was the killing of Shi'ites.

For the next two years, Yousef involved himself in a whirlwind of terrorist operations. The same year he injured himself when he tried to kill Pakistan's then prime minister, Benazir Bhutto, with a car bomb. A detonator exploded prematurely and he had to go to hospital with serious eye injuries.

According to the Pakistan police, who were determined to crack the case, Khalid was also involved in the assassination attempt:

> During interrogation of one of the conspirators of the assassination attempt on Ms Benazir Bhutto in the early '90s, he disclosed that the weapons to be used for the assassination of the lady were provided by Khalid al-Sheikh. The conspirator also disclosed that he himself had transported these weapons from Peshawar to Karachi, which were provided by Khalid al-Sheikh.[14]

Dr Rehman Malik, who was head of Pakistan's Federal Investigation Agency at the time says: 'It seemed to us that the entire family were involved in this business. Ramzi and Khalid were both out to make a name for themselves. They had close connections with the jihadis, but it was unclear whom they were working for. They were both extremely dangerous men and to us in the FIA, it always appeared that they had protection at a higher level. When we raided Ramzi's house in Quetta, he had been warned. Likewise with Zahid in Peshawar.'[15]

For his diligence and determination to smash the ring of conspirators around Khalid and Ramzi Yousef, Dr Malik – who was the person who finally arrested Yousef in Pakistan – was himself arrested on trumped-up charges. Later he was able to escape and make his way to Europe. 'Given the right backing, I have no doubt that we could have broken them at that time,' says Dr Malik.

In the spring of 1994, Ramzi Yousef moved to Thailand where he tried to blow up the Israeli Embassy. In June 1994, along with his own father and his younger brother, Abdul Muneem, he set out to bomb the shrine of the Prophet's grandson, Reza, in Mashad, close to the Afghan border in eastern Iran. This is one of the holiest sites for Shi'ites and it was an openly sectarian attack. The small bomb they used caused extensive damage to the shrine's prayer hall and killed 26 people.[16]

Yousef's activities at this time were those of a desperately angry man. He moved from one outrage to another, with little strategic thought. But under the influence of his uncles Khalid and Zahid he was growing closer to bin Laden's organisation, agreeing to a request from al-Qaeda to return to the Philippines to launch new operations alongside the Abu Sayyaf organisation. While there he once again re-established contact with Khalid.

By this time the Philippines, whose southern islands had been in the grip of a radical Muslim insurgency for several years, was seen as an important new area of operations for the now rapidly expanding al-Qaeda organisation. In addition to Ramzi Yousef, Khalid and their team, other groups of Arab fighters had been sent to the islands. One of them, Umar al-Faruq, had arrived in early 1994 in the company of al-Mughirah al-Gaza'iri, who had been the Amir at the Khalden training camp in Afghanistan. Faruq, who was later captured in Indonesia, says he was sent by Abu Zubaydah, one of al-Qaeda's most senior organisers, to instruct fighters at a camp run by the radical Moro Islamic Liberation Front. The camp, called Camp Abubaker, had a special section for Arab fighters called Camp Vietnam.[17]

Khalid arrived in the Philippines in August 1994 on a Pakistani passport issued in Abu Dhabi on 21 July under his full name of Khalid Shaikh Mohammed Ali Dustin al-Balushi.[18] He had also used at various times a Saudi Arabian passport and a Brazilian visa, issued in the name of Ashraf Refaat Nabih Henin in Kuala Lumpur, Malaysia.

Khalid was known to use a variety of disguises and one report from the Philippines lists nearly 30 aliases for him including, Salem Ali, Abdul Majid, Mohammed Khalia al-Mana, Ashraf Ahmed, Khalid Abdul Wadood, Babu Hamza, Khalid the Kuwaiti and Fahd bin Abdallah bin Khalid.[19] At the Tiffany apartments in Eisenhower Street, San Juan, Metro Manila, where he lived with Ramzi Yousef in August and September 1994, he used the name Salem Ali. Yousef called himself Dr Adel Sabah.

Khalid was frequently seen hanging around the VIP restaurant inside the Harrison Plaza Complex in Malate, Manila. One of the waiters at the restaurant said that he would arrive around ten in the morning and stay for an hour or so, often accompanied by an Arab known as Anton Hannania. But Khalid and Yousef never stopped thinking about why they had come to the Philippines, diligently working on a new 'spectacular'.

Their first attack was the bombing of the Greenbelt Theater in Manila on 1 December. A week later, on 8 December, they moved to the Dona Josefa apartments in Malate, Metro Manila, where they were soon joined by another old friend and former jihadi, Wali Khan Amin Shah, an Afghani with an Uzbek background.

On 11 December 1994, Khalid and Yousef successfully placed a bomb on a Philippines Air (PAL) airliner bound for Japan, killing a Japanese national and seriously wounding 11 others. The bombing was in revenge for the arrest of Ramzi Yousef's accomplices in the 1993 bombing of the World Trade Center.

The conspirators were very cool. As they planned their attacks in Manila, they took plenty of time out to enjoy themselves. After bombing the PAL airliner they went to Puerto Galera, a beach resort south of Manila, to take a week-long scuba-diving course. One of Khalid's girlfriends later told police that he had portrayed himself as a rich Qatari businessman. One of their meetings took place in a five-star hotel in Makati, Manila's financial district. The two men also frequented nightclubs and hotel bars. On one occasion Khalid set out to impress a lady dentist by hiring a helicopter and flying it over her clinic while talking to her on the telephone.

This story is significant, if true. It demonstrates that Khalid could fly. Where and how he learned is a mystery. One clue might lie in the background of Abdul Hakim Murad, the childhood friend from Kuwait who arrived in Manila on Boxing Day 1994 and was arrested at the Dona Josefa apartment in Manila two weeks later. Murad had obtained a commercial pilot's licence after training at a flying school in Dubai in 1981 and then at three flying schools in the USA. He started off at the Alpha Tango Flying School in San Antonio, Texas, before moving on to Richmore Aviation in Albany, New York, and then the Coastal Aviation Flying School in New Burn, North Carolina, where he acquired his commercial pilot's licence.[20] To his close jihadi friends he was known as 'Captain Majid'. Two years later, Khalid turned up at university in North Carolina, although little is known about what he did during the two previous years. Could he too have learned to fly in North Carolina?

All along, Khalid was developing his ideas, knowing that his young nephew would be willing to take almost any risk to carry out his relative's requests. Little by little he began to develop an incredible strategic document – codenamed Oplan Bojinka, a Bosnian word for explosion – which had a number of different elements, including a plan to assassinate Pope John Paul II, US president Bill Clinton, Philippines president Fidel Ramos and other dignitaries by using a remote-controlled bomb and snipers during a papal visit to the country between 12 and 16 January 1995.[21]

Ramzi Yousef had already trained Murad in mixing explosives while staying in Lahore, Pakistan, the previous August. Khalid's idea was to explode the bomb near a stage where the Pope would be saying Mass in front of tens of thousands of worshippers. In the pandemonium that followed, snipers were to open up at random on the fleeing crowd.

Oplan Bojinka also involved hitting various targets in the Philippines including the US Embassy, the International School, Catholic churches and government installations.[22] But the heart of the plan was a plot to blow up 11 airliners simultaneously as they flew over the Pacific. In each case a bomb would be planted under a seat and the bomber would leave the plane during a stopover. Khalid was the main organiser.

All these plans were thrown into confusion on 7 January 1995 when a fire broke out in the Dona Josefa apartment, forcing the men to flee for their lives. Police arrested Murad and Shah and later recovered a laptop computer, diskettes and other materials that allowed them to piece together the full extent of the Oplan Bojinka. Khalid and Yousef got away, the latter fleeing to Pakistan, where a month later, on 7 February 1995, he was arrested at the Holiday Inn, Islamabad, by Rehman Malik, director-general of Pakistan's Federal Investigation Agency.[23]

According to a senior computer analyst from a company in Manila who was asked to examine the hard disk of the computer seized at the Josefa apartment, there were some sections written in Arabic using an Arabic version of a word-processing package. 'If you tried to read it using an English program, it would look encrypted,' says the analyst.[24]

He also found something much more remarkable: 'One report, which suggested an alternate plan to the blowing up of 11 airliners, mentioned crashing the airliners into the World Trade Center in New York, the White House and Pentagon in Washington DC, the John Hancock Tower in Boston, Sears Tower in Chicago and Transamerica Tower in San Francisco. Note that the original plan was the bombing or blowing up of 11 airliners. The crashing was an alternate plan (at that time).'[25]

The analyst had effectively stumbled over the blueprint for the 2001 attacks on America. It was confirmed later by Murad, who told interrogators that he had also discussed with Khalid the idea of flying an aircraft into CIA headquarters in Langley, Virginia. Khalid, who had worked out these plans, had not forgotten the failure of 1993. He was determined to go back to New York and finish off the Towers. And once you had decided to use suicide bombers, why stop at one tower or two? Why not go for a dozen? The plan was drawn in outline. The logistics and the funding had not been fully thought out and only he and Murad were trained as pilots. The plan would take a few more years to perfect, but Khalid never let it drop.

There were other indicators that Khalid was intent on attacking the USA, including a letter in the name of the 'Fifth Battalion of the Liberation Army under the leadership of Lt General Abu Baker Almaki', which threatened to attack American targets 'in response to the financial, political and military assistance given to the Jewish State in the occupied land of Palestine by the American Government'.[26]

When he was arrested on 7 February 1995 in Islamabad, Ramzi Yousef also had in his possession a draft letter headed, 'We Demand his Release', written by the 'Liberation Army' and claiming the 'ability to make and use chemicals and poison gas . . . for use against vital institutions and residential populations and the sources of drinking water and others'.[27]

'It was a strong network, continually hatching plots. After seven years, they were able to do what they started here. That's the story,' said Colonel Rodolfo Mendoza, who led the original investigation in Manila.[28]

The computer disks were passed on to the US authorities, who later used their contents to convict Ramzi Yousef. In the light of these plans, it is very difficult for the US intelligence agencies to claim that they did not have any kind of a warning about the attacks. Had they correctly identified the plans Khalid had been developing in Manila, and the way in which he rose to the top of al-Qaeda's military committee during the next four years, it is unlikely the 2001 attacks could have taken place.

While Ramzi Yousef fled to Pakistan, Khalid appears initially to have stayed put in the Philippines. He was not immediately a suspect and Murad and Shah had not talked about him to their interrogators. Shah said he had been given the bomb-making materials for the plot against the Pope by 'Adam Ali', a man whom he had first met in Karachi in 1992. He said he had been introduced to him as 'Abu Khalid' and that he was a doctor by profession. From the description given by Shah, it is likely that this was Khalid.

Philippines police reports say that Khalid was in the country until September 1995, probably under the protection of the Abu Sayyaf group. From there he moved to the Gulf. Some reports say he was living openly under his own name on a farm in Qatar owned by Abdullah bin Khallad al-Thani, then the emirate's religious affairs minister. Many former Afghan jihadis stayed on the farm, but interest in Khalid was growing. He had now been secretly indicted for the 1993 World Trade Center bombing and could not be ignored.

The FBI pondered on how to deal with the situation. The FBI director, Louis J. Freeh, met with Qatari officials to discuss various options but could come to no agreement. Any attempt to seize Khalid by force could result in a gun battle, with unknown consequences. Eventually Freeh formally wrote to the Qatari government, but by the time permission was granted Khalid had fled.[29]

By the late autumn of 1996, the CIA was receiving reports that Khalid was travelling in South America. Once again, despite trying to make arrangements with the local security services to arrest him, he was able to flee. He was now rapidly rising up the ranks of al-Qaeda, having conclusively thrown in his lot with bin Laden, who had by this time arrived in Afghanistan, having been expelled from Sudan. From the beginning of 1997 onwards, there is hardly a single al-Qaeda operation that Khalid was not involved in and there was also the unfinished business of the Twin Towers, to which he would surely return.

Nor did he let rest his desire to kill the Pope. Khalid had kept up his connections with the Abu Sayyaf group in the Philippines and when he heard of another planned visit by the Pontiff to Manila in 1999, he once again began planning.[30] Philippines intelligence documents confirm the plans for a second attempt on the Pope's life, which was only thwarted when the visit was called off due to his ill health.[31]

Documents captured when the Pakistani authorities arrested Ramzi Binalshibh in Karachi in September 2002 show that Khalid visited the Philippines several times to finalise the assassination attempt. The aim was to use local Abu Sayyaf militants to detonate explosives while the Pope was saying Mass.[32]

By February 1998, when the International Islamic Front for Jihad Against Jews and Crusaders was publicly announced to the world, Khalid was head of al-Qaeda's military committee, a trusted lieutenant to bin Laden and a man who by that time already had years of experience under his belt.[33]

Even after the planning for the 11 September attacks began in 1999, Khalid was still working on other projects. He travelled to Hamburg on several occasions to meet with Ramzi Binalshibh and Mohammed Atta, but he retained his close links in the Far East and started building a large regional network, based on four territorial organisations: Malaysia, Singapore and southern Thailand; Indonesia, except for Sulawesi and Kalimantan; the southern Philippines, the eastern Malaysian states of Sarawak and Sabah, Kalimantan and Sulawesi, Borneo and Brunei; and Irian Jaya and Australia.

Al-Qaeda considered the Far East to be particularly important and had always trained large numbers of fighters from these areas at its camps in Afghanistan. Several of the organisation's most senior figures visited the area, including Ayman al-Zawahiri, bin Laden's deputy. Escorted by al-Qaeda member Umar al-Faruq and a local Islamist, al-Zawahiri visited Aceh in Indonesia in mid-2000 to explore the possibility of assisting the secessionist movement on the island.

But Khalid was the key man who built alliances with Indonesia's Jemaah Islamiah organisation and the Abu Sayyaf group and the Moro Islamic Liberation Front in the Philippines. He built connections with Indonesian Islamists living in exile in Malaysia and sent them to the southern Philippines for training. In particular, Riduan Isamuddin Hambali was designated as the main contact person for al-Qaeda.

The results were devastating. On Christmas Eve 2000, twenty bombs exploded simultaneously in ten Indonesian cities. Six days later five simultaneous bombs rocked Metro Manila, killing twenty-two people. Khalid then attempted to organise suicide bombings of the US and Israeli embassies in the Philippines and Singapore in early 2001, providing funding for the operations. Under his instruction, Mansour Jabarah, a Kuwaiti-born Canadian citizen, and Ahmed Sahague, a Saudi, worked with Hambali on the plan.[34]

Umar al-Farq was captured in Indonesia in 2002 and later revealed to the FBI that al-Qaeda had provided funding for the Bali bomb in October 2002, which killed almost 200 people, mostly Australians, in the popular holiday destination.[35]

Khalid became more active than ever after the 11 September attacks, living clandestinely with Ramzi Binalshibh in a safe house in Karachi. When Abu Zubaydah, al-Qaeda's chief of operations, was arrested in Pakistan in March 2002, Khalid took over from him. Besides continuing to direct operations in Indonesia and the Philippines, he was closely involved in the planning of the suicide attack on the ancient Djerba synagogue in Tunisia in April 2002, which killed 21 people, including 14 German tourists. Nizar Nawwar, the al-Qaeda member who drove a truck laden with natural gas into the synagogue and engulfed it in flames, called Khalid just three hours before the attack. The truck attack was claimed by the Islamic Army for the Liberation of the Holy Sites, the same name initially used by al-Qaeda to claim the bombings of the US embassies in Nairobi and Dar-es-Salaam in 1998. It was also the same name found on Khalid's computer in Manila and on the draft letter found on Ramzi Yousef when he was captured. The Islamic Army, which is run through al-Qaeda's military committee, is Khalid's personal creation.

NOTES

1. http://www.fbi.gov/mostwant/terrorists/terkmohammed.htm
2. See Simon Reeve, *The New Jackals: Ramzi Yousef, Osama bin Laden and the Future of Terrorism* (London, Andre Deutsch, 1999), p. 114.
3. 'Suspected 9/11 mastermind graduated from US university', CNN, 19 December 2002.
4. Peter Bergen, *Holy War Inc.: Inside the Secret World of Osama bin Laden* (London, Phoenix, 2002) p. 53.
5. Ramzi Yousef also had close relations with Zahid al-Shaikh. He was interviewed by the Pakistani police in New York after his extradition. 'Mr Ramzi further stated that after his arrest, he wanted to talk to Zahid al-Shaikh, but he was not permitted. This indicates the involvement of Zahid al-Shaikh and the level of protection which was provided to Mr Ramzi by him.' 'Interrogation of Mr Yousef Ramzi and Abdul Hakim', Federal Investigation Agency, Pakistan, July 1995.
6. Federal Investigation Agency, report on Zahid al-Shaikh, nd.
7. *The Herald*, Islamabad, 1993.
8. Bergen, *Holy War Inc* ., p. 120.
9. *Ibid.*, p. 140.
10. *Washington Post*, 14 May 2002.
11. One of the main contacts was Abdul Majeed Madni/Munir Ibrahim Ahmed, a Saudi who had set up a business in Karachi importing holy water from the well of Zam-Zam in his home country. Madni is alleged to have provided the funds to purchase the weapons used in an assassination attempt on Benazir Bhutto.

12. Reeve, *The New Jackals*, p. 149. A radiological bomb has a conventional core of high explosive, around which is packed radioactive material. Its effect is to scatter this material over a wide area, contaminating it for many years.

13. Police report, authors' copy.

14. *Ibid.*

15. Authors' interview with Dr Rehman Malik, London, December 2002.

16. Reeve, *The New Jackals*, p. 66.

17. 'Umar Faruq: Summary of Information', Philippines Secret Intelligence Report, 5 November 2002.

18. Philippines Secret Intelligence Report, 5 November 2002.

19. *Ibid.*

20. 'Abdul Hakim Hashim Murad: Tactical Interrogation Report', Philippines Police, 9 January 1995.

21. When he was arrested on 11 January 1995, Wali Khan Amin Shah had in his possession detonating cord, mercury, a quartz timer, two sets of handcuffs, springs for a pistol and a firing pin. These items were to be used for the attempt on the Pope's life. He told interrogators that he had been given them by Khalid Shaikh Mohammed. See Tactical Interrogation Report, Philippines Counterintelligence Group, 13 January 1995.

22. 'OBL/Al Qaeda – Philippines Secessionist Group's Links', Philippines Counterintelligence Group, nd.

23. On 12 February 1997, after he had been extradited to the United States, Ramzi Yousef was sentenced to 240 years imprisonment on 11 counts, including the bombing of the World Trade Center. Unusually, the judge recommended that he should be kept in solitary confinement for the rest of his life. He is now being held at the Supermax Prison in Florence, Colorado, and will never be released. Khalid Shaikh Mohammed was later indicted for the same crimes, which are listed in the Indictment issued by the District Court for the Southern District of New York. See Indictment S93 Cr.180 (KTD). The FBI put a $5 million reward on his head.

24. Exclusive interview with anonymous source, Philippines, July 2002.

25. *Ibid.*

26. Southern District of New York, Indictment S93 Cr.180 (KTD)., p. 30.

27. *Ibid.*, p. 32.

28. 'Dancing girls and romance on the road to terrorist attacks', *Los Angeles Times*, 25 June 2002.

29. See 'Terror chief keeps scheming, escaping', *Chicago Tribune*, 24 December 2002. Robert Baer, a former CIA agent, recounts a similar story, but adds that an Egyptian, Shawqi Islambuli, whose brother had assassinated Egyptian president Anwar Sadat in 1981, was also living on the same farm. See Robert Baer, *See No Evil, op. cit.*, p. 404.

30. Nick Fielding, 'Mastermind of 9/11 plotted to kill the Pope', *Sunday Times*, 10 November 2002.

31. Philippines Secret Intelligence Report, 5 November 2002.

32. 'Al-Qaeda in plot to assassinate the Pope', *The Times*, 11 November 2002.

33. The original signatories were Egyptian Islamic Jihad, Islamic Group of Egypt, Jamiat-e-Ulema of Pakistan and the Jihad Movement of Bangladesh. Other groups are thought to have been secret signatories. See Rohan Gunaratna, *Inside al-Qaeda* (Hurst & Co., London, 2002), p. 45.

34. Jabarah was arrested in Oman in January 2002, after details of the plot were found in a wrecked al-Qaeda house in Afghanistan.

35. Philippines Secret Intelligence Report, 5 November 2002.

CHAPTER SIX

Unlocking the Masterminds

'End of the matter: consult with no one when it comes to the killing of Americans.'

Osama bin Laden

Deep asleep on the floor of room five, Fouda felt a gentle, repetitive nudge on his shoulder. 'Brother Yosri, brother Yosri,' a calm, persistent voice whispered, 'it is dawn.'

Day two in that Karachi safe house got off to an expected start: prayers again led by Ramzi Binalshibh. Still drying his wet arms with the tail of his kameez, Khalid rushed in and took his place next to Fouda. With him there was a new face.

'Stand straight – shoulder to shoulder and foot to foot,' Ramzi kindly commanded, 'may Allah have mercy on you.' During the prayers, Ramzi recited parts of Surah 9 from the Koran, known as *At-Taubah* (Repentance).

Revealed in the ninth year of the *Hijrah*,[1] it is the only surah that does not start with the formula *Besmellahi rahmaani raheem* – In the name of Allah, the Beneficent, the Merciful – for it is a declaration of war. When it was written in the seventh century, the Christian Byzantine Empire based in Constantinople had begun to move against the expanding Muslim tribes streaming out of Arabia, and this surah contains mention of a greater war to come and instructions with regard to it. It refers to the ghazwah of Tabuk, and especially to those Arab tribes who failed to join the Muslims in that raid:

O ye who believe! What aileth you that when it is said unto you: Go forth in the way of Allah, ye are bowed down to the ground with heaviness? Take ye pleasure in the life of the world rather than in the

Hereafter? The comfort of life of the world is but little in the Hereafter. If ye go not forth He will afflict you with a painful doom, and will choose instead of you a folk other than you. Ye cannot harm Him at all. Allah is Able to do all things.[2]

The 'Hypocrites', as the half-hearted supporters of Islam were called, had long been a thorn in the side of the Muslims. It is a moving and commanding section of the Koran and Ramzi was entranced by it. In a fearful, shaken but beautiful voice, Ramzi wept as he went on reciting more of the same surah:

Lo! Allah hath bought from the believers their lives and their wealth because the Garden will be theirs: they shall fight in the way of Allah and shall slay and be slain. It is a promise which is binding on Him in the Torah and the Gospel and the Koran. Who fulfilleth His covenants better than Allah? Rejoice then in your bargain that ye have made, for that is the supreme triumph.[3]

It is this very surah, it has since become known, that the hijackers were instructed to recite as they carried out the hijackings on 11 September, along with Surah 8, *Al-Anfal*, known as 'The Spoils'. From the content of the latter, its date of revelation can be established as the time that elapsed between the ghazwah of Badr,[4] the first in the history of Islam, and the division of the spoils, both of which occurred in the second year of the Hijrah.

According to the Koran, a Meccan caravan was returning from Syria. Its leader, Abu Sufyan, feared he would be attacked by the forces of the Prophet in Medina, and sent a camel-rider on to Mecca with a frantic appeal for help. In response, the tribe of the Qureysh[5] mounted an expedition and headed north towards Medina.

Mohammed's little army of 313 men, ill-armed and roughly equipped, travelled across the desert for three days until they halted near the waters of Badr. It was here that they heard news that the army of the Qureysh from Mecca was approaching on the other side of the valley.

When thy Lord inspired the angels (saying): I am with you. So make those who believe stand firm. I will throw fear into the hearts of those who disbelieve. Then smite the necks and smite of them each finger. That is because they opposed Allah and His messenger. Whoso opposeth Allah and His messenger (for him) lo! Allah is severe in punishment. That (is the award), so taste it, and (know) that for disbelievers is the torment of the Fire. O ye who believe! When ye meet those who disbelieve in battle, turn not your backs to them. Whoso on that day turneth his back to them, unless manoeuvring for battle or intent to join a company, he truly hath incurred wrath from Allah, and his habitation will be hell, a hapless journey's end.[6]

The army of Qureysh outnumbered the Muslims by more than two to one. When the Prophet saw them streaming down the sand dunes, he cried: 'O Allah! Here are the Qureysh with all their chivalry and pomp, who oppose Thee and deny Thy messenger. O Allah! Thy help which Thou hast promised me! O Allah! Make them bow this day!'

> O Prophet! Exhort the believers to fight. If there be of you twenty steadfast they shall overcome two hundred, and if there be of you a hundred (steadfast) they shall overcome a thousand of those who disbelieve, because they (the disbelievers) are a folk without intelligence. Now hath Allah lightened your burden, for He knoweth that there is weakness in you. So if there be of you a steadfast hundred they shall overcome two hundred, and if there be of you a thousand (steadfast) they shall overcome two thousand by permission of Allah. Allah is with the steadfast. It is not for any Prophet to have captives until he hath made slaughter in the land. Ye desire the lure of this world and Allah desireth (for you) the Hereafter, and Allah is Mighty, Wise.[7]

The implication of this surah is clear. It relates to other battles in other times, but this is the period in the history of Islam that provides inspiration to al-Qaeda and their followers. They too see themselves as a small, isolated band fighting against impossible odds. They look back in history and see how during the earliest days of Islam a small group of Muslims were able with their new faith to turn the injustice and oppression exercised against them by ignorant Qureysh into an overwhelming spiritual power that enabled them in the end to create and defend their own state.

Irresistibly, this period in the history of Islam has a unique flavour of magnetic nostalgia: its own aroma, rituals, myths, visions, metaphysics, and even its own vocabulary. People are rigidly divided, according to this way of thinking, into believers and disbelievers or hypocrites. No one can have a personal philosophy, for there is no such thing as philosophy.

According to the distinctions adopted by bin Laden and his followers, Muslims are divided into one of two categories: *Muhajiroun*[8] or *Ansar*.[9] The Muhajiroun are those who are urged to flee injustice and infidelity until such a time that they can come back and deal with it, while the Ansar are urged to receive them and support them until such a time that they can all unite in a common fight. This, for example, is how the London-based al-Muhajiroun group chose its name. Its leader, Syrian-born Sheikh Omar Bakri Mohammed, who 'fled' via Saudi Arabia to London on a fake Lebanese passport, deeply believes in this. Avoided by mainstream Muslims, he divides the world into either *Dar Harb* (house of war) or *Dar Silm* (house of peace). Ironically, London, where he lives on social support, is Dar Harb.[10]

Many of the mujahideen in the hills and mountains of Afghanistan would certainly like to think of themselves in these terms. Members of bin Laden's al-Qaeda and Ayman al-Zawahiri's Islamic Jihad who moved to Afghanistan from other countries are thus defined as Muhajiroun; while members of Mullah Omar's Taliban and other indigenous groups in Afghanistan are Ansar. Interestingly, when bin Laden rented a house in Sayed Jalaluddin Afghani Road in Peshawar, Pakistan, he called it *Beit al-Ansar* (Place of the supporters of the Prophet). Likewise, when Mohammed Atta, Ramzi Binalshibh and the rest of the Hamburg cell moved in 1998 to their flat in 54 Marienstrasse, they called it *Dar al-Ansar* (House of the supporters of the Prophet).

With this background, it comes as no surprise to find that the innermost circle of bin Laden and al-Qaeda refer to the 11 September attacks as the 'Manhattan ghazwah',[11] for they truly believe they are in a phase of jihad to establish the Islamic state, similar to that one of the early age of Islam. The ten-year period between 622, the year of the Prophet's flight from Mecca, and 632, the year of his death, becomes the mythical environment in which the masterminds and the hijackers view themselves.

Over the centuries the frequency of raids in the name of Islam rose and fell. They came to an end in the early twentieth century with the collapse of the Ottoman Empire and the rise of a strong central authority under the House of Saud. According to two notable Islamic scholars, 'The reconstituted ghazwahs directed at the World Trade Center and the Pentagon and other targets are intended to overturn that history and bring men back to the example of the Prophet.'[12]

A chilling five-page handwritten document was found in the luggage Mohammed Atta left behind at Boston Logan Airport as he rushed to catch his connecting flight – doomedm American Airlines Flight 11. The document, released by the FBI,[13] gave spiritual guidance to the hijackers as they approached the climax of their mission:

> As you set your foot into (T)[14] and just before you enter, recite your prayers and remember that it is a ghazwah in the way of Allah, for the Prophet, peace be upon him, said: 'A ghazwah . . . in the way of Allah is better than the World and what is in it'.

As they were just about to challenge mighty America, the document reminds the 19 hijackers of the angels that supported the Muslims in the ghazwah of Badr, when the unbelievers outnumbered the ill-equipped believers: 'Smile and feel secure, Allah is with the believers, and the angels are guarding you without you feeling them.'

Dreams and visions and their interpretation are also an integral part of these spiritual beliefs. They mean that the mujahideen are close to the Prophet, for whatever the Prophet dreams will come true. In a videotape recorded shortly after 11 September, al-Qaeda spokesman Sulaiman Abu Ghaith is seen and heard speaking in the company of bin Laden, who was playing host to a visitor from Mecca: 'I saw in my dreams that I was sitting in a room with the Sheikh [bin Laden], and all of a sudden there was breaking news on TV. It showed an Egyptian family going about its business and a rotating strap that said: "In revenge for the sons of al-Aqsa [that is, the Palestinians], Osama bin Laden executes strikes against the Americans." That was before the event.'

Bin Laden then interprets: 'The Egyptian family symbolises Mohammed Atta, may Allah have mercy on his soul. He was in charge of the group.'

Ramzi Binalshibh would later tell Fouda long stories about the many dreams and visions of the 'brothers' in the run-up to 11 September. He would speak of the Prophet and his close companions as if he had actually met them.

In a phone call shortly before the zero hour, Binalshibh asked Atta 'persistently' to pray to Allah during the attack that He may forgive him (Binalshibh) if he did wrong or was imperfect. 'Mohammed [Atta] used to assure me that we shall meet, God willing, in Paradise, and that our meeting shall be soon,' said Ramzi. 'I asked him [that] if he was to see the Prophet Mohammed, peace be upon him, and reach the highest place in Heaven, he should convey our *salaam* [greetings] to him as well as to Abu Bakr, Omar and the rest of the companions, followers and mujahideen.'

Atta promised so to do, but also told Ramzi a little anecdote about 'brother' Marwan (al-Shehhi) that he knew would please him. 'Mohammed told me that Marwan had a beautiful dream that he was [physically] flying high in the sky surrounded by green birds not from our world, and that he was crashing into things, and that he felt so happy.'

'What things?' Fouda asked.

'Just things,' answered Ramzi.

Green birds are often given significance in these dreams.

This mentality that dwells in the early age of Islam is also evident in the way the devotees of this new, almost heretical form of Islam refer to one another. All Muslims are 'brothers', this is not uncommon. What is uncommon is that each has a kunyah[15] that has got nothing to do with the person's real name. It borrows straight from the past, and it is meant to do so. Every member is assigned a kunyah that is actually the name of one of the Prophet's Companions, a faithful imam, a scientist, a military leader, a hero, etc.

This serves more than one purpose. It encapsulates a mountain of history into one name, and thus it is a great motivator. It is also a 'codename', crucial for underground activity, and this would please someone like Khalid Shaikh Mohammed. And it provides for a spiritual belonging and an emotional bond amongst the 'brothers' in a society of mujahideen in the way of Allah, and this would very much please someone like Ramzi Binalshibh.

A few weeks after the Karachi interviews, Ramzi sent Fouda a floppy disk answering some further questions. One of them was the exact kunyah for each of the 19 hijackers. Here is the way Ramzi himself put them in order, and the authors' research on each kunyah:

1. Mohammed Atta (Leader of the team that hijacked American Airlines Flight 11, which crashed into the North Tower of the World Trade Center): *Abu 'Abdu'l'Rahman al-Masri.* Literally, it means 'father of the servant of the Beneficent, the Egyptian'. One of the most famous Abdu'l'Rahmans in the early history of Islam is perhaps Abdu'l'Rahman Ibn 'Ouf. He is one of the ten to whom the Prophet gave glad tidings that they would go to Paradise. He donated much of his wealth to the army of the Muslims, and the Prophet once said to him: 'O! Ibn 'Ouf, you are one of the rich, and you will be entering Paradise toddling.'

2. Satam al-Suqami (AA Flight 11): *'Azmi.* The 'i' suffix in Arabic relates the meaning of the main body of the name to the caller. Thus, as you call him, you would actually be saying: 'My 'Azm'. Literally, the word 'Azm' means 'resolve' or 'determination'. There is no specific 'Azmi in history books, as this style of naming was not common in the early ages of Islam.

3. Waleed al-Shehri (AA Flight 11): *Abu Mos'ab.* Literally, it means 'father of the invincible'. One of the most famous Mos'abs in the early history of Islam is Mos'ab Ibn 'Omair. He was one of the most handsome, aristocratic, knowledgeable Companions. He also became the first ambassador in the history of Islam after the Prophet dispatched him to Medina to teach its inhabitants – the Ansar – the new religion.

4. Wail al-Shehri (AA Flight 11): *Abu Salman.* Literally, it means 'father of the intact'. It was Salman al-Farsi, originally from Persia, who suggested that the Muslims should dig a large trench around Medina to protect the believers against the armies of the disbelievers. A novelty in Arab warfare, it later proved crucial. The Prophet said of him: 'Salman is one of us, people of the House.' He was gifted with great wisdom and the Prophet's cousin, 'Ali Ibn Abi Talib, bestowed on him the laqab (title) of 'Luqman the wise'.

5. Abdul Aziz al-Omari (AA Flight 11): *Abu'l'Abbas al-Janoubi.* Literally, it means 'father of the one who frowns a lot, the southern'. The third state in the history of Islam was established in Baghdad by the Abbasids. But it is probably long before this that we find an association between this kunyah and the Prophet's uncle, al-Abbas Ibn 'Abde'l'Mottaleb.

6. Marwan al-Shehhi (Leader of the team that hijacked United Airlines Flight 175, which crashed into the South Tower of the World Trade

Center): *Abu'l'Qaqa'a al-Qatari.* The word 'Qaqa'a' in Arabic means 'the sound of clashing swords'. But al-Shehhi was not from Qatar. He was actually born in the United Arab Emirates. The most famous Qaqa'a is certainly al-Qaqa'a Ibn 'Amre al-Tamimi, a legendary military leader. The first Caliph, Abu Bakr al-Seddiq, said of him: 'Lo! The voice of al-Qaqa'a in battle is better than one thousand men.'

7. **Fayez Rashid Banihammad (UA Flight 175):** *Abu Ahmed al-Emarati.* The second part of the kunyah means that he comes from the United Arab Emirates, but the first part is too common. It probably refers to his grandfather, Ahmed Hassan al-Qadi. Generally speaking, however, the Prophet advised that the best names are those constructed of the letters 'ABD' or 'HMD'.

8. **Hamza al-Ghamdi (UA Flight 175):** *Julaibeeb al-Ghamdi.* Julaibeeb is the diminutive for Jilbab, which is the one-piece, traditional Arab dress. Al-Ghamdi is, literally, the one who manufactures scabbards for swords. A great companion of the Prophet, Julaibeeb al-Ansari disappeared during the ghazwah of Uhud, the second in Islam and the most disastrous. The Prophet said: 'But I miss Julaibeeb.' They later found his body next to the bodies of seven slain unbelievers.

9. **Ahmed al-Ghamdi (UA Flight 175):** *Ikrimah al-Ghamdi.* Ikrimah is a very old and common name among pre-Islam Arabs. A man of influence in Qureysh, Mecca, 'Amre Ibn Hisham, who was a sworn enemy of the Muslims, was later given the kunyah of Abu Jahl (literally: father of ignorance) and the laqab of 'enemy of Allah'. He had a son called 'Ikrimah' who later embraced Islam and became a close companion. The Prophet said to him: 'Welcome, riding immigrant.'

10. **Mohannad al-Shehri (UA Flight 175):** *Omar al-Azdi.* Apparently named after the second Caliph, 'Omar Ibn al-Khattab. Like 'Amre Ibn Hisham, he was a sworn enemy of the Prophet in the early days of Islam until the Prophet prayed to Allah to strengthen Islam with either of them. As it turned out, it was 'Omar who embraced Islam and became the symbol of justice with his kunyah, al-Farouq.

11. **Hani Hanjour (Leader of the team that hijacked American Airlines Flight 77, which crashed into the Pentagon):** *'Orwah al-Ta'ifi.* Named after 'Orwah Ibn Massoud al-Thaqafi who embraced Islam in the very early days and asked the Prophet that he be allowed to go back to his folk in Ta'if with the new faith. As he approached them on top of a hill they fired arrows at him until he fell to the ground. As he was dying he said: 'This is such an honour Allah has bestowed on me, and such a martyrdom Allah has given to me.'

12. **Nawaf al-Hazmi (AA Flight 77):** *Rabi'ah al-Makki.* Named after Rabi'ah Ibn Ka'ab, a close companion and a devoted servant of the Prophet. Impoverished and not so handsome, he was taken care of by the Prophet

himself who told him: 'Ask me anything and I will give it to you.'

13. **Salem al-Hazmi (AA Flight 77)**: *Bilal al-Makki.* There is only one Bilal in Islam. It is Bilal Ibn Rabah al-Habashi. A black slave in pagan Qureysh, he embraced Islam and had to endure fierce torture. He was left in the boiling desert with a large stone on his chest. Every time they checked on him, they found him repeating one phrase that was to resonate throughout the history of Islam: '*Ahadun, Ahad* (the One and Only).' He was bought and freed by Abu Bakr al-Siddiq. Gifted with a beautiful voice, he was chosen by the Prophet to be Islam's first caller for the prayers.

14. **Khalid al-Mihdhar (AA Flight 77)**: *Sinan.* Linguistically, Sinan is the spear, and sometimes specifically the front edge of it. It can also be used to mean the stone on which one sharpens a sword. There are many Sinans in the history of the Arabs, including Rashad-ul Din Sinan, the 'Old Man of the Mountains' who was leader of the sect of Assassins in the twelfth century.

15. **Majed Moqed (AA Flight 77)**: *al-Ahnaf.* Named apparently after one of the Prophet's closest companions, al-Ahnaf Ibn Qais. He was credited for his enlightened opinions, patience and tolerance.

16. **Ziad al-Jarrah (Leader of the team that hijacked United Airlines Flight 93, which crashed in Pennsylvania)**: *Abu Tareq al-Lubnani.* Literally, it means 'father of the one who knocks on the door, the Lebanese'. It is very likely that he was named after Tareq Ibn Ziad. One of the greatest military leaders in the Ummayad age, he conquered North Africa and the Andalus (now Spain). As he crossed the Mediterranean from Africa into Europe he burnt his ships and cried at his soldiers: 'The enemy is in front of you, and the sea is behind you.' Until today, the rock where he crossed still bears his very name, Gabal Tareq, Gibraltar (Mountain of Tareq).

17. **Saeed al-Ghamdi (UA Flight 93)**: *Mo'ataz al-Ghamdi.* The name 'Mo'ataz' is derived from the noun 'izzah' which means 'might, pride, invincibility'. This style of naming started to be common during the Abbasid age, but no one with this name is outstanding.

18. **Ahmed al-Haznawi (UA Flight 93)**: *Ibn al-Jarrah al-Ghamdi.* Al-Jarrah in Arabic is 'the surgeon'. It is almost certain that he was named after Abu Ubaidah 'Amer al-Jarrah, a great Companion of whom the Prophet said: 'Every nation has a trustee, and the trustee of this nation is Abu Ubaidah.' He is also one of the ten to whom the Prophet gave glad tidings that they would go to Paradise.

19. **Ahmed al-Na'ami (UA Flight 93)**: *Abu Hashem.* Ramzi Binalshibh said that al-Na'ami was a descendent of the Prophet. If true, the kunyah then makes sense. The Prophet's family was related to the Hashemite family. His grandfather, Hashem Ibn 'Abd Manaf was one of Qureysh's most distinguished, honourable and influential men. He took charge of the *Ka'aba* (the House of Allah which Muslims believe was built by the Prophet Abraham in Mecca) and played host to pilgrims.

Ramzi Binalshibh under arrest in Karachi after a two-hour gun battle with police, exactly a year after the attacks on America.

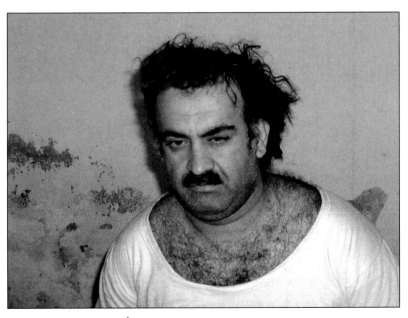

Khalid Shaikh Mohammed pictured hours after his arrest in Rawalpindi.

 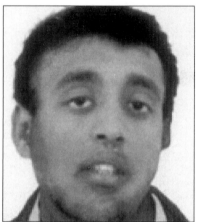

Until their arrests, these were the only known photographs
of the two main planners of the hijackings.

TOP: Khalid Shaikh Mohammed
BOTTOM: Ramzi Binalshibh

In both cases the pictures on the right have been
electronically manipulated from the pictures on the left.

Mohammed Atta as a young boy with his parents in Cairo.

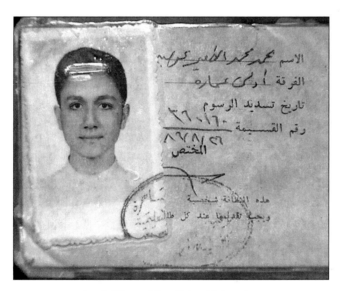

Atta's ID card for Cairo University.

Mohammed Atta senior at his house in Giza, Cairo.

Atta's picture on the wall of his parents' house.

Mohammed Atta shortly before
leaving Egypt for Germany.

Atta in Cairo shortly after he
graduated from Cairo University.

Atta on a building site in Egypt.

Atta in Istanbul, Turkey, in 1994 on his way to Aleppo in Syria.

The first-floor apartment at 54 Marienstrasse, Hamburg,
where Atta lived along with other members
of the Hamburg cell.

The entrance to the al-Kuds mosque in Hamburg where Atta
and others are thought to have been recruited to al-Qaeda.

Professor Dittmar Machule in his office
at Hamburg's Technical University.

The first page of Atta's thesis, with its quote from the Koran.

Osama bin Laden interviewed in
Afghanistan in October 2001.

Osama bin Laden and Ayman al-Zawahiri in February 1998 as they
announced the formation of the International Islamic Front for the
Jihad against Jews and Crusaders.

Omar Sheikh outside a Karachi courthouse during his trial for kidnapping *Wall Street Journal* reporter Daniel Pearl.

INSET: An al-Qaeda military unit undergoing training in Afghanistan.

Atta and al-Shehhi's house in Nokomis, Florida.

ABOVE: Flight instructor Arne Kruithof with his student, Ziad al-Jarrah.

INSET: The Comfort Inn Hotel in Portland, Maine, where Atta spent his last night.

BELOW: The 'Manual for a Raid', written by al-Omari and found in Atta's luggage.

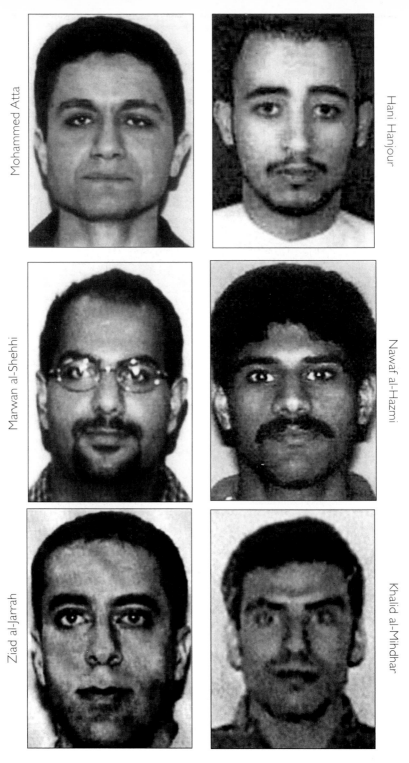

The pilots plus Atta's deputy, al Hazmi, and al-Mihdhar, who were all members of the senior planning group for the attacks, the *majlis al-shura*.

AMERICAN AIRLINES FLIGHT 11

Mohammed Atta (Abu 'Abdu'l'Rahman)

Abdul Aziz al-Omari (Abu'l'Abbas al-Janoubi)

Satam al-Suqami ('Azmi)

Wail al-Shehri (Abu Salman)

Waleed al-Shehri (Abu Mos'ab)

UNITED AIRLINES FLIGHT 175

Marwan al-Shehhi (Abu'l'Qaqa'a al-Qatari)

Hamza al-Ghamdi (Julaibeeb al-Ghamdi)

Mohannad al-Shehri (Omar al-Azdi)

Ahmed al-Ghamdi (Ikrimah al-Ghamdi)

Fayez Rashid Banihammad
(Abu Ahmed al-Emarati)

AMERICAN AIRLINES FLIGHT 77

Hani Hanjour ('Orwah al-Ta'ifi)

Khalid al-Mihdhar (Sinan)

Nawaf al-Hazmi (Rabi'ah al-Makki)

UNITED AIRLINES FLIGHT 93

Ziad al-Jarrah (Abu Tareq al-Lubnani)

Ahmed al-Haznawi (Ibn al-Jarrah al-Ghamdi)

Ahmed al-Na'ami (Abu Hashem)

Saeed al-Ghamdi (Mo'ataz al-Ghamdi)

Majid Moqed (al-Ahnaf)

Salem al-Hazmi (Bilal al-Makki)

Ahmed al-Haznawi's final will, issued
as a video by al-Qaeda.

Al-Qaeda intended to issue video wills for all the
hijackers, as this advert makes clear. Only al-Haznawi's
and al-Omari's have so far emerged.

After the prayers it was time for breakfast. Ramzi went to the kitchen, Khalid to his SMS messages. Curious about the newcomer who was following Khalid wherever he went, Fouda questioned Ramzi. 'Our brother is a close companion of Shiekh Abu Abdullah [bin Laden], God protect him,' Ramzi said as he started to boil about a dozen eggs, 'he has a nice anecdote for you.'

Reaching out for some plates, he added: 'And by the way, you better think of a name for him as he is not going to give you one.'

Fouda decided to call the man 'Abu Anas'. Ramzi liked it. 'Does this remind you of Hamburg?' Fouda asked.

'What? The kitchen?' Ramzi smiled as he went on. 'Hamburg! The good old days – of course it is always on my mind. All the brothers with whom I shared every moment, especially those who paid with their lives in the way of Allah. May Allah count them all amongst the martyrs.' Against Ramzi's wish, Fouda insisted that he was going to make tea this time. It was the friendliest moment so far.

'But, brother Ramzi, they also killed innocent civilians.' Fouda threw in the remark as diplomatically as he could. Ramzi was not impressed, although it was obvious that he had been bracing himself for such a question.

'This is a big issue,' he said firmly, 'and I do not wish you to confuse it in your programme, like many have done.' Trying to sidestep the question, he then asked: 'Did you see that programme on the BBC which was filmed in Hamburg and America?'[16] Fouda nodded as he continued to listen. 'It was good – very good, was it not?' Ramzi said, 'but only from a Western point of view.'

The doorbell rang and yet another new face came in. Fouda thought it was one of Khalid's many messengers. Ever since he had arrived they had been coming and going, some bringing messages, some bringing food and all leaving with instructions. This time, however, it was one of al-Qaeda's cameramen. Abu Yousef, as Khalid called him, was holding a small plastic bag when Fouda shook his hand and took him to a corner in room two. He had a Sony mini DV Handycam, a cable-neck microphone and five 60-minute DV cassettes, but no tripod. 'Do not worry about that,' Khalid said as he indicated to Abu Yousef to go to room one. 'He will find a way round it.'

Now it was the turn of Khalid and Ramzi to interview Fouda about their interviews. They were always going to be in control of the situation, and Fouda knew that. But he also knew that when Abu Bakr had picked up the phone on behalf of al-Qaeda, both parties had entered an unwritten agreement. They knew very well the investigative nature of Fouda's programme, *Sirri Lilghaya*. They knew that it was all about facts, information and details. Fouda would have been prepared to put up with a week of rhetoric as long as he got out of there with a few minutes of facts and straight talking. And for that, he listened and listened.

From the beginning he had wondered whom he would be meeting. Bin

Laden, maybe? Or his deputy, the inscrutable Egyptian, Ayman al-Zawahiri? But they were figureheads, the public face of al-Qaeda, the spiritual leaders. Khalid and Ramzi were here to take credit for what they had *organised*. They were the two master planners of 11 September – relaxed, calm and willing to speak. The men behind the Twin Towers operation had decided to break their silence.

As they sat cross-legged on the floor in room five they swiftly began to explain the planning and execution of 'Holy Tuesday' – or the 'New York and Washington Raids', as they also call them, using the old Arabic word, ghazwah.

'About two and a half years prior to the holy raids on Washington and New York,' said Khalid, who was clearly taking the lead and speaking rapidly in his colloquial Gulf Arabic, 'the military committee held a meeting during which we decided to start planning for a martyrdom operation inside America.'

He continued: 'As we were discussing targets, we first thought of striking at a couple of nuclear facilities but decided against it for fear it would go out of control.'

Fouda was dumbfounded. Nuclear targets? Could he be more specific?

'You do not need to know more than that at this stage, and anyway it was eventually decided to leave out nuclear targets – for now.'

'What do you mean "for now"?'

'For now means for now,' Khalid said, silencing Fouda. He continued: 'The attacks were designed to cause as many deaths as possible and havoc and to be a big slap for America on American soil.'

'Who would carry this out?'

'We were never short of potential martyrs. Indeed, we have a department called the Department of Martyrs.'

'Is it still active?'

'Yes it is, and it always will be as long as we are in jihad against the infidels and the Zionists. We have scores of volunteers. Our problem at the time was to select suitable people who were familiar with the West,' said Khalid, his stern face inflexible as the details poured out.

Now it was Ramzi's turn to interrupt the story with another surprise. He had gone to room three and returned with a small, dirty grey suitcase. He caught Fouda's eye as he unzipped it. 'Yes, it is my Hamburg souvenirs,' he smiled, handing Fouda a cup of tea. 'You are the first outsider to have a look at this.' He carefully began to unload his 'souvenirs', one by one. Soon, strewn on the floor in front of Fouda, were the bulk of the planning materials used by Mohammed Atta and the other hijack pilots as they plotted their attacks.

This was extraordinary. Fouda had not doubted that Ramzi was involved in the cell in Hamburg and had played a major role in planning the attacks in America. But here, now, in front of him, the very items used by Ramzi were being lifted nonchalantly out of the old suitcase.

There were dozens of items: a glossy Boeing brochure and flight manuals, a thick 'how-to-fly' textbook, an air navigation map of the American eastern seaboard, English language textbooks, floppy disks – lots of them, flight simulator CD-ROMs. It had all been in the Hamburg apartment that Ramzi shared with Atta, al-Shehhi, Bahaji and Essaber on the first floor of 54 Marienstrasse. And once the operation was in place and he had to leave, Ramzi had been confident enough to leave Germany with it all and travel to Pakistan, knowing that the contents of his suitcase would have created panic had a curious airport official chosen to open it.

'Wait, wait,' Fouda said as Ramzi tried to line up even more souvenirs. Next to a series of sophisticated illustrations on 'How to perform sudden manoeuvres', Fouda's eye had caught a page with paragraphs underlined and appended with handwritten notes. 'It is brother Abu 'Abdu'l'Rahman's handwriting,' said Ramzi, referring to Atta by his al-Qaeda kunyah. It did not look much like the rather prettier handwriting in the chilling 'Manual for a Raid' document that had been found in the luggage Atta had left behind at Logan Airport and which up to this point had always been attributed to him.

The note in Atta's luggage read:

> Force yourself to forget that thing which is called world. The time for amusement is gone and the time of truth is upon us. If Allah grants any one of you a slaughter, you should perform it as an offering on behalf of your father and mother, for they are owed by you. Do not disagree among yourselves, but listen and obey.

Ramzi explained the discrepancy in the handwriting. Atta was not the author of the instructions and prayers found in his luggage. They had been written by Abdul Aziz al-Omari, Atta's fellow hijacker and companion during the last hours of his life. Al-Omari, although one of the youngest of the hijackers, was recognised by the rest as having an exceptional knowledge of Islam – and a neat hand.

This discovery confirmed what Mohammed Atta senior had been saying since the emergence of this document. 'My son's is a funny handwriting,' he said, 'and I am announcing this for the first time. You could not tell if it belonged to a small kid or to a city planner.' When Fouda, however, challenged him to show the world some of his son's handwriting, he refused on the ground that 'the Americans would take it, scan it into a computer and programme it so as to compose whatever they like to attribute to my son'.[17]

Ramzi now spoke of how he had himself been eager to take part in the attacks. He had applied three times for a visa to enter America for flight training, but he had been turned down on security grounds.[18] He insisted, and Fouda believed him, that he was desperately sad not to have taken a more direct part in the operation. 'We have to pay a tax to go to Paradise,' Ramzi had said at one point.

He revealed that his souvenir suitcase and its contents were mostly material brought by Atta from America for him to study and learn during the period when he was still expecting to be one of the 'martyrs'. He had learnt the annual flight schedules for American Airlines by heart and still had at his fingertips the minutiae of the esoteric symbols used in the schedules to explain flight variations. He explained that this knowledge had been used to plan the aircraft seizures.

On the floor of room five, where they all sat, talked, ate and slept, Fouda helped Ramzi spread out his souvenirs. He would later film them himself from every possible angle. He could hear Ramzi's voice every now and then suggesting something or another, but he went on and on, filming what amounted to 60 minutes of footage.

But first it was room one in which the interviews would be conducted. Abu Yousef, the cameraman, gave the impression that he knew what he was doing. Thanks to Sony, the mini DV camera can be operated by just about anyone. However, he showed great imagination in trying to solve the problems caused by the lack of a tripod. He simply placed his camera on the edge of a large, empty box. Fouda began to brief him on the style of the programme, but then thought again. 'Just fix your camera on a medium close-up shot,' he said, as Khalid roamed around looking up and down and in every direction before checking the image in the viewfinder again and again. 'Forget about over-the-shoulder shots. Just fix it and let it run.'

Fouda sat in front of the camera and invited Khalid to have a look into the viewfinder. 'What do you think?'

But Khalid was not yet comfortable. He yelled at Abu Anas, the visitor: 'Bring me that brown cloak, will you?' He then stretched it with the help of Ramzi, pinned it to the wall in front of the camera and had another look. Still, he was not comfortable. He disappeared for a moment and came back dressed in a large, loose brown cloak, almost identical to the other one, covering him from neck to toes. As everybody was laughing, he took it off, placed it on Ramzi's shoulders and asked him to sit in front of the camera so that he could have yet another look into the viewfinder. 'It is okay now,' he declared, having checked that it obscured his body shape and hid any particular characteristics. 'We can begin. Sit in front of me.'

When the camera was switched on, Khalid Shaikh Mohammed's appearance changed. He tried to look like a religious leader or the leader of a political party. But his shallow knowledge of both religion and politics caught up with him. He tried to sound authoritative, but he stumbled in his desperate attempts to compose a couple of decent sentences in classical

Arabic. And he tried to address an imaginary audience of Muslims like an old-fashioned orator, at the same time managing to confuse what Allah said with what the Prophet said.

On several occasions Fouda had to correct him and on others they both had to consult with Ramzi. By this time, whether it was due to the heat or embarrassment, Khalid was sweating profusely. Filming had to be interrupted several times so he could dry himself down. The whole experience appeared to have shrunk him, to have drawn his claws. Suddenly he was no longer aggressive.

During the 70-minute interview, Khalid referred to his boss, bin Laden, sometimes as 'Sheikh Abu Abdullah', sometimes 'Sheikh Osama' or simply 'the Sheikh', but always in the present tense, and always praying to Allah to protect him. Once, though, he made what Fouda thought was a 'slip of the tongue', referring to him in the past tense. How much we could, or should, make of this it is hard to say. One audiotape issued in November 2002 appeared to suggest that bin Laden had survived American bombing at Tora Bora in Afghanistan, as did two others that surfaced in February 2003.[19]

During this whole affair, Khalid projected himself as a man of action rather than a man of thought. If they had business cards, bin Laden would be the 'Chairman' of al-Qaeda, Ayman al-Zawahiri the 'Vice Chairman' and Khalid Shaikh Mohammed the 'CEO'. Ramzi would perhaps be the faithful employee who comes in first and leaves last – the sort of employee whose name would jump into his boss's mind in emergencies, one willing to help out with everything.

Ironically, al-Qaeda is a 'company' in more than one sense and, interestingly enough, this is how it had been referred to in al-Zawahiri's correspondence with some of his close followers. A letter found in his computer after the fall of the Taliban was designed to look innocent should it fall in the wrong hands. Dated 3 May 2001 and signed 'Dr Nour, Chairman of the Company', it said:

> We have been trying to go back to our main, previous activity. The most important step was the opening of the school. We have made it possible for the teachers to find openings for profitable trade. As you know, the situation down in the village has become bad for the traders. Our relatives in the south have abandoned the market, and we are suffering from international monopoly companies. But Allah enlightened us with His mercy when the Omar Brothers Company was established. It has opened new markets for our traders and provided them with an opportunity to re-arrange their accounts. One benefit of trading here is the congregation in one place of all the traders who came over from everywhere and began working for this

company. Acquaintance and cooperation have grown, especially between us and Abdullah Contractors Company.[20]

Decrypt this message and it reads as follows:

> We have been trying to go back to our military activities. The most important step was the declaration of unity with al-Qaeda. We have made it possible for the mujahideen to find an opening for martyrdom. As you know, the situation down in Egypt has become bad for the mujahideen: our members in Upper Egypt have abandoned military action, and we are suffering from international harassment . . . But Allah enlightened us with His mercy when Taliban came to power. It has opened doors of military action for our mujahideen and provided them with an opportunity to re-arrange their forces. One benefit of performing jihad here is the congregation in one place of all the mujahideen who came from everywhere and began working for the Islamic Jihad Organisation. Acquaintance and cooperation have grown, especially between us and al-Qaeda.[21]

Then there is the fact that al-Qaeda has always been engaged in commercial activity for one reason or another. Bin Laden himself built huge businesses in the Sudan in the early 1990s, winning large government road-building and construction contracts. In Afghanistan he had also helped to build bunkers in the mountains, while his many Arab followers often described themselves as employed in the honey business when entering or leaving Afghanistan. In East Africa, al-Qaeda had created very good business opportunities by cornering the market in tanzanite, a rare precious mineral used in the jewellery trade.

Now, in the opposite corner of room one, it was Ramzi's turn to speak. As he sat in front of the camera, the wall behind him was covered with a multi-coloured plastic rug. Unlike Khalid, he was not interested in covering his shoulders and hands with a cloak. 'It is better to be natural,' he said, 'and anyway we will keep the tapes for editing purposes before you have them in a few weeks.'

'A few weeks?'

'You see, brother Yosri, we have to introduce some alterations to our voices, cut out parts that are not appropriate and perhaps also blank out our faces.'

Fouda, anxious to obtain as much material as possible, suggested that this could all be done using Al-Jazeera's facilities in Qatar. But Khalid interrupted. 'You guys usually use the mosaic effect,' he said, referring to the technique often used in TV programmes to disguise someone's face. 'But this could be easily decoded,' he said firmly. Ramzi added: 'We have our own production company, al-Sahab (The Clouds), and we can easily deal with that.' It was true. In fact, when Binalshibh was arrested in September 2002, investigators found hundreds of blank CD-ROMs in the apartment.

To make the point more clearly, Khalid went off to room three and came back with a small box. 'These are for you,' he said as he opened the box and started to hand Fouda some CD-ROMs and mini DV cassettes. 'This is brother Ibn al-Jarrah's[22] will in Arabic; this is the same in English for your friends in London; this is a documentary we made on the new crusades, which you guys did not broadcast;[23] and this is the beheading of Pearl the Zionist. You may use as much as you wish, and we would actually like you to distribute them to news agencies and Western TV channels, especially the French.'

As Abu Yousef lined up his shot with the video camera, Ramzi now sat on the floor in front of Fouda, calm, gathered and relaxed. 'So, brother Abu . . . ' Fouda did not finish his first question when Ramzi interrupted.

'Stop!' he ordered the cameraman, 'No kunyahs, please.' It did not, however, take him long to get in the mood. Now, he was different. The Ramzi who always needed a nudge or two could not stop talking.

'*Al-hamdu li'llah* [thank God] who said in His Glorious Book: "Fight them! Allah will chastise them at your hands, and He will lay them low and give you victory over them, and He will heal the breasts of folk who are believers",'[24] he started off. 'No sane Muslim should doubt the fact that [the day of] the Holy Tuesday operations in Washington and New York on 11 September was one of the great days of the Muslims. It brought back to them the memory of the days of the ghazwahs and battles of Badr, Hitteen, al-Qadiseyyah, al-Yarmouk and 'Ain Jalout' – referring to great historical battles won by Islamic forces.[25]

Ramzi continued on and on in beautiful Arabic, speaking in religious terms and phrases, before he began to answer Fouda's first question. 'As for the question of coordination,' he said of his own role as co-ordinator of 11 September, 'it is, in short, a process of linking the cells to one another, establishing a communication hub between these cells on the one hand and the General Command in Afghanistan on the other hand, and defining priorities of action for these cells. It also means following up on their work throughout the different phases, until the hour of execution. It is also about solving the problems that might face the brothers in these cells and devising an appropriate security umbrella under which the brothers can move around.'

For an 'Islamic activist' who lives in the West, how wide can this 'appropriate security umbrella' be? And how far, in their eyes, can a believer go in his efforts to deceive a non-believer?

Well, it would appear, as wide and far as necessary. Back in the Karachi hotel room, Abu Bakr had already said that it was acceptable for Fouda to miss the Friday prayers. A good Muslim should never lie, but Binalshibh lied several times to the German authorities. Atta too lied several times. He lied to his professor in Hamburg when, in justifying his absence, he told him he had 'family problems'. He lied to his flight instructor in Florida when, in covering up their past, he told him he was al-Shehhi's uncle. And he lied to the whole world when, in laundering his identity, he changed basic details in his passport. Nor did the deceptions finish there.

Al-Qaeda's members, while preaching one morality for others, were as inconsistent as those about whom they preached. In the mountain of documents left behind in al-Qaeda's training camps in Afghanistan, one Yemeni, Khalid, wrote to his brother describing the people he had just joined:

> I am in a whirlpool of contradictions. You cannot trust anyone here. Imagine that I have to hide the copy of the Koran you gave me for fear it might get stolen like my watch. They train us here on how to mix with the Christians and how to emulate their life style. We have to learn how to drink alcohol and to shave off our beards.[26]

Like missing prayers, drinking alcohol is one of Islam's most hated *Kaba'ir* (major sins). But it seems that one of the most senior hijackers, the Lebanese Ziad al-Jarrah, was encouraged, or at least licensed, to do just that. He blended in nicely with Westerners, lived with a girlfriend, according to his family, went out to pubs and clubs, and drank alcohol up to the very last moment on his way to 'paradise'.

As his good friend and flight instructor in Florida, Arne Kruithof, confirmed, 'Ziad was just an all-round fun guy to be with, whether that was on the ground or in the air, or off-campus when we went out. We had barbecues, played volleyball on the beach, and he used to drink the occasional bottle of Bud.'[27]

Call them sins of omission, but by the ultra-high standards that al-Qaeda set itself, these were major sins, the small lies that covered up the big lie.

Ramzi began to explain in more detail the events in Germany. By the time he had set about laundering his own identity, the stage in the Hamburg theatre was all but set. Each 'brother' had already embarked on his role, reconnaissance units had been dispatched, and bin Laden had already sent very open and public messages to Washington. They all fell on deaf ears. 'They never understand,' bin Laden had said, with a shrug of the shoulders, in one interview, 'until they are hit on the head.'

NOTES

1. The Islamic calendar follows from the year of the Hijrah, when the Prophet Mohammed had to flee from Mecca to Medina with his early followers. The first year corresponds with 622 in the Christian calendar.

2. *The Glorious Qur'an*, Surah 9, Verses 38–39.

3. *Ibid.*, Verse 111.

4. Also known as *Yathreb*.

5. The biggest tribe of Mecca, from which the Prophet Mohammed came.

6. *The Glorious Qur'an*, Surah 8, Verses 12–16.

7. *Ibid.*, Verses 65–67.

8. Early followers of the Prophet who fled Mecca with their new faith to Medina.

9. Inhabitants of Medina who welcomed the Prophet and his early followers and supported them.

10. Exclusive interview with Sheikh Omar Bakri Mohammed, London, August 2002. His justification for this classification of the UK is that the British government is helping the Americans in their 'war on terror'.

11. They also call them 'the two ghazwahs of Washington and New York', and sometimes 'the Holy Tuesday operations'.

12. Hassan Mneimneh and Kanan Kakiya, 'Manual for a Raid', *New York Review of Books*, 17 January 2002.

13. See www.fbi.gov/pressrel/pressrel01/letter.htm

14. The authors believe that the letter (T) indicates the Arabic word for aeroplane, '*Ta'irah*'.

15. An Arab, even before the birth of Islam, would usually have a given name followed by ancestry names. But he would also have a *laqab* which is normally a description of a physical feature, a behaviour, an attitude, the work that he does, an anecdotal situation that has stuck with him, etc. Many Arabs nowadays can find the roots of their family names/surnames in this laqab.

He would also have a kunyah. It literally means 'hidden name' and is usually given as one progresses from boyhood to adulthood. It mostly starts with either Abu (father of) or Ibn (son of), followed by a given name different from his original one. From then on he would be called as such as a matter of respect. For example, a famous Arab poet from the Abbasyd age had the laqab Abu'l'Ataheyah, and the kunyah Abu Ishaq, but not many would know that his real name was Ismail Ibn al-Qasim Ibn Suwaid Ibn Kaysan.

The contemporary meaning of kunyah is in a sense 'less hidden', though it slightly differs from one part of the Arab world to the other. In Egypt, for instance, it would be a straight 'Abu + eldest son's name', whereas in the Gulf countries it would be a straight 'Abu + father's name'. Some names in particular are always associated with specific kunyahs: a Mohammed would also usually be called Abu'l'Qasim, a Hassan Abu Ali, an Ibrahim Abu Khalil, a Mostafa Abu Darsh.

16. Referring to Jane Corbin's *Panorama* broadcast on BBC, December 2001.

17. Interview with Mohammed Atta senior, *op. cit.*

18. The security grounds were the suspicion of his involvement in the attack on the American destroyer USS *Cole* off the coast of Aden, Yemen, 12 February 2000.

19. Broadcast on Al-Jazeera Channel on 11 November 2002, the 145-second voice recording referred to recent events including the Bali bombing in Indonesia and

the theatre hostage crisis in Moscow, all of which took place after Fouda's interviews with Mohammed and Binalshibh. The Americans initially accepted the tape as genuine, but Swiss investigators later said they were 90 per cent certain it was faked. The authenticity of the two later tapes has not been challenged.

20. *Al-Sharq al-Awsat*, issue no. 8784, 16 December 2002, p. 3.

21. A similar type of coded talk was used around the same period between Atta and Binalshibh as they approached the zero hour of 11 September.

22. Kunyah for Ahmed al-Haznawi, one of the so-called 'foot soldiers' on board United Airlines Flight 93, which was piloted by the Lebanese Ziad al-Jarrah and crashed over Pennsylvania. Parts of his will had already been broadcast for the first time on Al-Jazeera Channel shortly before the meeting in Karachi.

23. Al-Jazeera did receive a copy of the documentary that was little more than a tribute to the 'martyrs' of the mujahideen during their struggle against the Soviet Army in Afghanistan and subsequent infighting. Al-Qaeda later sent a copy to the Saudi-owned Middle East Broadcasting Corporation (MBC), which, surprisingly, ran parts of it.

24. *The Glorious Qur'an*, Surah 9, Verse 14.

25. In Badr the Muslims defeated Qureysh of Mecca, in Hitteen the Crusaders, in al-Qadiseyyah the Persians, in al-Yarmouk the Byzantines and in 'Ain Jalout the Mongols.

26. *Al-Majallah*, issue no. 1188, 23 November 2002, p. 24.

27. Exclusive interview with Arne Kruithof, Venice, Florida, August 2002.

CHAPTER SEVEN

'The Hour is Nigh, the Moon is Split'[1]

'I wish I could raid and be slain, and then raid and be slain, and then raid and be slain.'

Osama bin Laden, quoting the Prophet

It was the breakthrough that German investigators had been waiting for. A red brick building with 21 employees in Wentorf, Hamburg, provided the evidence that seven now-infamous men, including Binalshibh, Atta and al-Shehhi, definitely knew each other as early as 1997. Earning 15 Deutschmarks per hour, their job at the Hay Computing Service Company – where they worked for two years – was to re-pack computers sent by IBM or Phillips before transporting them to a storage hall at the Hamburg free port for repair or modification.

At the end of 1997 Mohammed el-Amir (Atta) suddenly vanished for several months from the Technische Universitat Hamburg-Harburg. The university knew nothing about his whereabouts. 'In Atta's records,' said university spokesman, Rudiger Bendlin, 'we see between 1997 and '98 a gap of several months. We do not know where he was or what he did.'[2] Much as he tried to stress that his son was 'always calling him', Mohammed Atta senior also failed to provide an answer to the same question.

Just a few months before bin Laden and his deputy, Ayman al-Zawahiri, declared in February 1998 the creation of a new International Islamic Front for the Jihad against the Jews and the Crusaders, certain dates and locations lead to one conclusion: Atta travelled for the first time to Afghanistan. He would have stayed in what Khalid Shaikh Mohammed told Fouda was called *Beit al-Ghumad* (House of the al-Ghamdis) in the dusty, arid city of Kandahar in southern Afghanistan, effectively the capital of the Taliban. Bin

Laden had a large compound nearby and there were several similar houses – many of them built like fortresses – in the vicinity. The gathering place for Atta and the others was a building often used by volunteers from Saudi Arabia and named after the Saudi al-Ghamdi clan – four of whose young members, Hamza, Ahmed, Saeed and Ahmed al-Haznawi, would be foot soldiers in the hijackings.

Atta did not go to Afghanistan alone. A few months before his disappearance, Ramzi Mohammed Abdullah Omar, as Binalshibh was known to the German authorities, had also disappeared. He had learnt that the final verdict on his asylum application appeal had gone against him. Realising that he was now likely to face deportation, he secretly deported himself, only to re-enter Germany once more in December 1997 on a Schengen visa.[3] This time, his name was Ramzi Binalshibh.

According to al-Qaeda intermediary Abu Bakr, both Atta and Ramzi arrived in Afghanistan at the same time. 'They came together,' he said. 'I did not know who they were, but they arrived together. Brother Ramzi was very active and very much into media, and brother Atta was very kind.'[4]

When he arrived back in Hamburg after several months, Atta had acquired a new kunyah. From then on, he would be known among al-Qaeda members as Abu 'Abdu'l'Rahman al-Masri. 'When I asked him: Mohammed, what happened? Where have you been?' said his professor, Dittmar Machule, 'he explained that he had some family troubles, and I believed him – I believed him.'

But he was different. 'When I went to see him,' said his Egyptian friend, Nader el-Abd, 'he appeared dazed. He kept his good manners and respect, but not much humour any more.'

By the time Atta travelled to Afghanistan, bin Laden and the senior leadership of al-Qaeda had already agreed on the need for a strike against America. Bin Laden's companion, Abu Anas, who had arrived at the Karachi apartment and joined the others during Fouda's interview, made a point of drawing his attention to a television broadcast from February 1998: 'Did you notice, brother Yosri, something in Sheikh Abu Abdullah's [bin Laden's] interview with ABC when he announced the formation of the new organisation?' he asked. 'He sat in front of a map of Africa with Kenya and Tanzania behind his shoulders. That was his message to the Americans, but they did not get it. They are stupid.'

Later, Fouda made a point of checking the ABC interview. Dressed in a camouflage jacket, sitting on the floor and cradling an AK-47 rifle across his knees, a preoccupied but confident bin Laden said in the context of the interview: 'But, Inshallah, our forthcoming victory in Hijaz and Nejd[5] will make America forget the horrors of Vietnam, Beirut and other places.'[6]

It was a warning that an attack was imminent and on 7 August 1998 two simultaneous explosions rocked the American embassies in Nairobi and

Dar-es-Salaam, killing 263 people and wounding 4,500 others. The attacks took al-Qaeda's operations to a new level. The idea of synchronised strikes, which has since become an al-Qaeda trademark, had been born in blood and gore. It was the same idea behind Oplan Bojinka in the Philippines – massive, indiscriminate and merciless.

Nine days later, German authorities in Munich arrested Mamduh Mahmoud Salim and started to investigate Syrian-born businessman Mamoun Darkazanli. They were both suspected of financial involvement with al-Qaeda's activities in the West. That was followed, two weeks later, by the discovery in an apartment in Turin, Italy, of weapons, ammunition and plans to attack American institutions in Europe. At the same apartment, Italian investigators also found a Hamburg address of one Mohammed Haydar Zammar. Some sources have speculated that it was Zammar who recruited Atta and the others to al-Qaeda. There is no doubt that he was an important figure amongst the Islamic radicals in Germany and acted as a conduit to the burgeoning al-Qaeda organisation busily establishing itself in Afghanistan.

From 1997 onwards, the Syrian-born German citizen was often seen by Atta's neighbours carrying boxes up to the Egyptian student's first-storey walk-up. Only after 11 September, however, would the Americans come to realise the importance of the 135-kg Zammar. As he arrived in Morocco from Germany on 27 October 2001, having fled Hamburg, Zammar was arrested and shipped to his native Syria, the US's latest ally of convenience.

'He is like Abu Zubaydah,' said a US intelligence source. 'He is cooperating. Or he is cooperating without realising that he is doing it.'[7] Zammar was not the only al-Qaeda suspect sent by the Americans to an Arab state, where the local secret police could be relied upon to use techniques to extract information that would be banned in the USA.

Although al-Qaeda had carried out several actions prior to the twin attacks in East Africa, these were the first major actions planned and carried out by the organisation under the control of Khalid Shaikh Mohammed. The organisation was feeling confident and determined to flex its muscles. Now it was time to begin preparation in earnest for a much more spectacular event. It was time to activate the Hamburg cell.

In mid-July 1998, Ziad al-Jarrah and Zakariya Essaber both joined the Volkswagen plant in Wolfsburg as interns. Before the end of the same month Atta granted a Tunisian, Bachir B., power of attorney to take care of his affairs 'just in case'. And a few months later, on 1 November 1998, Atta, Ramzi Binalshibh and Said Bahaji all moved in together to the tiny 58-square-metre apartment on the first floor of a three-storey, mid-terrace, post-war building at number 54 Marienstrasse. They were later joined by Marwan al-Shehhi and Zakariya Essaber. Al-Jarrah maintained a discreet distance from the group, staying in a separate apartment with his girlfriend.

Ideally located just a few minutes' walk from the Technical University in

Hamburg-Harburg, the apartment in Marienstrasse was to become the al-Qaeda headquarters in Europe where the attacks on America would be planned. When they rented it, they had only one request from the landlord: a high-speed communications line.

Now deserted and eerie, it holds few attractions for any potential tenants. It was a functional place: 'I remember that I went into Said's room and into the kitchen,' said one friend of Bahaji who spoke on condition of anonymity. 'In Said's room I saw a small table and a computer; in the kitchen the normal stuff: cupboards, plates and pans. We had some food and tea, and I also met Omar [Binalshibh] and Mohammed el-Amir [Atta].'[8]

On New Year's Day 1999, the half-German Said Bahaji was called up for military service with the Bundeswehr but it took him only a few months to convince the German Army to exempt him on medical grounds. His escape was cause for celebration amongst the brethren and shortly afterwards Atta approached the university's administration with a unique request. He wanted permission to establish an 'Islamic working group' and funding for a prayer room within the secluded students' union building.

Permission was granted and soon the group were able to make use of the room as a discreet meeting point. The BBC's *Panorama* programme even claimed that Atta used the telephone line and the computer in room number 10 to communicate with Afghanistan.[9] This is, however, inaccurate, as the computer was not installed until long after Atta had departed. 'The computer was installed in February 2001,' says elected students' union officer Hendrich Quitmann. 'That was six months before the event and more than a year after Atta had left.'[10]

This must have been the busiest time in Atta's life – so far at least. As he re-doubled his efforts to get his long-awaited Masters degree out of the way, he was once more called to Afghanistan. This time he was accompanied by Marwan al-Shehhi, who would shortly begin to carry his new kunyah of Abu'l'Qaqa'a al-Qatari. The idea of a 'martyrdom operation' inside America was beginning to crystallise in the minds of the al-Qaeda leaders.

During their visit, they took their military instructions from Khalid Shaikh Mohammed and their promise of Paradise from Osama bin Laden. 'Then realise and appreciate what it is that the best of mankind [the Prophet], peace be upon him, wishes for himself,' bin Laden told them. 'He wishes to be a martyr.' According to Abu Anas, bin Laden would then quote the Prophet Mohammed as saying: 'I swear in He who Mohammed's life is in His Hands [Allah], I wish I could raid and be slain, and then raid and be slain, and then raid and be slain.'

It must have been quite an experience for the members of the Hamburg cell, none of whom had ever done military service. But Khalid's men would take them through what was required step by step. Though it was clear that they had been chosen for their 'brains', they had to enrol in the training camps for familiarisation with weapons, explosives, martial arts and combat skills.

A document discovered after the fall of the Taliban outlined the rules and instructions of the training camp. These included:

- Listening and obedience (is a must) in all your activities.
- Commitment to the Camp's programme, in part and in whole (is a must).
- It is forbidden to discuss controversial matters or criticise any Islamic group or organisation or any individuals, be they imams, thinkers, leaders or politicians.
- It is forbidden to step outside the boundaries of the camp without prior permission.
- It is forbidden to give lessons and general advice without prior arrangement with the administration.
- It is forbidden to play with ammunition, weapons, explosives or anything you do not know about.
- Guarding is a religious exercise and a responsibility. Do it to the best of your knowledge and ability.
- If you do not adhere to these clauses of the Camp's Rules and Instructions, you will be blamed and may ultimately be exempted from training.[11]

It was about this time, during the second half of 1998, that reconnaissance teams were sent to scout out potential targets in America. Although the idea of the attack had been agreed in principle, the specific targets remained to be chosen. That would eventually become Atta's job. Having studied potential targets on the ground, the military committee of al-Qaeda decided, as Khalid had already explained, to 'take nuclear targets off the list – for now'. The reconnaissance teams also recommended that 'we forget about the White House for navigation reasons'. The comparatively small building was not easily spotted from the air and was known to be well protected, so it was replaced by another spectacular target: Capitol Hill.

Later, when Atta was studying at flight school in America, he devised code words to refer to each of the selected targets. 'The cover-up context would be students hoping to join different universities in America,' Ramzi explained, 'We agreed on calling the World Trade Center – the Faculty of Town Planning; the Pentagon – the Faculty of Fine Arts; and Capitol Hill – the Faculty of Law.' The irony of giving the codename of Faculty of Town Planning to the World Trade Center would not have been lost on Atta, who had spent years studying the subject and often expressed his disgust at high-rise buildings.

Had the aircraft United Airlines Flight 93 not been brought down over

Pennsylvania, it would therefore have been Ziad al-Jarrah's mission to crash into Capitol Hill. In November 1999 al-Jarrah himself had disappeared from Hamburg for three months, during which he earned his kunyah in Afghanistan: Abu Tareq. In an attempt to explain his abscence he told a classmate that he wanted to learn how to fly in Pakistan 'because it was cheaper than America'.[12]

Ironically, the easy-going, alcohol-drinking al-Jarrah was one of the most dedicated trainees. 'Quite often he would go on guarding the camp beyond his shift,' an emotional Abu Bakr told Fouda, 'and every time I offered to relieve him, he would say to me: "You live here, but I live among the infidels. Please let me wash off some of my sins." He was a real Muslim, unlike what has been said of him.'

When the future pilots had completed their training in Afghanistan they all returned to Germany to begin a new phase of the operation. 'With regard to the brothers, the pilots, they returned from Afghanistan to Germany between February and March 2000,' said Ramzi. 'Last came our brother Abu Tareq al-Lubnani, that is Ziad al-Jarrah, may Allah have mercy on his soul.'

Flying out of Pakistan, al-Jarrah had to change flights in Dubai in the United Arab Emirates. It now appears that he was being watched. As he made his way through one of Dubai International Airport's busy transit halls, he was stopped at a security barrier. Someone at the CIA station based in the US Embassy in the Gulf state wanted to know a little more about this unusual character. He was questioned by security staff, but following consultations with the US Embassy, he was released.

From Dubai, a preoccupied al-Jarrah flew to Lebanon to dance at a family wedding party, which was filmed on video.[13] As the voices of well-known Lebanese singers Taroub and Najwa Karam were pumped through huge loudspeakers, pretty women took turns dancing around him in a circle in a typical Lebanese manner. There, right in the middle of the circle was Ziad al-Jarrah dancing, clapping, pulling and being pulled, and appearing to enjoy himself. But the camera would catch al-Jarrah from time to time looking as if he was trying too hard. He now had short hair, a frail body and a pair of unfocused eyes. This was not the al-Jarrah who had left Lebanon four years earlier. Something had happened to him, but it was, according to a Lebanese psychologist, far from brainwashing.

'The technique of referring to the glories and tragedies of the past, and persuading someone to use their time to provide for a better future for themselves and for the group they belong to,' explained Dr Ahmed Ayyash, 'this is mental programming, not brainwashing. Brainwashing is eradicating what you have in your mind and planting new ideas and beliefs. These people do not believe in this.'[14]

Al-Jarrah's friend, Ramzi Binalshibh, who later turned out to be his commanding officer, knew just what al-Jarrah was going through. 'I spoke with brother Ziad and asked him: "How do you feel?" He said: "My heart is at ease, and I feel that the operation will, Inshallah, be a success.'"

During al-Jarrah's absence Atta had finally finished his thesis. Many months later, in May 2002, Professor Machule sat Fouda exactly where Atta had sat during the oral examination. Machule was impressed with Atta and gave him a high-grade pass. His thesis was prefaced with this verse from the Koran:

> Say: Lo! My worship and my sacrifice and my living and my dying are for Allah, Lord of the Worlds. He hath no partner. Thus am I commanded, and I am first of those who surrender (unto Him).[15]

Though uncommon, the choice of dedication did not draw much attention at the time. But now Professor Machule sees the significance of it. A few weeks after the oral examination in August 1999, he was surprised to discover that Atta was still around. 'I remember one day he passed once or twice in front of my office door. He glanced in and when he saw me busy with students he disappeared. Then he came back to look again. He said "Hello!" and I remember very well his eyes. I said "Oh! Hello, Mohammed! How are you? Wait!" I shouted as he went off. "Wait a moment, let us have some coffee or something." But he did not wait. He vanished.'

These were the last words the German professor would speak to his dedicated student, Mohammed el-Amir. The next time he would hear of him would be on TV – under a different name. 'Maybe he wanted to say goodbye. I do not know,' he said.

By this stage, Atta was very short of time. He and al-Shehhi now devised a plan to clean up their identities. They both reported their passports stolen. As their final destination was being prepared, it was crucial to get hold of passports devoid of 'weird' visas, showing them clean-shaven and preferably with fresh names. On the day the new passports arrived, Mohammed el-Amir became history, making way for a new person whose name would in less than two years resonate around the world: Mohammed Atta.

No one knew where Binalshibh was or what he was up to. The likelihood now is that he was in Malaysia. Three of the 11 September hijackers – Khalid al-Mihdhar, Nawaf al-Hazmi and his brother Salem al-Hazmi were seen attending a meeting in Kuala Lumpur, Malaysia, where they were put under observation by intelligence agents on 5 January 2000. They are known to have met with two men suspected of involvement in the suicide bombing of the USS *Cole* in Aden Port in Yemen, which occurred in October the same year and resulted in the death of 17 American sailors. These were the one-legged Yemeni national Tawfiq bin Attash – usually known as Khallad – and Fahad al-Quso.

Also believed present at the same meeting were Khalid Shaikh

Mohammed, head of al-Qaeda's military committee and the man in overall charge of planning the attacks on America. In addition, there was Ahmad Hikmat Shakir, an Iraqi member of al-Qaeda, and Riduan Isamuddin, known as Hambali, who was a high-ranking member of Jemaah Islamiah, the group that in October 2002 would carry out the Bali bombing, killing nearly 200 tourists, mostly Australians.

The meeting lasted for four days and is thought to have been primarily concerned with planning the USS *Cole* attack, preparations for the 11 September attacks and a review of several failed operations, including the attempts to bomb Los Angeles International Airport during the millennium celebrations. Despite the fact that al-Mihdhar and al-Hazmi were both followed by Malaysian intelligence officers and had their computers searched, no evidence was found to indicate that they were involved in planning terrorist attacks and they were allowed to depart unhindered. They returned to Los Angeles via Bangkok and Hong Kong respectively, arriving back on 15 January 2000. Both then enrolled in a flight school in San Diego under their real names.

Despite the fact that both men had been spotted at the meeting in Kuala Lumpur, neither was prevented from entering the United States. Al-Mihdhar was even able to leave the country again in June 2000, travelling to Frankfurt, while al-Hazmi's visa was extended in July 2001 without any problem.

Immediately after his return from Afghanistan, Ziad al-Jarrah followed in the steps of Atta and al-Shehhi. On 9 February 2000, he went to the registration office in Hamburg and reported his Lebanese passport, number 1151479, stolen and had a clean one issued.

Meanwhile, Atta started to correspond with flight schools in 'enemy territory' and set about studying every little detail from every possible angle and every possible source. Khalid had worked out the basic details of his 'spectacular' operation and all he needed now was a team and a leader capable of carrying it out. He had found the perfect leader in Atta. It was a match made in 'heaven'. The mastermind who had waited so long for revenge for the failed 1993 attack and who was now full of hatred for America would soon lodge his masterpiece with history. And the perfect soldier who had just excelled in his thesis on how to build in the Arab world would soon excel at destruction in America.

Intentions, targets, means, codes, logistics and personnel were all now clearly defined. The planning and preparation were in full gear when a new US administration led by President George W. Bush took over in the White House. In bin Laden's eyes it was far more evil than its predecessor. 'In their first months of rule they said they will move their embassy [in Tel Aviv] to Jerusalem, and that Jerusalem will always be Israel's eternal capital. They were applauded by the Congress,' said bin Laden. 'This is sheer hypocrisy and utter injustice, and they will never understand until they are hit on the head.'[16]

Fifteen months before the zero hour, Atta and al-Shehhi together, and al-Jarrah by himself, arrived in Miami, Florida. They made their way to the west coast of the sunshine state where they unpacked in a quiet little town called Venice. Just as it was in Hamburg, Atta and al-Shehhi maintained the pretence of not knowing al-Jarrah in Florida, and that would remain the case until the very last day before the attacks.

In the first week of June 2000, Ziad al-Jarrah began his course at the Florida Flight Training Center near the local airport.[17]

'He communicated with us via email,' said owner of the school and instructor, Arne Kruithof. 'He took care of his visa and when he arrived he checked out okay on every question I asked him. He was the perfect applicant. He had considerable background on aviation and he spoke very good English, perfect French as well as some other languages.'[18]

Displayed on the walls of the flight school are hundreds of students' photos, including several of al-Jarrah. He appeared to be an integral part of the school's small society. 'Ziad was easy to talk to,' said Kruithof of the Arab trainee who quickly became his friend. 'He had a great sense of humour and a big heart. When I was ill once he was the only one who visited me, bringing a gift of a plant.' Kruithof also remembers that in the beginning al-Jarrah was not very comfortable with his female instructor, but soon adapted and would often go out to bars and clubs to enjoy himself and drink 'the occasional bottle of Bud'.

About 150 metres down the road from al-Jarrah's school there was another called Huffman Aviation, Inc.[19] It was here, on 1 July 2000, that Atta posed as al-Shehhi's uncle as they were being shown around. Two days later they came back with a decision. They wanted to join the course, but they also wanted the school to find them a place to live as they were still staying in a hotel.

'We found them a room with our bookkeeper, Charles,' said CEO Rudi Dekkers, 'but that lasted only one week as they were very anti-social and very rude to Charles's wife . . . Here in the school, we had kind of a problem with Atta. He was not nice. He was very arrogant. He was showing that he was on top of everybody . . . He was very unpleasant. Al-Shehhi was nice, very nice. I believe till today that he did not know what was happening. Atta knew, in my opinion, what he was doing. He had a face of death. Unbelievable.'[20]

As they gradually honed their flying skills, al-Jarrah shared a house in South Venice with two Dutchmen and a German couple who were training at the same school, whereas Atta and al-Shehhi chose to rent a house by themselves in the nearby town of Nokomis, about ten miles north of Venice. Within days of starting, money began to arrive from abroad in their local bank accounts. By September 2000 more than $110,000 had arrived, transferred from banks in the United Arab Emirates by a mysterious Saudi banker called Mustafa Ahmed Adam al-Hawsawi.

By the end of the course, Atta's bill had reached $18,703.35, while al-Shehhi's bill was $20,711.07. They paid in instalments with Sun Trust bank cheques, each paying $1,000 every other week. But it was Atta who always signed the cheques.

'When I asked al-Shehhi how come Atta was paying for him,' said Rudi Dekkers, 'he said: "He is my uncle, and he takes care of the money."'

Talking of those days, Ramzi Binalshibh said he had no problem with this deceit, which, in his opinion, was necessary. 'Every brother decides on the extent of his disguise according to his age, educational level and looks, so that they can misguide security agents and the people around them.'

On 26 July, Ramzi, the coordinator who had to be left behind in Hamburg, transferred 3,853 Deutschmarks to al-Shehhi's account in America. This was followed on 25 September by a bigger transfer of 9,629 Deutschmarks. During the next two months Ramzi is thought to have travelled to his home in Yemen, where it is likely he was involved in more planning for the attack on the USS *Cole*. The other planners included Khallad and Qaed Sinan al-Harithi, who was killed by a missile fired from a CIA-operated drone in November 2002. The most important member of the group in Yemen was the Saudi Abd al-Rahim al-Nashiri, head of al-Qaeda's Gulf operations, who was also captured in November 2002 in an undisclosed country (probably Yemen) and is now in US custody. Al-Nashiri was also involved in planning the attacks on the US embassies in East Africa in 1998.

As set out in the original plan, Ramzi himself was still hoping to join his 'brothers' in America to die as a martyr on one of the aircraft. He made his first attempt in May 2000 using his own passport. Later, there is some suggestion he tried twice to get a visa using the passport of Agus Budiman, an Indonesian student studying in Hamburg. Ziad al-Jarrah also tried at least twice to use his friend, Arne Kruithof, owner of the flight school, to obtain an entry visa for Ramzi. 'He approached me right in this room as we were drinking coffee,' said Kruithof. 'He told me that he knew somebody who was also interested in getting a Commercial Pilot Licence . . . He said his name was Ramzi something . . . When we found out that his English was poor, we referred him to a language school through which he tried to obtain a visa . . . When I asked Ziad why, if he knew, his visa was denied, he said: "No, I do not know that." We did then make a few phone calls, but nobody could tell us anything.' Apparently American intelligence had by then highlighted Ramzi as someone with possible involvement with al-Qaeda.

Another desperate applicant was Zakariya Essaber. He too had a new passport issued and on 12 December 2000, applied for an entry visa at the American consulate in Hamburg, but was turned down. He tried again, and again he failed.

Six days later, on 18 December 2000, having sent two warning letters to his home address, the Technical University in Hamburg-Harburg decided to strike Marwan al-Shehhi from its rolls. 'There is no single hint, no record whatsoever that he ever attended any of his classes,' said university spokesman, Rudiger Bendlin. 'In the summer of 2000 we sent a letter to his Marienstrasse address asking him to pay the insurance fee . . . When there was no answer, we sent a warning letter to the same address informing him that if he did not pay he would be out of the university. To our surprise, we found out much later that this second letter was found in Afghanistan.'[21]

Al-Shehhi could not have cared less. By now he and Atta had moved from single-engined to multi-engined aircraft. 'They were working very hard,' said their French instructor, Thierry Leklou. 'They committed themselves to learning, but lacked the love and passion for flying. They were not very patient, but in the end they were good enough to get their licences.'[22]

On 21 December 2000, Atta and al-Shehhi got their Private Pilot Licences as did, just down the road, Ziad al-Jarrah. Was that enough for them to pilot the Boeings into their targets just nine months later?

'First of all, we do not know exactly what he [al-Jarrah] did when he was in the cockpit,' answered Arne Kruithof. 'But to crash an aircraft you do not need any experience.' Kruithof also confirmed that, when asked by the FBI, he was able to recognise al-Jarrah's voice on the cockpit voice recorder as he took charge of United Airlines Flight 93 before it was brought down over Pennsylvania.

'They were not going home to their wives or families,' said Rudi Dekkers. 'They knew they were going to kill themselves. You can do a lot more when you know you are going to kill yourself. Second, you drive a car – you have a private car licence. Can you steer a big truck on the highway? Yes, you can. Can you back it up? Can you park it backing up? You cannot.'

In January 2001, al-Jarrah's girlfriend came over from Hamburg to spend a couple of weeks with him, after which he vanished. 'He was supposed to come back and finish his Commercial Pilot Licence,' said Kruithof, 'but he did not. Later, I found out that he did it somewhere else. He never contacted me once he left.' The trio then made their way from the western to the eastern coast of Florida, al-Jarrah still travelling separately from the others.

'This all happened while none of the closest friends of Mohammed, Marwan or Ziad knew of their whereabouts or what they were planning to do,' said Ramzi Binalshibh in Karachi, 'but brother 'Orwah al-Ta'ifi [Hani Hanjour] had already been in America, and he was a trained pilot. At that point of time, there was no communication between him and the Atta group. Contact was to be established later.'

On 4 January 2001, as al-Jarrah was enjoying some time off with his girlfriend, Atta was on his way from Miami Airport to Madrid. There are unconfirmed reports that he was looking for training on commercial aircraft simulators near the Spanish capital's airport. From there, he went back to Germany for a short visit.

'He used to look very healthy,' remembered Atta's Egyptian friend in Hamburg, Nader el-Abd, 'but I found him very frail when he came back. I asked him where he had been. He said he was looking for somewhere to do his Ph.D.'

Atta only needed six days in Europe. On 10 January 2001 he returned to Miami via Berlin. Thirteen days later, a Frenchman of Moroccan origin, Zacarias Moussaoui, who it has been reported was a possible standby in case Ramzi could not get into America, flew out from London Heathrow to Minnesota for training on a Boeing 757 simulator, even though he had no previous knowledge of flying. Ramzi had by then lost all hope of joining his 'brothers' in America.

'What they now needed was more flying hours,' said Ramzi, 'more training on simulators of large commercial planes such as Boeing 747s and 767s, as well as studying security precautions in all airports.'

As Marwan al-Shehhi followed Mohammed Atta to Dakota, Georgia, for more flight lessons, Ziad al-Jarrah hastily flew to Beirut and on to Zahla hospital where his father was undergoing open-heart surgery. He knew that this would be the last time he would see his father before he himself would die on his mission in America.

Until the interviews in Karachi, the hardest evidence in the public domain of al-Qaeda's involvement in 11 September was in the form of a videotape of bin Laden boasting to his supporters in Afghanistan. But the fact that the video was found in Afghanistan and later handed over to the US forces there was enough to make many people sceptical of its contents. In the video bin Laden is seen telling a visitor from Saudi Arabia how they planned for the attacks:

> We thought it over and planned [for it]. We sat down to calculate the [expected] size of the enemy's losses. We thought if [we had] four aeroplanes then we would have a lot of passengers on board. As for the towers, we thought that the number of storeys for one aeroplane to crash into would be three or four. That was our calculation, and I was the most optimistic among them in light of the nature of the business. I said that the fuel in the aeroplane would also make the iron melt . . . This was one of the best expectations – that the storey above would also collapse.[23]

The debate immediately after the release of this tape was at times farcical and gave rise to all kinds of conspiracy theories. 'First, the videotapes are contradictory,' said French writer, Thierry Meyssan. 'Bin Laden said he sent a Boeing to the Pentagon. This is false. No Boeing attacked the Pentagon. It was a cruise missile. So, why would bin Laden, or the man known as such, say such a thing?'[24]

'Even if it is materially proven that al-Qaeda had the principal role in this operation,' said Egyptian scholar, Dr Zaghloul al-Naggar, 'then it must have been infiltrated by American and Israeli spies. They are clever at this, and I know that they had their records of the Afghan mujahideen, especially the Arabs, and that they had been watching them.'[25]

'I have not seen any evidence that these guys were actually flying the planes,' said American conspiracy theorist, Edward Spanaus, 'and certainly no evidence that bin Laden was conducting and running the operation . . . The important thing is who controlled it from the top. If you try to focus too much on the people on the ground . . . you lose sight of who the mastermind is, who ran the operation from the top, and that is the important question.'[26]

Later, when Fouda asked his intermediary in Karachi about the veracity of the tape and whether or not it had been doctored, Abu Bakr was disarmingly frank, quickly dismissing any idea of a conspiracy.

'No,' he said. 'The tape, the brothers said – I am not sure whether they left it behind on purpose or not – but the Sheikh [bin Laden], yes, was talking to someone from Mecca.'

Yet there were many unexplained facts in the run-up to the attacks. For example, as America was celebrating its 4th of July Independence Day in 2001, when security is usually at its tightest, Khalid al-Mihdhar, who was a 'most wanted terrorist', easily found his way into the country.

'Al-Mihdhar was put on a watch list,' said former CIA Counter Terrorism chief, Vincent Cannistraro, 'but this was not recognised and nothing was really done until after he was in the United States. I mean there was about a two-week period before 11 September when the Immigration and Naturalisation Service was looking for him, and the FBI was looking for him. They should have been looking for him for a year. There was a disconnect.'[27]

Ramzi Binalshibh confirmed to Fouda that members of the Hamburg cell, who by then were in the final phases of the operation in the run-up to zero hour, were frequently being tailed. 'For example,' he said proudly, 'brothers Marwan and Ziad were tailed by security officers throughout their reconnaissance flight from New York to California – all the way through. But Allah was with them.'

It is also now known that senior intelligence officials were officially informed of what is now referred to as the 'Phoenix Memo'. Drawn up on 10 July 2001 by Arizona FBI agent Ken Williams, it expressed concern for the sudden rise in the number of Arabs taking flight lessons. Hani Hanjour, who two months later crashed American Airlines Flight 77 into the Pentagon, was there, training in Arizona, within easy reach.

On 2 July 2001, another FBI report warned of the increasing likelihood of an attack in the US and a CIA report received by the president on 6 August 2001 – only five weeks before the disaster – warned that the likely attack might involve an airliner.

It is also known that on his way back from al-Qaeda camps in Afghanistan, Ziad al-Jarrah was stopped in Dubai Airport at the behest of a CIA official to answer a few questions and then allowed to go on his way. Five months before the zero hour, Atta himself was stopped in Miami Airport on his way back from one of his many trips to Europe. His US visa had run out, but nonetheless he was allowed to enter the country.

A few days later, Atta was stopped for speeding while driving his car near Miami. He was given a ticket and an order to appear before court. He did not, and nobody asked why. But he would learn from his lesson. On 2 May 2001 he obtained a local driving licence number A300540-68-321-0. Within two weeks, six of his 'brothers' had also applied for and received their own US driving licences.

By then the 'foot soldiers' had already begun to arrive in the US individually and in twos until they totalled 15. These were to be the 'muscle' for the operation. 'As for the other brothers, the executors, who totalled 15, they came at a later stage except for brother Rabi'ah al-Makki, better known as Nawaf al-Hazmi, who had already been living in America for a long time,' said Binalshibh. 'At a later stage, contact was established between him and our brother Mohammed [Atta]. Nawaf was deputy to our brother, Mohammed Atta, who was in command of all the brothers.'

Khalid Shaikh Mohammed was less than forthright with the men he selected for his dream operation. 'They knew they were in for a martyrdom operation,' he said. 'But, to prevent any leakage of information, they were not informed of many details. We told them that brother Abu 'Abdu'l' Rahman [Atta] would provide them with details at a later stage.'

Some intelligence sources believe that had al-Hazmi and al-Mihdhar in particular not been lost after they entered the USA, the entire al-Qaeda network in the US could have been unravelled. The two 'buddies' from Saudi Arabia took their flight lessons in southern California and gradually improved their skills as commercial airline pilots. Neighbours found it odd that they would rarely use the telephone in their apartment. Instead, they routinely went outside to make calls on mobile phones.[28]

People who knew the men recall that they could not have been more different. Al-Hazmi was outgoing and cheerful. He once posted an ad online seeking a Mexican mail-order bride. By contrast, al-Mihdhar was dark and brooding, and expressed disgust with American culture. One evening, he chided a Muslim acquaintance for watching 'immoral' American television. 'If you're so religious, why don't you have facial hair?' the friend shot back. Al-Mihdhar patted him condescendingly on the knee. 'You'll know someday, brother,' he said.

After flying into New York on 4 July 2001, al-Mihdhar spent some of the time leading up to September travelling around the East Coast and, at least once, meeting with Mohammed Atta and other 'brothers' in Las Vegas.[29]

Al-Hazmi had moved on from California in early 2001 having flunked out of two flight schools. Next he decided to try his luck in Phoenix, Arizona, where he hooked up with Hani Hanjour. It was Hanjour who eventually piloted American Airlines Flight 77 into the Pentagon. In May 2001, al-Hazmi, now Atta's deputy, showed up with Hanjour in New Jersey and opened shared bank accounts with two others, Ahmed al-Ghamdi and Majed Moqed. The following month, al-Hazmi helped two others, Salem al-Hazmi (his brother) and Abdul Aziz al-Omari, open their own bank accounts. Two months after that, in August 2001, the trail would have led to the 'field commander', Mohammed Atta himself, who had bought plane tickets for Moqed and al-Omari.

Ramzi Binalshibh told Fouda that the Las Vegas meeting in the summer of 2001 was a meeting of the *majlis al-shura*, or consultative council. According to him it consisted of the four pilots, Atta, al-Shehhi, al-Jarrah and Hanjour, plus al-Mihdhar and Atta's deputy, al-Hazmi. The rest did not have much to do other than wait for instructions. They spread along the east coast of Florida north of Miami, praying, reciting the Koran, and building their strength. 'They were all courageous and well behaved,' said Binalshibh. 'Everybody remembers them all the time. They were never influenced by the corrupt way of life in America, although they were all young men surrounded everywhere by temptations.'

Five months before the zero hour, three Arab-looking faces hired a taxi for an unusual 400-km journey from south Germany to Hamburg in the north. They asked the driver to take them to the railway station where a friend would be waiting for them to settle the taxi fare. That friend was none other than Mohammed Atta. Khalid Shaikh Mohammed would not confirm or deny that he was one of the passengers, nor would he comment on speculation that linked his name to a vital 'summit' that was held three months later in Spain.

At the start of the second week of July 2001, Atta flew to Madrid where he hired a rental car and drove to Tarragona in north-east Spain. On 9 July he arrived at the four-star Monica Hotel accompanied by an Arab-looking man investigators now believe was Said Bahaji, Atta's former flatmate in Hamburg. Under the name he used to go by in Germany, Mohammed el-Amir, Atta checked into the Saint Jordi Hotel in the same town. The next morning he met with Ramzi Binalshibh who was also accompanied by another man, possibly Khalid Shaikh Mohammed. The four, according to Spanish investigators, were later joined by Marwan al-Shehhi and two others. The 'summit' went on from 10 to 17 July. Neither Khalid nor Ramzi would discuss this meeting with Fouda.

Two days later, Atta made his way back to Atlanta via Madrid and Berlin. And two weeks later, Zacarias Moussaoui's bank account in America received two financial transactions: one from Dusseldorf on 1 August for 23,571.59

Deutschmarks, and the other from Hamburg on 3 August for 9,487.80 Deutschmarks. The man who transferred the money used a made-up name and a fake passport. German investigators still don't know his identity, and Ramzi Binalshibh would not comment.

Twenty-five days before the zero hour – although at this point the final date had not been decided – Zacarias Moussaoui was suddenly arrested. The arrest was initially kept secret, so it is still unclear how the other conspirators learned of his arrest. Possibly enquiries made by FBI agents as they tried to find out what Moussaoui was doing tipped them off. Whatever the reason, Atta knew it was either now or never. Preparations were nearly complete, but this was the incident that triggered the final events. Through yet another meeting of the majlis al-shura, Atta assigned tasks and divided roles as follows:

Ziad al-Jarrah's team (Abu Tareq): Ahmed al-Haznawi (Ibn al-Jarrah), Ahmed al-Na'ami (Abu Hashem), Saeed al-Ghamdi (Mo'ataz), were assigned the task of blowing up Capitol Hill, codenamed the 'Faculty of Law'.

Hani Hanjour's team ('Orwah): Khalid al-Mihdhar (Sinan), Nawaf al-Hazmi (Rabi'ah), Majed Moqed (al-Ahnaf), Salem al-Hazmi (Bilal), were assigned the task of paralysing the military nerve centre of the greatest power on earth, the Pentagon, codenamed the 'Faculty of Fine Arts'.

Marwan al-Shehhi's team (Abu'l'Qaqa'a): Hamza al-Ghamdi (Julaibeeb), Mohannad al-Shehri (Omar), Ahmed al-Ghamdi (Ikrimah), Fayez Rashid Banihammad (Abu Ahmed), were assigned the task of destroying the South Tower of the World Trade Center, symbol of US trade and economic power.

Mohammed Atta's team (Abu 'Abdu'l'Rahman): Abdul Aziz al-Omari (Abu'l'Abbas), Satam al-Suqami ('Azmi), Wail al-Shehri (Abu Salman), Waleed al-Shehri (Abu Mos'ab), were assigned the task of destroying the North Tower of the World Trade Center, codenamed the 'Faculty of Town Planning'.

With just three weeks to go before the attacks were launched, Atta decided to contact Ramzi in Germany and confirm to him the final targets and timings and that all was well. He used the Internet, pretending to be a young man sending a love message via a chat room to his German girlfriend, Jenny. This is the exact message as it crossed the Atlantic in broken German:

Hello J....>

Wie geht's Dir? Mir gehts gut ....
    Wie ich Dir letzte mal gesagt habe die Erstsemester wird in drei wochen beginn keine Aendrungen!!!!!!!Als laeuft gut>Da ist gute Hoffnung und heftiges Wundschdenken!!! zwei Hochschulen... und

zwei Universitaeten... als geht nach plan dieser Sommer wird bestimmt haeiss warden.Ich will mit dir ueber einge Kleinchkeiten unterhalten 19 scheine fuer das Spezialstudium,und 4 klausuren>>>>>>>shoene Greusse an deine Professor...

Bis dann . . .[30]

The message was innocuous to anyone reading it as it stood, even in English translation:

The first semester commences in three weeks. There are no changes. All is well. There are good signs and encouraging ideas. Two high schools and two universities. Everything is going according to plan. This summer will surely be hot. I want to talk to you about some details. Nineteen certificates for private education and four exams. Regards to the Professor. Goodbye . . .

Its actual meaning was something else:

The zero hour is going to be in three weeks' time. There are no changes. All is well. The brothers have been seeing encouraging visions and dreams. The Twin Towers, the Pentagon and Capitol Hill. Everything is going according to plan. This summer will surely be hot. I want to talk to you about some details. Nineteen hijackers and four targets. Regards to Khalid/Osama. I will call you nearer the time.[31]

In a letter, along with an audiotape of their interview, sent to Fouda after he had returned to London from Karachi, Binalshibh provided further details about Atta's message.

First, the notice of the zero hour [three weeks] is a long one and no one can predict what might happen in between. This refutes all allegations by the American security agencies that they managed to intercept messages that spoke of the zero hour. Otherwise, where had they been all that time?

Second, the message indicated the targets in a simple, clear, unsophisticated language – two high schools and two universities. This contradicts the American security agencies' claims that the executors used sophisticated encryption programmes. The message also included reassurances that everything was going according to plan and that there were good signs and encouraging ideas – meaning visions and dreams of the brothers which filled them with confidence.

Third, Atta mentioned that that summer was surely going to be hot! This language of confidence, so long before the operations, indicates how strong [his] confidence in Allah's victory was.

Fourth, the way he spoke of the 19 brothers and, once more, the targets, is another crippling challenge for the security agencies with all their facilities and equipment. This is a holy gratuity from Allah.[32]

The die was now cast and Atta moved fast, as fast as he could. He first decided on two American airline companies: United Airlines and American Airlines. Of the planes, he picked the largest: Boeing 757s and 767s. Then he decided on the longest routes with maximum volume of fuel and best punctuality. Finally, he ordered his 'brothers' to disperse and to take different routes on their way to the assigned airports.

Binalshibh's final message about the attack came at 2.30 a.m. on 29 August 2001 when the phone rang in his Hamburg flat. When he picked it up, it was a voice he recognised, someone with a few Egyptian jokes and riddles for him. 'He told me in an Egyptian dialect: "A friend of mine has given me a riddle that I am unable to solve, and I want you to help me out",' an extremely emotional Ramzi remembered.

'I said to him: "Is this really the right time for riddles?" He said: "Yes, I know, but you are my friend and no one else but you can help me solve it." I said: "Okay, go ahead then." He said: "Two sticks, a dash and a cake with a stick down – what is it?" To which I replied: "Did you really wake me up to tell me this riddle?"'

Still slightly befuddled, Ramzi could not grasp the riddle. Suddenly, however, he cracked it. He got the message. 'Sounds like a sweet riddle. Let your friend know he has nothing to worry about,' he reassured his caller.

Sitting in front of Fouda on the floor of room five in that Karachi safe house, Ramzi turned his head away with a proud smile and then said in his serious tone: 'That caller was none other than brother Abu 'Abdu'l'Rahman [Atta]. He was unbelievable! Unbelievable! May Allah bless his soul and put Paradise under his feet, for he is, Inshallah, among the *shuhadaa* [martyrs].'

Then, with a rare flash of mischief, Ramzi explained: 'Two sticks is the number 11, a dash is a dash, and a cake with a stick down is the number 9. And that was the zero hour – 9/11.' Ironically, the only two numerals which look almost exactly the same in both Arabic and English are the numerals 1 and 9. Even more ironic is the fact that the American way of referring to the month before the day makes the writing of the date identical in both languages, as Arabic is written from right to left. Thus, 9/11 would have been easily solvable if anyone had been listening.

Ramzi was the first person outside the group in America to know the exact details of the zero hour. Even 'the Sheikh' himself, bin Laden, would not know until five days before the event. Ramzi wasted no time. He had less than two weeks to tie up all the loose ends and make all necessary arrangements. First he had to order active cells around Europe, America and elsewhere to evacuate. He began to gather his things, packed his souvenir suitcase and wiped the Hamburg apartment clean. He also made sure that his flatmate, Said Bahaji, had left Germany via Turkey and arrived ahead of him in Karachi on Tuesday, 4 September. Ramzi left Germany for Pakistan via a complicated route the day after.

Soon after he arrived, a messenger was dispatched across the border to bin Laden. 'Then all camps and residential compounds [in Afghanistan] were put on high alert,' said Ramzi. 'Brothers were dispersed, and the message was great news for Sheikh Abu Abdullah, may Allah protect him.'

According to Khalid Shaikh Mohammed, all 19 hijackers had videotaped their wills before leaving for the US, except for one. Khalid would not name him, but explained why: 'He feared it might be hypocritical and Allah, then, might not accept his sacrifice.' When Fouda asked if it would be possible to have a look at Atta's video will, Ramzi said: 'We shall treasure it for a while.'

The 19 hijackers now had only three days to live. Atta made his way with a member of his own team, Abdul Aziz al-Omari, to Boston where they stayed at the Swiss Chalet Hotel, now called the Park Inn. The morning after, Atta paid one more visit to Boston Logan Airport, looking closely at the runway, entry points and security arrangements. He then went down-town to return the remaining money he had no need for.

'I told him to keep the money for emergencies, but he said: "No, I have enough, and you guys need it more than me,"' said Ramzi. Atta sent a total of about $8,000 back to the mysterious Saudi financier, Mustafa Ahmed Adam al-Hawsawi, in Dubai, who collected the money hours before the attacks and vanished.

As the rest of the foot soldiers took up their assigned positions, Atta took al-Omari on one last road journey. The targets were in New York to the south and his departure airport was here in Boston, but he drove north to Portland, Maine. Subsequently there was some speculation that the two men had a rendezvous with an unknown ally who had crossed the border from Canada to meet them, but the real reason was much simpler. Atta, who was well aware that two teams of hijackers would be assembling at Boston Logan, knew that transit passengers from another airport would not be subjected to such serious security checks and that, therefore, at least one group had a chance of getting through.

Advising himself and his 'brothers' on their conduct during the hijacks, the eloquent al-Omari wrote in his 'Manual for a Raid':

> You must believe in the destiny of death, remove extra body hair and apply perfume. Wash yourselves. Learn your plan well and expect reaction or resistance from the enemy. Recite the surahs of At-Tawbah

and al-Anfal and understand what they mean, and learn about Paradise that Allah has reserved for martyrs.[33]

Fifteen hours before the zero hour, Atta and al-Omari arrived at the Comfort Inn Hotel near Portland local airport. They asked for one room for one night.

> Remember the words of Almighty Allah: 'And verily ye used to wish for death before ye met (in the field). Now ye have seen it with your eyes!',[34] and then remember: 'How many a little company hath overcome a mighty host by Allah's leave!'[35]

After checking in to room 232, the two men went out for a short walk in the small town. As they withdrew some money from a cash machine, a CCTV camera captured their image.

It must have been distracting, and ironic at the same time, for them to hear the continuous sound of aeroplanes taking off and landing near their window in Portland. By now all the hijackers knew what they were about to do. They would have taken to heart the verses of the Koran spelled out for them in the 'Manual for a Raid'. Slowly, the hours were counting down and the 19 men, after days of religious and mental preparation, knew they were facing death. Their minds would have gone back, time and again, to the verses of the Koran they had been instructed to read, comforting themselves during the last night of their lives as they thought of the glories of Paradise that awaited them in the afterlife:

> Think not of those who are slain in the way of Allah, as dead. Nay, they are living. With their lord they have provision. Jubilant (are they) because of that which Allah hath bestowed upon them of His bounty, rejoicing for the sake of those who have not joined them but are left behind: that there shall no fear come upon them neither shall they grieve.[36]

Early in the morning of 11 September 2001, as inhabitants of the two most important cities in the US headed as usual for work, the 19 foreigners had already embarked on their final journey. In twos, no more, they headed straight for their targets.

'These were very apprehensive moments,' said Ramzi. 'You are going into battle, a very large military battle, an unconventional battle against the most powerful force on earth. You are facing them on their own soil, among their forces and soldiers with a small group of 19.'

To Newark Airport near New York City headed Ziad al-Jarrah and his team. Awaiting them was United Airlines Flight 93, due to depart at 8 a.m. for San Francisco.

Smile and relax. Allah is on the side of the believers, and angels
protect you without you knowing.[37]

'People are often morally defeated,' said Ramzi Binalshibh. 'They have a
complex towards the CIA and Mossad [but why should they] when Allah has
instilled this nation with the duty of jihad, as we see [from the example of]
these rare heroic and courageous operations?'

To Dulles Airport near Washington DC, headed Hani Hanjour and his
team. Awaiting them was American Airlines Flight 77, due to depart at 8.10
a.m. for Los Angeles. But something almost went wrong. 'This person goes
through the metal detection machine and it starts buzzing,' said Vincent
Cannistraro. 'They call the person out so that they can do a hand search. Just
as the person was beginning to do that, a pretty woman walks by and the guard
looks at her and waves the guy on. Well, that person happened to be Hani
Hanjour, and he basically had box cutters and razor blades in his pockets.'[38]

And say: 'Oh Almighty Allah, set a bar before them and a bar behind
them, and (thus) have them covered so that they see not.'[39]

'And, as I told you, the enemy is stupid,' said Ramzi, with an air of disdain,
'and Allah does protect the mujahideen. Of course you need after all to be
alert and wise.'

To Boston Logan Airport headed Marwan al-Shehhi and his team.
Awaiting them was United Airlines Flight 175, due to depart at 7.58 a.m. for
Los Angeles.

Young man, smile in the face of death, for you are on your way to
Heaven.[40]

To the same airport, Boston Logan, headed Satam al-Suqami and the two al-
Shehri brothers, Wail and Waleed. Awaiting them, along with Atta and al-
Omari, was American Airlines Flight 11, due to depart at 7.45 a.m. for Los
Angeles. When they first arrived though, there was no trace of Atta and his
companion. A CCTV camera captured them still stuck at Portland Airport
at 5.45 a.m. Their flight had been delayed. As soon as they arrived at Boston
Logan, they rushed to catch their connection flight. The two men made it,
but Atta's luggage did not. There was simply no time for the airport workers
to transfer it from one flight to the other. A copy of Abdul Aziz al-Omari's
document of prayers and instructions was later found in the abandoned bag.

As you set foot onto (T), recite your prayers and remember that it is
a ghazwah in the way of Allah . . . The time for amusement is gone
and the time of truth is upon us.

'This was not just a single hijacking operation, but four,' said Ramzi. 'It was crucial, then, that all were executed simultaneously, and that all the brothers were on board at the same time.'

Atta took his place in business class seat number 8D. It was not an accident. 'They were all booked in advance,' confirmed Ramzi. 'They studied it, and they selected seats, mostly via the Internet, which would allow for maximum mobility and manoeuvrability. Depending on the interior of the plane and the distribution of members of the crew and security men, the brothers formed, in the way they spread themselves, either the letter L or the letter H. Each team had three wings: a pilot sitting in business class, two members sitting as close as possible to the cockpit door to break in at a certain point of time, and two[41] at the back to keep the passengers at bay.'

> Then, when (T) taxis and begins to ascend in the direction of (Q),[42]
> recite the prayers of travel, for you are travelling to Almighty Allah.
> (And enjoy your travel.)

The hijackers were instructed to take control of the aeroplane either during the vulnerable process of take-off, or not at all. 'It was crucial to consider the first 15 minutes as the golden opportunity to take control of the aeroplane and steer it to its target,' said Binalshibh. 'Each brother knew exactly what he was supposed to do. The break-in team would seize the earliest opportunity to rush into the cockpit and get rid of everyone inside, whereas the protection team would deal with passengers and security men – slaughtering them if necessary, and moving all passengers to the back. Meanwhile, the pilot would be taking his place inside the cockpit, steering the aeroplane. At worst, all this should be done within a maximum of six minutes – the sooner the better. All the brothers did a great job with the help of Allah, and there was constant contact among the four aeroplanes to reassure each other and coordinate their action as the pilots were finally on their way.'

Little is known about what happened in the air. Very few of the existing cockpit voice recordings have been released by the FBI. But in the case of Ziad al-Jarrah, it is known that he attempted to terrify the passengers into giving up all ideas of resistance. 'This is the captain speaking,' he said. 'I would like you all to remain seated. There is a bomb on board.'

> Then, each of you must be ready to perform his role in the manner
> that would please the Almighty Allah. Maintain your courage and
> resolve.[43]

'As for weapons, yes, the brothers were armed,' confirmed Ramzi. 'Their first weapon after their faith in Allah was *al-Takbeer* [the chanting of the words Allah-u-Akbar! – God is Great!], for this is the Prophet's first weapon in his ghazwahs. Of course, they also carried material weapons necessary to maintain absolute control over the aeroplanes. As for their clothes, there was nothing special, and you can make sure of this from other sources.'

The only sign that the hijackers wore any kind of special clothing were reports from passengers who called friends and family on their mobile phones to say that at least some of the hijackers emerged with red bandanas tied around their heads as they screamed at everyone on board.

> When battling, hit like a hero who has no desire to return to the World. Chant: 'Allah-u-Akbar', as Takbeer throws fear into the hearts of the disbelievers . . . If Allah grants any one of you a slaughter, you should perform it as an offering on behalf of your father and mother, for they are owed by you.[44]

'It is enough that I tell you that our brother, *Azmi* (Satam al-Suqami) slaughtered a security officer on his flight with brother Mohammed Atta which hit the first tower in New York,' said Ramzi Binalshibh. By 'slaughtered', he meant that the security officer's throat was slit with a knife or box-cutter.

At 8.44 a.m., Tuesday, 11 September 2001, Mohammed Atta had only one thing on his mind as he approached Manhattan: he was now just a single minute away from Paradise.

'We were in one of the mountainous paths having had the news on Thursday [6 September] that they would strike on Tuesday [11 September],' said bin Laden on that famous tape released by the FBI. 'We had the radio on, anticipating that it was going to be in the morning, as they would be going to work – that is 5.30 p.m. our time.'

As the hour drew near, bin Laden and his close companions, including Abu Anas, were attentively listening to the BBC World Service Arabic Section. It was an Egyptian presenter, Mahmoud al-Mosallami, Fouda's former colleague, reading the news: '. . . The Revolutionary Front for the Liberation of the People revealed today that the man who carried out the suicide operation in Istanbul is Ugor Bulbul who was one of the participants in the hunger strike . . .'

Bin Laden then turned to a Dr Ahmed Abu'l'Khair who was listening with him and said: 'If he [the newsreader] says: "We have just received this . . ." it means that the brothers have struck.'

They all listened on to al-Mosallami: 'This news comes to you from the BBC in London. And I have just received this news: Reports from the United States say that an airliner was destroyed upon crashing into the World Trade Center in New York . . .'[45]

145

NOTES

1. *The Glorious Qur'an*, Surah 54, Verse 1.
2. Exclusive interview with Rudiger Bendlin, Hamburg, June 2002.
3. Schengen visas were introduced on 26 March 1995 by the following member-states of the European Union who are signatories of the Schengen Agreement: Austria, Belgium, Denmark, Finland, France, Germany, Greece, Iceland, Italy, Luxembourg, the Netherlands, Norway, Portugal, Spain, Sweden. The Schengen visa issued by an embassy or consulate of the above countries allows the holder to move freely in all of these countries.
4. Meeting with 'Abu Bakr' in a Karachi hotel, August 2002.
5. Comprises old Arabia.
6. Bin Laden for ABC, somewhere in Afghanistan, February 1998.
7. *Time* magazine, vol. 160, no. 1, 1 July 2002, p. 28.
8. Exclusive interview with anonymous source, Hamburg, June 2002.
9. *Panorama*, December 2001.
10. Exclusive interview with Hendrich Quitmann, Hamburg, June 2002.
11. *Al-Majallah*, issue no. 1188, 23 November 2002, p. 27.
12. Exclusive interview with anonymous source, Hamburg, May 2002.
13. A copy of the video was presented to Fouda by al-Jarrah's relatives in Beirut.
14. Exclusive interview with Dr Ahmed Ayyash, Beirut, July 2002.
15. *The Glorious Qur'an*, Surah 6, Verses 162–163.
16. Exclusive interview conducted with bin Laden by Al-Jazeera correspondent, Tayseer Allouni, somewhere in Afghanistan, October 2001.
17. For more information, see www.fftc.info
18. Interview with Arne Kruithof, *op. cit.*
19. For more information, see www.huffmanaviation.com
20. Exclusive interview with Rudi Dekkers, Venice, Florida, July 2002.
21. Interview with Rudiger Bendlin, *op. cit.*
22. Exclusive interview with Thierry Leklou, Venice, Florida, July 2002.
23. The son of an influential building contractor in Saudi Arabia, Osama bin Laden was himself a trained civil engineer.
24. Interview with Thierry Meyssan, *op. cit.*
25. Interview with Dr Zaghloul al-Naggar, *op. cit.*
26. Interview with Edward Spanaus, *op. cit.*
27. Exclusive interview with Vincent Cannistraro, Washington DC, July 2002.
28. Michael Isikoff and Daniel Klaidman, 'The hijackers we let escape', *Newsweek*, 10 June 2002, pp. 22–31.
29. *Ibid.*
30. Given to Fouda on a floppy disk by Ramzi Binalshibh.
31. Binalshibh's own decryption.
32. A subsequent message sent later with the audiotapes of his interview.
33. Abdul Aziz al-Omari, 'Manual for a Raid', a document of prayers and instructions found in Atta's luggage.

34. *The Glorious Qur'an*, Surah 3: The Family of 'Imran, Verse 143.

35. *Ibid.*, Surah 2: The Cow, Verse 249.

36. *The Glorious Qur'an*, Surah 3: The Family of 'Imran, Verses 169–170.

37. Abdul Aziz al-Omari, *op. cit.*

38. Interview with Vincent Cannistraro, *op. cit.*

39. Abdul Aziz al-Omari, 'Manual for a Raid', based on *The Glorious Qur'an*, Surah 36: Ya Sin, Verse 9.

40. *Ibid.*

41. One in Ziad al-Jarrah's team.

42. The authors believe that the letter (Q) stands for the Arabic word Qiblah (the direction of Mecca towards which Muslims have to face during prayers). Incidentally, as all four flights were diverted in mid air, they were facing in the direction of the Qiblah.

43. Abdul Aziz al-Omari, *op.cit.*

44. *Ibid.*

45. The authors would like to thank the BBC World Service Arabic Section for providing them with a copy of the recording.

CHAPTER EIGHT

Grasping at Shadows

'Our words shall remain dead, like brides made of wax, stiff and heartless. Only when we die for them shall they resurrect and live among the living.'

Ramzi Binalshibh, quoting one of al-Qaeda's
most intimidating chants

It was late in the afternoon of Sunday, 21 April 2002 when Fouda finally packed his shalwar kameez with what little else he had in his suitcase, carefully placed Khalid's DVDs and CD-ROMs in his hand luggage and hoped for the best. He then joined in behind Ramzi for a last prayer before saying goodbye.

After nearly 48 hours, the last moments in that Karachi safe house were bizarrely emotional. Ramzi hugged him affectionately, Abu Anas shook his hand warmly, and Khalid handed him what looked like a statement, entitled 'The operation against the Jewish Synagogue in Djerba, Tunisia'. 'You can read it all later, on your own time,' he said, and then insisted on doing something that was very uncharacteristic of him. As Ramzi and Abu Anas stayed inside the flat, he led the way down the stairs.

'There is no need for you to come all the way down,' Fouda said.

'You know what!' Khalid answered, sounding like he was sending a text message. 'You would make the perfect terrorist.' He went on half-jokingly, 'I mean, look at yourself. You are a good boy, young, intelligent, highly educated, well organised, you speak good English, you live in London, and you are single.' Blindfolded, Fouda was deprived of the benefit of examining Khalid's eyes as he made his little 'joke'. A brief meaningless smile, however, spared him a serious answer. But Khalid was not satisfied.

'You remind me in a sense of brother Atta,' he said. Coming from Khalid, this was such a compliment and a great honour that it needed delicate handling.

'One of Allah's dearest blessings is that no human being can read the minds of their fellow human beings,' Fouda replied, playing the philosopher. 'It is our deeds that shall speak for us all in the end.' That was good enough for Khalid.

After guiding Fouda quickly to the waiting car, Khalid opened the door himself and shook Fouda's hands warmly. 'You are such a man. God bless you and protect you.' Those were the last words Fouda heard from al-Qaeda's military commander, words that would resonate in his ears for many days to come.

After about ten minutes in the car, the driver asked Fouda to remove his blindfold. The driver, a new face, then got out and hailed a taxi for him. On the way to Quaid-e-Azam International Airport, there was time to have a look at the Djerba statement. 'The Almighty said: "Fight them! Allah will chastise them at your hands, and He will lay them low and give you victory over them, and He will heal the breasts of folk who are believers,"'[1] it started.

Though bin Laden had touched on the Palestinian issue immediately after the US attacks on Afghanistan had begun in October 2001, this was the first clear statement of the new priorities. The emphasis had now changed towards Israeli targets, something that up to this point al-Qaeda had not focused on.

> In response to the atrocious Jewish campaign on the struggling Palestinian people, which the entire world is silently witnessing, so as not to upset the White House tenant . . . and the shame that has engulfed Arab and Muslim regimes . . . 1.3 billion Muslims are captives of their own corrupt regimes, loyal only to their masters in the West . . . and in light of these significant events . . . and in a positive change of direction to enlighten the Muslim peoples of the true role that they have to undertake, came the martyrdom operation against the Jewish synagogue in Djerba.

Within months, this 'change of direction' was to be affirmed through a double operation in Mombasa, Kenya, when al-Qaeda attacked the Israeli-owned Paradise Hotel on 28 November 2002, claiming the lives of fifteen people, including nine Kenyans, three Israeli tourists and the three suicide bombers. They also failed in a spectacular attempt to bring down an Israeli charter flight with a missile as it took off from the local airport on the same day.

The statement on Djerba admitted al-Qaeda's responsibility for the deadly operation in Tunisia which cost the lives of 21 people, including 14 Germans, just days before Fouda's arrival in Pakistan:

On orders from the military committee of al-Qaeda, the hero martyr Nizar (Saif-ud-Din al-Tunsi) single-handedly prepared for this operation. He has given the entire nation a unique example of a young man from outside Palestine who attacked the Jews with such a magnificent operation. The hero had embarked on a reconnaissance mission to inspect the target, photograph it and define points of weakness.

Implicating Khalid personally, the statement added: 'After discussions and consultations, the hero moved on to perform his duty towards his religion and his nation. We ask Allah to accept him amongst the martyrs.'

Just as he arrived at the International Departures gate at Karachi Airport, Fouda realised he was being watched. Amid the chaotic crowd saying their farewells stood two familiar Arab faces. When their eyes met, Abu Bakr nodded while Hassan, one of the drivers who had taken Fouda to his interview with Ramzi and Khalid, put his right hand on his heart. Then, just as suddenly, they disappeared.

On his way back to London, Fouda decided to stop in Dubai for a couple of nights. It was vital, as it proved later, to reflect on his bizarre meeting, to digest what had been a shocking and revelatory experience, and to develop a wall of resistance in the face of temptation. Living with the temporary 'guilt' of being the only person on earth – outside the highest levels of al-Qaeda – to know the story behind 11 September was ultimately more bearable than the unknown risks involved in a possible early leakage.

Now that he was back in one piece, and with a story to show for his experience, he took stock of the situation. Everything was here – except for the most important thing: the interview tapes. Suddenly, Fouda realised that he had no material evidence to prove that he had actually met anyone from al-Qaeda, let alone *the* masterminds.

A week later, armed with information he had picked up in Pakistan, Fouda threw himself into Binalshibh's world in Germany. With addresses, locations, phone numbers and contacts, seeing Hamburg through the coordinator's eyes proved to be both interesting and embarrassing. Some of those 'members of the Muslim community' recommended by Ramzi himself declined to become involved, some did cooperate, but all wondered where on earth Fouda got hold of their details and, of course, he was unable to reveal his source.

Back in London again on 4 June, his fax began to buzz late in the afternoon. It was a handwritten message from Abu Bakr.

> I met yesterday with the man who was with us at the airport. I mentioned the issue to him and, Inshallah, we will be sending you the stuff within days. Rest assured, I will be following up with them, and I will be in touch with you telephonically.

As he knew from a previous phone call that Fouda would soon be heading back to the Middle East, Abu Bakr also had a personal request. 'Since you are going to Egypt, would you please bring me some sweets from Tanta as well as some books? I will pay you back.'[2]

The list of the books included: *American Age from New York to Kabul* by Mohammed Hassanein Haikal, *War of Jilbab and Rocket* by Mahmoud al-Maraghi, *Memoirs of an Afghan Arab* by Dr Ayman Sabri Farag and *The Life of Mahmoud Mohammed Shaker's Pen* by Aida al-Sharif, as well as VHS copies of some of Fouda's previous investigations within the series, *Sirri Lilghaya*.

Two days later, on 6 June, Fouda was in Cairo for a meeting with Mohammed Atta senior. The next day, as he was taking part in a 'Media and Terrorism' seminar organised by his former Faculty of Mass Communication at Cairo University, Fouda's mobile phone rang with an urgent wire agency message. 'Al-Jazeera has just broadcast a videotaped will of Ahmed al-Haznawi, one of the 11 September hijackers,' it read. It was one of the tapes that Ramzi had mentioned to him in Karachi.

From Cairo, Fouda travelled, two days later, on 9 June, to Beirut for a meeting with Ziad al-Jarrah's family. While there, Abu Bakr called with a further reassurance. But the bottom line was still the same: he did not have a clue when or where or how the tapes would be delivered.

By that time, Khalid and Ramzi had dispersed, each going their own way. Khalid went back underground, running his vast, albeit wounded, network, probably from somewhere in Karachi, while Ramzi got busy with al-Qaeda's video production arm, al-Sahab. They were preparing their own documentary and statements to mark the forthcoming first anniversary of 11 September.

From Beirut, Fouda flew on 14 June to Doha, Qatar, where for the first time he told his boss, Mohammed Jasim al-Ali, what had happened in Karachi. 'No way!' was his first reaction. 'I think you better tell Abu Abdel-Aziz [the vice chairman, Mahmoud al-Sahlawi] yourself.'

After lunch at the Diplomatic Club, Fouda took Abu Abdel-Aziz aside and broke the news to him. 'Khalid Shaikh Mohammed?' he whispered in shock. 'I think you better tell Abu Abdullah [the chairman, Sheikh Hamad Bin Thamer Al Thani] yourself.'

The following morning, Fouda was in the chairman's office. One of the youngest and brightest members of Qatar's ruling family, Sheikh Abu Abdullah listened attentively for more than half an hour. Calm and gathered, he then asked the right questions: 'The tapes! When are you going to get hold of them? We must have them as soon as possible! How many people know about this so far? Keep it quiet, and take no chances. If you need any special arrangements for your own security, just let me know.'

For seven long days in Doha there was no news from Abu Bakr. There was always the chance that the tapes might never materialise. But, with or without them, the documentary, Fouda decided, was going to happen. He decided to head back to Karachi to get whatever he could, arriving early on 22 June.

He quickly hooked up with an Al-Jazeera camera crew coming down from Islamabad and began filming in the streets of Karachi and the surrounding areas. Fouda attempted to reconstruct on tape the events of two months earlier, doing much of the camera-work himself, as the crew did not know what they were filming for. The hope was that during the filming, which lasted for four days, Abu Bakr would get in touch. He did.

After a couple of small operations in Karachi, Abu Bakr had apparently decided to lay low for a while. 'They have been trying to tap our phones,' he said as he took his seat in Fouda's hotel room. 'I mean the Pakistani intelligence, as well as the French and US intelligence. I alone have four mobile phones, but the brothers have switched all their phones off, just in case, and I could not get in touch with them. But do not worry. You have done Germany, Britain, Egypt, Lebanon, UAE . . . and you still have America. Go ahead and when you come back I, Inshallah, will make sure that the stuff is delivered to Qatar – we'll find a way.'

Al-Qaeda's go-between then took his shoes off and went to the bathroom for a wash. When he came back he had another proposal. 'I always wanted you to include [Sulaiman] Abu Ghaith [al-Qaeda's spokesman] in your programme. You know he is an excellent orator and, by the way, he would not mind appearing under his real name.' But Fouda by then was only interested in the tapes. 'Yes, they told me it was going to take two weeks,' answered Abu Bakr. 'Khalid thought it was still far too early to deliver the tapes. And when one of the brothers went to see them they told him: "Give us two more weeks", and he told me to give you the transcription. I said: "Okay, let us finish with this."'

It was clear that Abu Bakr could not challenge a decision made by Khalid, the military commander of his organisation. Admitting this, he nonetheless felt guilty about not being able to fulfil his promise in time. 'The first fax that I sent you, it was Ramzi who wrote it. He said to me: "This couple of pages is our own point of view. If he [Fouda] would like to help us, we will help him." Now that you have met them yourself, they have provided you with the information and you are free to do whatever you please with it. If in the programme your point of view was pro- or anti-Islamist, they will not say anything to you. They could only say that "yes, we have helped the man. He is well known as an expert in his field and is not being used by either the Egyptian government, for instance, or America or the Islamists. He is just a professional."'

As they were agreeing on new ways of communication, Fouda brought out $200 and suggested that Abu Bakr should use it towards the cost of international calls – a normal practice in this business. Reluctantly, Abu Bakr accepted. Fouda would later learn that when he found out about the money, Khalid pushed Abu Bakr against the wall and threatened to kill him for accepting a 'reward for something he was supposed to be doing in the way of Allah'.

Fouda left Karachi on 26 June, only to embark a couple of weeks later on a hectic filming schedule in Miami, Venice, Hollywood, New York, Newark, Washington DC, Boston, Portland and other locations in the United States. While he was there, Abu Bakr finally called to break the good news: the tapes were in his hands.

Once again, Fouda then made his way back to Karachi, arriving from America via London on 27 July. He immediately made his way to the Regent Plaza Hotel and before long Abu Bakr was at the door. 'Please take your money back,' he said as he returned the $200 to a surprised Fouda. 'Thanks very much, but it was such a bad idea.'

Abu Bakr confirmed that he had been given the tapes, but, due to security reasons, had preferred to keep them with a 'brother'. As he was leaving to collect the tapes, he brought out of his deepest pocket a floppy disk. 'This is from brother Ramzi,' he said. 'I do not know what is on it.'

As he waited anxiously for Abu Bakr's return, Fouda put the floppy disk into his computer and began to go through Ramzi's two-page message:

> In the name of Allah, The Beneficent, The Merciful
> Dignified brother/ Yosri Fouda,
> As-Salaam-u-Alaikom . . .
> Considering the importance of the work that you undertake and the media message that you direct at both Arab and Muslim peoples, it is the obligation of he who works in a field capable of influencing public opinion to be faithful to Allah in this work. He should find his ultimate end in satisfying The Almighty Allah, and not satisfying human beings. He should not aspire to material benefit or fame, but consider his reward to be with The Almighty Allah. Taking into consideration facts of history, the reality that Muslims are presently living, and the amount of injustice and persecution exercised against them is fundamental in demonstrating your point of view within your programme. [You should] put the events of 9/11 and what subsequently occurred in this Crusade against Muslims in the historical and religious context of the conflict between Muslims and Christians, and in particular the struggle for survival by our Muslim brothers in Palestine. This link [between past and present] is very important so that the picture is complete in the minds of the viewers. This is a historical responsibility in the first place; for, unlike what has been promoted in the media, the ongoing war is not between America and the al-Qaeda organisation. It is in fact a clear Crusade against Islam and Muslims, and the pieces of evidence are

more than countless. You yourself are a man of experience in, and knowledge of, such issues.

Please forgive me for this long, yet important introduction which we had to clarify, may Allah make your present work of benefit for Muslims.

These are just some remarks:

● In case you are asked about the people you have met, it is vital that you do not give away details of their features or the change that occurred to their appearances. You should only stick to those features in the pictures they have.

● It is recommended that you interview Dr Abdullah al-Nafeesi[3] and Mr Abdul Bari Atwan.[4]

● There will be a new release by al-Sahab, coming up soon and we might provide you with a preliminary copy of it as soon as it is finished, along with some of the most important sound bites by Sheikh Osama and others from the leadership.

● The oath by Sheikh Osama would be important for your programme. I see that you should include it.

● There are some [Islamic] chants, like the videos *Caravans of the Martyrs I, II* and *III*, you can get from Islamic bookshops.

● Please note that music should not accompany the Glorious Qur'an or the Noble Hadith – absolutely not.

May Allah reward you with good things.

Close to midnight, Abu Bakr returned, looking agitated. 'I do not know, brother Yosri, how to tell you this,' he said, avoiding looking Fouda in the eye. It was obviously going to be bad news. But how bad?

Calming him down, Fouda took him by the arm and guided him to a chair. 'Take it easy. If it is the tapes, it is okay. Or is it something else?' Sitting on the edge of his seat with his left hand holding his forehead, a clearly disturbed Abu Bakr then put his right hand into the small pocket of his kameez and brought out a folded piece of paper. Saying nothing, he handed it over. Fouda quickly unfolded the dirty piece of paper. Immediately, he spotted a deliberately made hole after the phrase 'Dear brother . . .' Written in bad Arabic in bad handwriting, the message went on:

> We, the mujahideen, have been recently put under a lot of pressure. Although we are fighting in the way of Allah, we are not getting enough support at a crucial time of our jihad. Therefore, we ask for the amount of US$1m as a donation to help the brothers continue their work in the way of Allah. This is not an exaggerated sum of money as there are ten of us holding on, and the media people can surely afford it.

Stunned, Fouda kept reading as Abu Bakr looked apprehensive.

> The money should be provided in cash, put in a Samsonite briefcase,
> securely locked with a combination code. The briefcase should be then
> handed over to brother . . . who works at . . . pharmacy located at . . .
> This brother does not know about this matter, but we trust him. This
> is the mobile phone number you should then call to leave the
> combination code. It will be on only for the next two days.

The lower Fouda's eyes went down the page the more nervous Abu Bakr was
getting.

> The tapes will remain with us until we get hold of the briefcase. Only
> then we will find a way of delivering them to you. We, the brothers,
> would like to underline it to you that we will not tolerate any possible
> games, and that we are capable of dealing with any betrayals.

The unsigned Mafia-style message then ended with a last instruction: 'Having
read this message, you should memorise the mobile phone number, and burn
it to ashes.'

Without a second thought, Fouda handed the letter back, grabbed his
suitcase and started packing. Abu Bakr followed him. 'Please forgive me,' he
begged, 'it is all my fault.'

Smelling a rat, Fouda realised that this was a game being played behind the
backs of Khalid and Ramzi. Fouda did not even look at the man. 'Why don't
you tell your friend that he stands a chance of a better deal with the American
Consulate?' he said.

Suddenly, the dignified Abu Bakr was reduced to tears. 'Please forgive me,'
he wept. 'How could I possibly show my face to Allah if you do not forgive
me?'

What made Fouda certain that neither Khalid nor Ramzi knew about this
latest turn of events was the fact that Ramzi's floppy disk message was clearly
written on the assumption that it was going to be in Fouda's hands at the same
time as the tapes. Also, from Khalid's reaction to his payment of $200 to Abu
Bakr, it was clear that money was never a part of the equation. He and Ramzi
had not risked everything in meeting with Fouda to throw it all away over the
question of money.

Now that both had disappeared, there was obviously someone from within
who wanted to take advantage of the disruption that had hit the organisation.
Whoever it was knew that it would probably take some time for a message to
reach them, and that they would not be able to take action before he got away
with it – or that was what he thought. But he was wrong.

Leaving Abu Bakr with some follow-up questions to pass on to Ramzi,

Fouda headed back to London on 28 July with yet another promise from the go-between that he would make sure that the tapes were delivered in the UK. Sooner or later, Khalid and/or Ramzi would surely learn of what had happened and Fouda knew it. But what good was that if by then he was struggling against a fast-approaching deadline?

Running out of time, Fouda embarked on the long process of scriptwriting, assuming that what he had by then was everything he was going to get. So far, the only people he had told of his interviews with Khalid and Ramzi were the chairman, vice chairman and the director general of Al-Jazeera, and his associate in the London office, Muftah al-Suwaidan.

But Tayseer Allouni, Al-Jazeera's former correspondent in Kabul, surprised Fouda with a phone call from Doha a few days later. 'Are you expecting some tapes from Pakistan?' he asked, and then explained that the Al-Jazeera correspondent in Islamabad, Ahmed Barakat, who was covering for Ahmed Zaidan, had received a phone call from someone who claimed he had tapes for Yosri Fouda. The caller, according to Allouni, told Barakat that 'if Al-Jazeera is not prepared to pay $17,000, others would be willing to pay much more'.

Though it was a lot less than the original $1m asking price, Fouda asked Allouni to pass the message through Barakat that 'we are not prepared to pay even one penny, and that they can do whatever they please with the tapes'.

During the last week of August, after he had finished editing Part I of his documentary, *The Road to 11 September*, Fouda received a mysterious phone call from Karachi. It took him a while to recognise the voice of Hassan, the young talkative Arab with a Palestinian dialect who had been one of his drivers on the way to meet Khalid and Ramzi over three months previously. From then on, Abu Bakr would be just a memory. Someone else was now in charge. 'Just wanted to apologise to you about the mess,' Hassan said as he cleverly made Fouda feel that the news had reached Khalid and/or Ramzi. 'Everything is fine now and the brothers have asked me to pass on their greetings.'

Chairman Sheikh Hamad Bin Thamer Al Thani, who was in London at the time, joined Fouda and al-Suwaidan for a preview screening of Part I of the documentary. The following morning a brown envelope arrived in the mail. When he had a quick look at the way his office address was written, Fouda had no doubt it was from someone in al-Qaeda. The address would have looked perfectly normal to anyone else inside or outside the office, but as he had previously agreed in a simple code, it had 'Floor 7' instead of '7th Floor'.

Inside the envelope, which had been re-posted from a European country, there was a CD-ROM on which was an audio copy of Fouda's interview with Ramzi Binalshibh, together with a typed message from the latter answering some of the follow-up questions as requested. 'These are answers to some of the questions you have sent us. Enclosed is an audio copy of our interview as we have been unable to get hold of the master tape for the reasons that you know.'

There was nothing else – nothing from the interviews with Khalid or Abu Anas and nothing from the 'Hamburg souvenirs' rushes. But at least the coordinator's voice was there, albeit electronically modified. As he locked himself up inside the edit suite, after several attempts Fouda was able to turn it back to its original form, but decided in the end to use Ramzi's version as he had sent it. That, after all, had been the deal.

As Fouda quickly began to re-shuffle his script for Part II to accommodate Ramzi's voice, Al-Jazeera had already begun to promote Part I. Still very cautious, the promotion did not give too much away too early. 'On the first anniversary of the so-called Manhattan Ghazwah, Al-Jazeera opens doors never opened before,' was as close as it got. Not until the last few seconds did the 45-minute Part I give anything away when it was broadcast with English subtitles on Thursday, 5 September. But the last minute made headlines across the world the morning after.

A Reuters report reflected how little the world knew a year on about the masterminds of the most devastating act of terror in history. 'Arabic television station Al-Jazeera says it has confessions from two men it identifies as members of Osama bin Laden's al-Qaeda network claiming the group is responsible for the 11 September attacks,' the report said in its understated way.

> An Al-Jazeera official identified the two men as Yemen-born Ramzi bin al-Shaibah [Binalshibh], a former roommate of Mohammed Atta. The other man, Khaled al-Sheikh Mohammed [*sic*], appears on a US Federal Bureau of Investigations website list of most-wanted 'terrorists'. The website however does not link him to al-Qaeda. Shaibah was not on the FBI most-wanted list.[5]

The Reuters initial report then quoted Fouda as saying towards the end of Part I: 'In the second part of this documentary, there will be the first direct confession as to how al-Qaeda planned and executed the 11 September attacks.'

In coordination with Al-Jazeera, the London-based *Sunday Times* carried on 8 September a front-page report by Nick Fielding and a three-page story by Yosri Fouda, entitled 'The Masterminds'. Now it was set out in plain English, heightening expectations for Part II due for broadcast on Thursday, 12 September. In his front-page *Sunday Times* story, Fielding summed up the main points of what the world had not known until Fouda came back from Karachi:

> • The fourth target of the plotters was Capitol Hill and not the White House . . .
> • The initial plan was to crash the hijacked jets into nuclear power plants . . .

- The decision . . . was taken by the al-Qaeda Military Committee in early 1999 . . .
- Atta . . . was called to a council of war with key hijackers in the summer of 1999 . . .
- At least four reconnaissance units were sent to America before Atta and the would-be hijack pilots crossed the Atlantic . . .
- Atta communicated with Binalshibh in German through the Internet. He posed as a student in America contacting his girlfriend 'Jenny' in Germany.
- They referred to the targets as university departments. The twin towers were the 'Faculty of Town Planning', Capitol Hill was the 'Faculty of Law' and the Pentagon was the 'Faculty of Fine Arts'.
- They recruited the 'muscle' for the hijacks from al-Qaeda's so-called 'Department of Martyrs' . . .
- Binalshibh wanted to be the 20th hijacker but was refused entry to the United States . . .
- In hiding, he still has a suitcase full of planning materials used to plot the attacks . . .
- The interviews are the first full admission by any senior figures from bin Laden's al-Qaeda network that they carried out the 11 September attacks . . .'[6]

In a futile attempt to avoid the overwhelming world interest in the story, Fouda left London for Doha, where he put the last touches to Part II. As he arrived, he discovered another reason why chairman Sheikh Hamad Bin Thamer Al Thani had been so keen to invite him over along with Abdul Bari Atwan: Al-Jazeera had just received a new al-Qaeda tape. Over photos of the hijackers, bin Laden's voice was heard naming some of them, including the four pilots. He praised the men 'who changed the course of history and cleansed the [Arab-Islamic] nation from the filth of treacherous rulers and their subordinates'. It was not clear, however, when exactly he recorded his message.

Fouda suddenly realised that this tape was the one Binalshibh had referred to during the Karachi interview as a 'new release by al-Sahab to mark the first anniversary'. It also included the will of Abdul Aziz al-Omari, codenamed Abu'l'Abbas, Atta's last-night companion and author of the chilling 'Manual for a Raid' document found in Atta's luggage. 'May Allah reward all those who trained me and made possible this glorious act, notably the fighter and mujahid Osama bin Laden, may Allah protect him,' the eloquent al-Omari said in his last message before travelling to America to join the team of 15 who made up the 'muscle'.

Filmed in Kandahar shortly before they left for America, other future hijackers from the team were seen pouring over flight manuals and aerial maps of the Pentagon and other targets. As Al-Jazeera editor-in-chief, Ibrahim Helal, closed the door of the edit suite, Fouda rewound the tape. The maps and manuals looked very much like those he had filmed in Karachi, and the voice of the narrator sounded very familiar. Fouda was sure that the 'training materials' were part of the 'Hamburg souvenirs' and that the narrator was none other than Ramzi Binalshibh himself.

An edited version of the al-Sahab tape was broadcast on Al-Jazeera on 9 September. Only Helal knew of Fouda's discovery in the edit suite, but everyone knew that Fouda deliberately did not include Binalshibh's voice in the adverts for Part II of his documentary that had been running several times a day since the broadcast of Part I. Not until the morning of 11 September 2002, the first anniversary of the attacks, did the world get to hear Ramzi's voice *officially* for the first time.

'The brothers [in Afghanistan and Pakistan] shouted: "*TAKBEER, TAKBEER*",' Ramzi said, excitedly. He described how they all watched on television as Atta crashed American Airlines Flight 11 into the North Tower of the World Trade Center:

> They all chanted: 'Allah-u-Akbar' and bowed to Allah in gratitude, and they all wept. An operation like this you see in front of your eyes in that manner! The brothers thought that this was the only operation. We said to them: 'Be patient, be patient', and all of a sudden there was brother Marwan ripping through the South Tower of the World Trade Center, so violently in an unbelievable manner. We were all watching [this] live and praying: '*Allahumma*, aim, aim, aim.'

One day later and Part II would be out, also with English subtitles. Now Fouda could finally have some rest. After five long months, he went back to the hotel that evening for an early night, promising himself a tranquil morning on Doha's serene beach. Or that is what he hoped. At 2.35 a.m. he was woken by a phone call. 'Sorry, Yosri, but would you like to take a quick shower and join us here?' Al-Jazeera night editor, Arar al-Shara, said in a serious tone. 'They have captured Ramzi Binalshibh.'

Stunned and befuddled, Fouda sat on his bed unable to speak. 'Please, come here as soon as you can. People have been calling us to say: "When are you guys going to turn bin Laden in?"' As soon as he put it down, the phone rang again. This time it was the editor-in-chief, Ibrahim Helal. 'Well, well,' he said as he sounded half-asleep, 'seems that we are in for some time. I have just spoken to Abu Abdullah [the chairman] and his advice is to take it easy until we meet in the morning.'

Realising that he would find it hard to blame anyone if they associated his documentary with the high-profile arrest of Binalshibh, Fouda decided that it was crucial to set the record straight and clarify a few facts. Part of the circumstances that surrounded the Karachi interviews was mentioned in the documentary, but another part was not. Much of the latter he knew was not to be disclosed. His hands would always be tied by the promises he had had to give before the interviews took place, and which he was determined to keep.

Having just produced his biggest ever scoop, an unwilling Fouda suddenly found himself part of the story. The *New York Times* blamed him for 'keeping the information secret for more than two months' (actually, more than four months), and for 'not contacting law enforcement or intelligence agencies before or after the interviews'.[7] The *Washington Post* took his words out of context and claimed that 'Fouda is afraid, in a real sense, that he is not so popular among Binalshibh's followers – for the moment, fearful enough not to return to the scene of the interview.'[8]

Egypt's most popular newspaper, the semi-official *al-Ahram*, speculated that Fouda 'would not have been allowed to film inside [American] airports, banks and flight schools in these circumstances without some direct or indirect interference from an intelligence institution'.[9]

Carrying a front-page headline: 'Al-Jazeera informed CIA of the date', a Lebanese tabloid amateurishly claimed that:

> Western sources believe that the Qatari channel played an effective role in the arrest of Binalshibh by informing US intelligence agencies of the date of the interview, making possible the trailing of its correspondent and thus knowing the area where Binalshibh was before his arrest last Wednesday.[10]

On the same day, the Saudi newspaper, *al-Yaum*, had it all worked out. 'US intelligence contacted a high-level official inside Al-Jazeera immediately after the broadcast of Fouda's programme, *Top Secret*. The Americans told the [Qatari] official that it was necessary to persuade the Egyptian journalist to cooperate.' The newspaper added:

> This came after the failure of previous attempts to persuade Fouda to talk as he maintained that he was not prepared to break his promises. Sources say that the high-level official then contacted Fouda to tell him that if he did not cooperate he would be fired, but if he did cooperate he would be promoted and given benefits. Fouda refused to talk about his sources.[11]

The CIA, the newspaper claimed, then began listening in to calls made to Fouda's mobile phone, and thus entrapped al-Qaeda's intermediary who was then arrested and forced to lead them to Binalshibh's hideout. That line of thinking prompted a German journalist with *Der Spiegel* magazine to interview Fouda on the colour, make and size of his mobile, his service provider and whether or not it had an ear piece.

Fouda could not resist a wry smile when the London-based, Saudi newspaper, *Asharq al-Awsat*, referred in a headline to the arrest of Ramzi Binalshibh and 'Abu Bakr, al-Qaeda's media official',[12] for the go-between himself never knew that Fouda had invented the name of Abu Bakr for easy reference.

It was all going mad. And as the Americans and Pakistanis quarrelled over who should take the credit for the arrests, al-Qaeda had other opinions. In the beginning, they categorically denied that Binalshibh had been captured. Widely believed to be speaking in al-Qaeda's name, the jihad online network, www.jihad.net, said: 'This farcical play has to a great extent distorted Al-Jazeera's credibility . . . and Yosri Fouda knows why . . . We challenge him to prove that he actually interviewed the brothers directly.'

Another message posted on the same website called Fouda 'a swine and a traitor', while a never-heard-of-before 'al-Jama'ah al-Takfeeriyah', ostensibly based in Jordan, issued a statement vowing that 'Yosri Fouda, with permission of Allah, will perish.'

Fouda knew that the real al-Qaeda people had not spoken yet. Khalid and Ramzi, and the people in their immediate circle, were the only ones who knew exactly what had taken place before, during and after the interviews. It was clear that different parties were now trying to take advantage of the situation.

Keeping a cool head here was no less crucial than it had been during the Karachi experience itself. As he went live for an interview on Al-Jazeera on 20 September, Fouda knew that Khalid would be watching. The much-publicised programme hosted by Mohammed Krichan also included Al-Jazeera's Tayseer Allouni in Doha, CNN's Sheila McVicar in London and *al-Hayat*'s Mohammed Salah in Cairo. The topic was 'al-Qaeda and the media'. During the two-hour live phone-in programme Fouda said that the interviews had taken place in Karachi in June 2002. As he well knew, however, they had actually taken place much earlier.

When, the morning after, a new statement was posted on www.jihad.net correcting the date of the interviews, Fouda knew it had come from the right people. This is a translation of the full text of the statement as it appeared on the website on 21 September 2002:

> In the name of Allah, The Beneficent, The Merciful
> (A Clarification from the al-Qaeda Media Office)
> Regarding the connection of Al-Jazeera Channel and Mr Yosri Fouda
> With the Karachi events
> Praise be to Allah, Lord of the Worlds, and peace be upon the most
> honourable of the messengers, our Master Mohammed, and all his
> house and companions. The Almighty said: 'O ye who believe! If an

evil-liver bring you tidings, verify it, lest ye smite some folk in ignorance and afterward repent of what ye did.' (*The Glorious Qur'an*, Surah 49: The Private Apartments, Verse 6).

As it is keen to clarify the truth and to put an end to speculations and rumours, al-Qaeda Media Office would like to assure everyone that neither Al-Jazeera Channel nor Mr Yosri Fouda had anything to do with the recent events in Karachi. All this was destined by Allah and His Wisdom.

In this context, we do not overlook the criminal role played by the Pakistani government headed by Pervez Musharraf, and its quick efforts to please America and the West at the expense of the faithful sons of the nation.

We would like to underline that Mr Yosri Fouda's meeting with brother Khalid al-Sheikh and brother Ramzi Binalshibh took place in the month of Safar [according to the Islamic calendar, coinciding with April/May] of the present year and not in the month of Rajab [September] as some think. The meeting was secured under our special security arrangements, and Mr Yosri Fouda adhered to all the promises he was asked to make. He was honest in relaying information that was given to him by our side, although we have our reservations on some parts of his programme.

We would also like to confirm that al-Sahab company for media production has introduced some alterations to the voice of brother Ramzi Binalshibh which renders as false any claim that the voice was electronically matched. This is an unfounded allegation, bare of the truth. All the material that Mr Yosri Fouda received was approved and sealed by us.

We would also like to confirm that, in broadcasting programmes, analyses and interviews regarding al-Qaeda, Al-Jazeera Channel has only been reporting the opinion and the counter-opinion at a time everyone else was reporting a single opinion – the forced American opinion.

al-Qaeda Organisation
(The Media Office)
Saturday 14 Rajab 14:3 – 21 September 2002

Finally, Khalid, who must have been following what was happening minute by minute, had spoken out. He must have judged Fouda and Al-Jazeera to have passed a tough test and to have deserved a word of support. But why should he bother? The messages in the statement were clear, although some were unspoken. First it was about al-Qaeda itself. By glibly passing over the news of Binalshibh's arrest, Khalid was making the point that the organisation was not likely to be affected by the loss of a single operative. If one 'brother' was captured, there were many others ready to take his place. It was also dampening down any speculation that the Americans had trapped Ramzi through the use of electronic eavesdropping. The blame was firmly placed at the doorstep of Pakistan. And finally it chastised Arab governments for trying to take advantage of the situation at the expense of Al-Jazeera.

Ramzi Binalshibh, of course, did not get to see Part II of *The Road to 11 September*. It's even unclear whether or not he saw Part I of the documentary he himself proposed and outlined. Fouda would have liked to know what Binalshibh thought of the final product. Khalid, as the statement suggests, had reservations about 'some parts', and was more impressed by Fouda's adherence to his promises.

And was it not the final point that Khalid was asserting himself? It was Ramzi who had made the arrangements about getting the tapes to Fouda in London. It had been uncharacteristic of Khalid to agree to the interviews in the first place and Fouda now had the strong suspicion that if Khalid had really wanted the handover to take place, he would have made it happen. Now, with the recent arrest of Ramzi, he was on his guard, and taking no chances with his security.

So how did the authorities track down Ramzi Binalshibh? Al-Jazeera's broadcasts probably confirmed what intelligence agencies already suspected, namely that Binalshibh and Khalid Shaikh Mohammed were hiding in the Karachi area. This information would have been enough to justify the deployment of massive electronic resources in the area.

The US National Security Agency based at Fort Meade in Maryland, just north of Washington, has the ability to concentrate great power into tapping communications in a particular region by keying into a chain of geo-synchronous satellites. US intelligence sources say that while such systems as Echelon allow spy satellites to watch for particular words, or even a particular voiceprint, the real strength of intelligence satellites is that they can concentrate huge resources into one specified area.[13]

With the hard intelligence that Binalshibh was somewhere in the Karachi area, the NSA would have been able to focus down and begin listening. One source close to US intelligence said: 'Binalshibh was apparently caught because he was a geek who was too willing to get onto his satphone and his email. He thought he was too clever and had been getting away with things for too long.'

Binalshibh's satellite calls would have been particularly vulnerable to interception. A satellite call from Pakistan would have been transmitted via Intelsat's satellite, which sits over the Indian Ocean region. Western intelligence agencies have arrangements to tap directly into the satellite and listen to every single call made from Pakistan. There are still relatively few users of satphones and so keeping track of all calls from the region is well within the NSA's capacity.

According to information obtained from declassified Russian intelligence reports, the US signals intelligence (SIGINT) satellites follow a special oscillating orbit in which they move upwards, downwards and sideways around their geo-synchronous position. These small movements allow the satellites to pick up the same signals from different angles and take bearings to identify the precise locations of the calls.

According to those same Russian reports, the information gathered is sent down to earth through a narrow beam signal directly to NSA-controlled ground stations. Technology developed in London would also have allowed US intelligence to install a base station in Karachi that could have specifically targeted satellite calls originating from the city.

The NSA's overhead capability also allowed them to monitor thousands of mobile phone calls in the Karachi area. Teams of Arab and Urdu-speaking translators, whose numbers were significantly boosted after 11 September, would have allowed them to monitor the calls.

It would be a mistake, however, to imagine that all calls would have been monitored. Instead the NSA would have been developing expanding 'trees' of numbers to monitor. An expanding list of target phone numbers is developed by looking at telephones dialled by a suspect, then the numbers called by those phone numbers, and so on. Public phone booths in the area would also be targeted for interception.

Email is much easier to target than phone calls because the NSA's massively powerful Cray computers have access to almost all international traffic and email is much easier to search automatically by computer. Binalshibh's fondness for email exchanges – even if encrypted – would have made him vulnerable.

Sources close to the NSA have dismissed the suggestion that Binalshibh was detected by some kind of electronic voiceprint, saying such an idea was 'not credible'. 'Don't imagine these interceptions are always very clear,' the source said. 'Think about a lot of hiss and crackle and you've got the idea, so it would be very difficult to get a clean voiceprint with this kind of technology.'

Suggestions that US intelligence had succeeded in placing a tracking device inside Fouda's equipment or had followed him to his rendezvous are not credible. First, Fouda was not allowed to bring any recording equipment with him to the interview. Al-Qaeda's experience in placing explosives inside a television camera is well-known. They used this technique to kill Afghan Northern Alliance leader Ahmed Shah Massoud just two days before the attacks on America. They would scarcely have allowed a journalist to carry out a similar attack on two of their top operatives. Khalid also took away Fouda's mobile as soon as he entered the apartment. Second, if they had followed Fouda, why would they have waited nearly five months before moving in on Binalshibh? It doesn't make sense.

The arrest of Ramzi Binalshibh was perhaps the most important action against al-Qaeda during 2002. He held many of the secrets about the planning of the hijacking and was directly connected to the higher reaches of the organisation. But it was only one success and it would take more than electronic surveillance to catch the remaining al-Qaeda leadership.

NOTES

1. *The Glorious Qur'an*, Surah 9, Verse 14.
2. Tanta is Fouda's birthplace, famous for sweets and nuts.
3. A prominent Kuwaiti professor of political science who has written a series of articles on 11 September entitled 'The Manhattan Ghazwah'.
4. Editor of the London-based newspaper, *Al-Quds Al-Arabi*, critical of many Arab governments.
5. 'Arab TV to air 11 September confessions', *Reuters*, 02:55 GMT, 6 September 2002.
6. Nick Fielding, 'Al-Qaeda leaders reveal 9/11 secrets', *The Sunday Times*, 8 September 2002.
7. Felicity Barringer, *New York Times*, 16 September 2002.
8. Daniel Williams, *Washington Post*, 16 September 2002.
9. Salah Muntasser, *al-Ahram*, 15 September 2002.
10. *Al-Kifaah al-Arabi*, 16 September 2002.
11. *Al-Yaum*, 16 September 2002.
12. *Asharq al-Awsat*, 15 September 2002, p. 3.
13. For a detailed analysis of the workings of the National Security Agency, see James Bamford, *Body of Secrets: How America's NSA and Britain's GCHQ Eavesdrop on the World* (London, Arrow, 2002).

CHAPTER NINE

The Aftermath

'If Sharon is a man of peace in the eyes of Bush, then we are also men of peace.'

al-Qaeda, November 2002

The danger the United States faced from bin Laden's al-Qaeda organisation was never a secret. A succession of devastating military attacks against American targets had occurred throughout the late 1990s, the most important of which were the embassy bombings in Kenya and Tanzania in 1998 and the attack on the USS *Cole* in October 2000. Bin Laden himself kept up a barrage of increasingly lurid propaganda speeches and videos expressing his hatred of America. In June 2001, for example, he stated: 'It's time to penetrate America and Israel and hit them where it hurts most.'

America had already attempted one strike against bin Laden, launching cruise missiles in 1998 against three suspected training camps in Afghanistan and the al-Shifa pharmaceutical plant in Sudan, saying it was producing precursors for chemical weapons. Both were unmitigated failures. In the latter case, the American government has since grudgingly admitted that its attack was based on faulty intelligence and that the plant was a vital source of much-needed medicines for a poor developing country.

In December 1998, CIA director George Tenet provided new guidance for his deputies, effectively declaring war on bin Laden. 'We must now enter a new phase in our effort against bin Laden . . . We are at war . . . I want no resources or people spared in this effort, either inside the CIA or the Community.'[1] But despite this robust statement, there was no shift in budget or reassignment of personnel to counter-terrorism until after the 11 September attacks.

Diplomatic efforts to rein in bin Laden were also unsuccessful. Despite passing UN Security Council Resolution 1267 in 1999, which called on the Taliban government in Afghanistan to hand over bin Laden for trial in connection with the embassy bombings for which he had been indicted in America, nothing was done. Even the imposition of stringent sanctions, freezing Taliban assets abroad and banning flights abroad by Taliban aircraft, had little impact. A further UN resolution was passed in December 2000 in the wake of the bombing of the USS *Cole* that called for an arms embargo against the Taliban, prevented its senior officials from travelling overseas and imposed a ban on the supply of the heroin precursor, acetic anhydride, to the country. The heroin trade provided a vital source of income for both the Taliban and al-Qaeda.

All of these measures underestimated the relationship between the Taliban leadership of Mullah Omar and bin Laden and his followers, which was based on the traditional Pukhtunwali code of providing succour and support for a guest, no matter what the consequences. By this time the al-Qaeda leadership was effectively running a government within a government, aided and abetted by strong support from Pakistan's intelligence service, the ISI.

In May 1998, bin Laden had formed the International Islamic Front for Jihad Against Jews and Crusaders and issued a statement saying that 'the killing of Americans and their civilian and military allies is a religious duty for each and every Muslim, to be carried out in whichever country they are until al-Aqsa mosque [in Jerusalem] has been liberated from their grasp and until their armies have left Muslim lands.'

Later, bin Laden stated explicitly: 'Our enemy is every American male, whether he is directly fighting us or paying taxes.' At the same time his organisation's plans for the attacks on America were well advanced. They had been approved by al-Qaeda's military committee under the leadership of Khalid Shaikh Mohammed, the teams had been selected and prepared in a thorough training programme and only the final targets and timing remained to be decided.

To what extent did the Western powers understand what al-Qaeda was planning, or even capable of? The full answer to that question will not be known until the FBI and CIA release more information about their own investigations into 11 September. But already some information has begun to emerge.

On 4 October 2001, shortly after the tragedies in Washington and New York, the British government, with President Bush's approval, issued a document in which it attempted to make a quasi-legal case against bin Laden. That it was based on intelligence material was clear from the statement at the top of the document:

> This document does not purport to provide a prosecutable case
> against Usama bin Laden in a court of law. Intelligence often cannot
> be used evidentially, due both to the strict rules of admissibility and
> to the need to protect the safety of sources. But on the basis of all the
> information available, Her Majesty's Government is confident of its
> conclusions as expressed in this document.[2]

The implication is that there was some evidence available, but that it was not
in the public domain as it had been collected by the intelligence services.

The document confirmed that there had been no specific intelligence
about the attacks before they had occurred: 'After 11 September we learned
that, not long before, bin Laden had indicated he was about to launch a
major attack on America', although there had been clear indications that
something was going to happen. In June 2001, for example, the United
States specifically warned the Taliban that it had the right to defend itself and
that it would hold the regime responsible for attacks against US citizens by
terrorists sheltered in Afghanistan, again implying that the American
authorities were possibly in possession of some information that indicated an
impending attack.

The report also says that in August and early September 2001 bin Laden's
close associates were warned to return to Afghanistan by 10 September – as
was confirmed during Fouda's interviews with Ramzi Binalshibh in Karachi
– and that since the attack the British government had learned that 'one of
bin Laden's closest and most senior associates was responsible for the detailed
planning of the attacks'. Did they mean Khalid Shaikh Mohammed?

It also declared that very specific evidence, which was 'too sensitive to
release', proved bin Laden was guilty of the attacks.

At first, bin Laden himself played a guessing game over responsibility. On
7 October 2001 he said:

> Here is America struck by Allah Almighty in one of its vital organs,
> so that its greatest buildings are destroyed. Grace and gratitude to
> Allah . . . I swear by Allah that the Americans will never be able to
> enjoy peace until we live it in Palestine, and before the army of
> infidels departs the land of Mohammed, peace be upon him.[3]

But in the end, in public at least, it could only build a a circumstantial case
against bin Laden and al-Qaeda. 'No other organisation has both the
motivation and the capability to carry out attacks like those of 11
September.'

It was not until the middle of 2002, as the US Joint Intelligence
Committee began hearings in Washington to determine what was known in
America before the attacks, that more information began to emerge directly

linking al-Qaeda. In June 2002, officials from America's National Security Agency, who testified to the committee, let it be known that they had monitored telephone conversations between Khalid and Mohammed Atta.

The officials admitted that they had failed to share the intercepts with the CIA or any other US intelligence agency and had even failed to translate some of the conversations.[4] The NSA watchers didn't recognise the significance of what they had heard. According to the intercepts of the conversations between the two men, which have never been released, Khalid was abroad and Atta was in the United States.

These leaks from the Joint Intelligence Committee hearings were the first inkling that Khalid Shaikh Mohammed was in some way connected to the attacks. Even in September 2002, when Eleanor Hill, staff director of the joint inquiry, issued her first statement, Khalid's name did not appear. 'The Director of Central Intelligence has declined to declassify two issues of particular importance to this inquiry,' she wrote. The second issue was 'the identity of and information on a key al-Qaeda leader involved in the 11 September attacks'.[5]

The hearings took evidence from all the major agencies in the United States, holding many of the sessions in secret. Throughout the summer and autumn of 2002 a succession of witnesses testified about what they had known before 11 September and what they had found out since. They revealed that since 1994 the intelligence community had received information indicating that terrorists were considering using aircraft in attacks. No effort had, however, gone into analysing this potential threat.

Hill's statement says that by late 1998 the intelligence community had gathered enough general information to know that bin Laden intended to strike against the United States. Concern began to grow in the spring and summer of 2001, with a growing number of reports suggesting an imminent attack. Just as these reports began to tail off in July and August 2001, three developments occurred which, had they been connected by analysts, could have led to a breakthrough. 'The Intelligence community apparently had not connected these individual warning flags to each other, to the "drumbeat" of threat reporting that had just occurred, or to the urgency of the "war" effort against Osama bin Laden,' said Hill.[6]

The three developments were a memo from an FBI officer in Phoenix, Arizona, sent in July 2001; the detention of Zacarias Moussaoui, the so-called 'twentieth hijacker', in August 2001; and the belated realisation by the intelligence community that Khalid al-Mihdhar and Nawaf al-Hazmi – two of the eventual hijackers – had arrived back in the United States. Both had known connections to al-Qaeda and their movements had been monitored on several occasions.

The 35–40 CIA officers and 17–19 FBI agents working in two especially dedicated bin Laden units proved to be largely ineffectual against the hijackers. None of them had been able to develop good human intelligence sources within al-Qaeda and appeared to have relied on electronic intercepts and the occasional snippet of information from CIA stations around the globe. Of these total staff, only three analysts at the CIA's Counter Terrorism Center were allocated to look at bin Laden's worldwide organisation full time and only one analyst was working for the FBI.[7]

There was no one on the ground in Afghanistan providing information. Even during the CIA's most active period of involvement in Afghanistan in the 1980s, CIA agents had been forbidden by Pakistan from entering tribal areas along the border. Most of the effort of the agents in the two US-based units went into work connected to the East African embassy bombings and the attack on the USS *Cole*.

The list of information produced by the committee about what was known before 11 September is frustrating to read. If only, if only, one is forced to repeat. For example, in April 2001 a source with terrorist connections told the CIA that bin Laden might be interested in commercial pilots as potential terrorists. This source warned that the US should focus not only on embassy bombings, but that terrorists sought 'spectacular and traumatic' attacks and that the first World Trade Center bombing in 1993 could be the type of event that was being planned. No timeframe was mentioned and because the information was graded as personal speculation, it was not disseminated.

In July 2001, the CIA became aware of one person who had recently been in Afghanistan and who had reported that 'everyone is talking about an impending attack'.[8] The detention of Zacarias Moussaoui on 16 August 2001 in Minneapolis, Minnesota, after his flying instructor had become suspicious of his strange behaviour while learning to fly large commercial airliners on simulators, should have provided more clues, but the significance of his arrest was never fully understood. Moussaoui was arrested on a passport violation charge and investigators later found information about crop duster planes and wind patterns on his computer, but nothing specifically linking him to the attacks. According to information supplied by Binalshibh after his arrest, Khalid Shaikh Mohammed provided Moussaoui with the names of contacts in the United States, while Binalshibh gave him an email address and wired him money to advance the plot. Moussaoui has since tried to call Binalshibh as a defence witness at his conspiracy trial in federal court in Alexandria, due to begin in late 2003.

Binalshibh has also told investigators that he and Khalid ultimately lost confidence in Moussaoui's discretion and decided to use him in the plot only as a last resort. He also described an aborted plot to attack London's Heathrow Airport. This is partly confirmed by information that Binalshibh spent a week in London just before Christmas 2000, where he probably met with Moussaoui, who was then living in Brixton, south London. It is likely he was preparing him as his understudy for the planned suicide hijackings in America.

Arriving on 2 December, Binalshibh left exactly a week later to return to Hamburg. Moussaoui flew to Pakistan where he met Khalid Shaikh Mohammmed. But the two men kept in touch.

Moussaoui spent about two months in Pakistan, before leaving for London again on 7 February. Two weeks later, according to his US indictment, he flew from London to Chicago, declaring at least $35,000 in cash to US Customs. From there he travelled on to Norman, Oklahoma to join a flight school. But after failing to qualify for solo flight he quit and on 23 May 2001 emailed the Pan American International Flight Academy in Minnesota. Sources say that Binalshibh has told his interrogators that he once again met up with Moussaoui in Karachi in June 2001.

After a few weeks Moussaoui returned to the United States, joining the Minnesota flight school. In July and August 2001 Moussaoui called Hamburg to speak to Binalshibh from call boxes near his flight school. Almost immediately, on 1 August and 3 August 2001, Binalshibh, using the name Ahad Sabet, wired approximately $14,000 in money orders to Moussaoui from Western Union offices in Dusseldorf and Hamburg train stations to pay for his flying lessons. The money had in turn been sent to Binalshibh from someone using the name Hashim Abdulrahman in the United Arab Emirates.

But Moussaoui's erratic performance at the flight school had already come to the notice of his instructors and he was arrested shortly after when they contacted the FBI. Binalshibh has since told his interrogators that when he and Khalid met in Kandahar, Afghanistan, a month after the attacks, they discussed Moussaoui's arrest and congratulated themselves for keeping him at arm's length from the other hijackers.

The way in which the FBI dealt with the Moussaoui case became the subject of controversy in May 2002, when FBI agent Coleen Rowley wrote a 13-page memo to FBI director Robert Mueller, accusing the bureau of deliberately obstructing measures that could have helped prevent the 11 September attacks. She details how senior officials blocked requests to examine Moussaoui's laptop, to share information with other agencies or to link his arrest to Ken Williams' memo from Phoenix.[9]

At the end of August 2001 the CIA had asked for al-Mihdhar and al-Hazmi to be put on the Department of State's watchlist, only to be informed by the Immigration and Naturalisation Service that they were probably already in the United States. Searches in Los Angeles and New York failed to find them. According to Ramzi, by then both were taking part in meetings of the hijackers' majlis al-shura, which met in Las Vegas and other locations to plan final details of the operation. The meetings were made up of the four pilots plus al-Hazmi and al-Mihdhar, with al-Hazmi already selected as Atta's deputy. Numerous briefings around this time to senior figures within the Washington administration warned of a possible attack, but no one had appreciated, even at this stage, the full extent of what was planned.

The so-called 'Phoenix memo', written by FBI special agent Kenneth Williams, excited a great deal of interest from the press during the joint intelligence committee hearings. Williams received information about a group of students at the Embry Riddle Aeronautical University in Prescott, Arizona, in particular about Zakaria Soubra, a Lebanese member of the UK-based al-Muhajiroun organisation, who had lived in London and Manchester until 2000. At this time, Hani Hanjour, who was to pilot American Airlines Flight 77 into the Pentagon, was taking flight simulator lessons at the Sawyer School of Aviation in Phoenix, where he was later joined by Atta's deputy, Nawaf al-Hazmi, although Williams was not aware of this.

Soubra had converted to a fundamentalist form of Islam promoted in London by Sheikh Omar Bakri Mohammed, leader of the al-Muhajiroun organisation. After moving to the United States to study aviation engineering early in 2000, he had been interviewed by the FBI after only three months in the country, when he was reported to have visited a shooting range with another Muslim.

By the summer of 2001 Soubra was actively organising anti-US and anti-Israeli rallies and calling for jihad. Williams decided to compile his report on Soubra and six of his al-Muhajiroun associates, all of whom were involved in aviation training. Reports on three other people were also included. In his 10 July memo, Williams recommended that FBI headquarters should draw up a list of American flying schools, establish liaison with them, discuss his theories with the intelligence community and consider getting permission to start monitoring the students at such facilities. It contained no warning of an impending attack. Williams also warned that there could be an attempt by bin Laden 'to send students to the United States to attend civil aviation universities and colleges'.

Williams sent the memo via email to the FBI's counter-terrorism division, who believed their task was to 'read and clear' the document. They did so and then passed it on to the bureau's Osama bin Laden Unit in New York. An officer there sent it on to the FBI's Portland, Oregon, office, where it effectively disappeared.

Once again, investigators believe there is no evidence that had Williams' memo – which has still not been published in full – been taken seriously, it would have changed anything about 11 September. It simply highlights the low level of resources devoted to fighting al-Qaeda by the FBI and the shortage of high-quality intelligence.

By the time the joint inquiry published its final report on 10 December 2002, it had become less squeamish about naming Khalid Shaikh Mohammed. Fouda's story had already been published and broadcast around the world and so there was little point in continuing to hide his name.

Eleanor Hill's final report makes numerous references to Khalid and affirms that he was the principal planner.

> Prior to 11 September, the intelligence community had information linking Khalid Shaikh Mohammed (KSM), now recognised by the intelligence community as the mastermind of the attacks, to bin Laden, to terrorist plans to use aircraft as weapons, and to terrorist activity in the United States.[10]

But, says the report, the FBI analysts relegated Khalid to 'rendition target status' following his 1996 indictment in connection with the Oplan Bojinka plot in the Philippines and, as a result, focused 'primarily on his location, rather than his activities and place in the al-Qaeda hierarchy'. Information was not collected on him and his role in the attacks came as 'a surprise to the intelligence community'.

Hill's report is a massive indictment of American counter-terrorism prior to 11 September 2001. 'The quality of counter-terrorism analysis was inconsistent, and many analysts were inexperienced, unqualified, under-trained and without access to critical information.' There was a dearth of 'creative, aggressive analysis targeting bin Laden and a persistent inability to comprehend the collective significance of individual pieces of intelligence'. There were backlogs, a shortage of language specialists, conflict between agencies, lack of collaboration, an absence of a central counter-terrorism database and a lack of information from human sources close to bin Laden himself.

The FBI could not even claim success over the arrest of al-Qaeda operative Ahmed Ressam, who had been captured on the US–Canadian border in December 1999 trying to smuggle a bomb for use at Los Angeles Airport during the millenium celebrations. Ressam, who had also spent time in London, was arrested almost by accident by a curious border guard.

The testimony of one anonymous FBI special agent to the committee highlighted the problems confronting the security services.

> A concept known as 'The Wall' has been created within the Law Enforcement and Intelligence Communities. From my perspective and in its broadest sense 'The Wall' is an information barrier placed between elements of an intelligence investigation and those of a criminal investigation.[11]

The problem, put simply, is that law enforcement agencies such as the FBI are not allowed to use material collected during intelligence operations as evidence in a court of law.

Specifically, this special agent, a member of the FBI's New York-based

Osama bin Laden Unit who had spent many months investigating the attack on the USS *Cole*, says he was prevented from obtaining information about a meeting attended by Khalid al-Mihdhar and Nawaf al-Hazmi in June 2001. It was the Kuala Lumpur meeting and at least one of those present had been involved in the attack on the ship. This was another significant episode in the lead-up to the September operation, followed a month later by another summit in Tarragona, Spain.

It seems that the rules in this instance meant that when it was known at the end of August that al-Mihdhar was back in the United States, no one from the special agent's department involved in the criminal case could try to track him down, as it was now an 'intelligence' case. Despite his protests with FBI headquarters, he was overruled. He revealed that information on the two hijackers had first been passed to the FBI by the CIA in 'either January 2000 or January 2001', but had not been given to the teams working on the live inquiries.

He finished his testimony with a very moving story about his own experience on 11 September:

> On September 11, 2001, I spent the morning on the streets with other agents and Joint Terrorism Task Force personnel around the World Trade Center, providing whatever help we could. I and several of my co-workers were within blocks when both towers came down. Within minutes of the second strike on the Southern Tower, we asked a senior fireman heading towards the South Tower what we could do. At the time, he was getting out of his fire truck and looking at the towers. By the Grace of God he turned to us and replied that he did not know what we could do – but that we were not going anywhere close to the buildings without a respirator. I do not know who he was but I truly believe he saved our lives. I also believe that based on the direction that he was looking, towards the Southern Tower, that moments later he entered that tower and perished in the attack . . .[12]

While no one can doubt the bravery of those who went to the assistance of others during the attacks, many of whom died for their efforts, the overall picture is of a system that had become deskbound and cynical. And yet, there is evidence that in Germany the security forces came much closer to breaking the plot.

Evidence emerged during the trial of Munir al-Motassadeq in Hamburg that he had been under surveillance for at least three years due to suspicions about his Islamic radicalism. Others were also under surveillance for long periods of time, including Mohammed Haydar Zammar, who is thought to have recruited Atta to al-Qaeda. According to court documents, German investigators had identified all the main 11 September hijackers living in

Hamburg by 1998. Their phones were bugged, they were being followed and their details were entered into the criminal intelligence computer network. It was thought highly likely that their visits to Afghanistan were undertaken for the purpose of training in guerrilla warfare.

The German domestic intelligence service launched 'Operation Tenderness' against Zammar, monitoring his calls and contacts. On 29 August 1998 they noted, for example, that he had been at a meeting in Buntaweitestrasse in Hamburg, along with al-Motassadeq and Said Bahaji. Bahaji, a close associate of Ramzi Binalshibh, left Hamburg eight days before the attacks on America and is still at large. Zammar's name also figured in a 1998 report of an Italian police raid on a property connected to members of Jihad Islami living in Turin. Three men were arrested after police found handguns, ammunition and disguises. Zammar's details were found in an address book in the property.

More information about the Hamburg cell emerged after Mamduh Mahmoud Salim was arrested in Germany in 1999 on an American warrant. Salim, from Sudan, was involved in organising al-Qaeda's finances and had had many meetings in Germany, in particular with Syrian-born Mamoun Darkazanli, a Hamburg businessman. Salim was extradited to the United States and despite a degree of scepticism, the German authorities agreed to put Darkazanli under observation.

This revealed that Darkazanli was in touch with fellow-Syrian Zammar and that both men were regular visitors to the apartment at 54 Marienstrasse, then occupied by future hijackers al-Shehhi and Mohammed Atta.

In one conversation the police tapped, Zammar's wife was recorded telling his father he could be reached on another number, which was the 'meeting place of Said [Bahaji], Mohammed el-Amir [Atta], Munir [al-Motassadeq] and Omar [Ramzi Binalshibh]'. In 1999 the CIA decided the case was so important that it assigned a case officer to the US Consulate in Hamburg. He pushed for Darkazanli to be approached with an offer to turn informer.[13] The offer was rejected. Darkazanli continues to live in Hamburg and has not been charged with any offence.

Within a few months, in November 1999, the future pilots then living in Hamburg – Atta, al-Shehhi and al-Jarrah – left for training in Afghanistan. They returned early in 2000, but decided to keep a very low profile and not raise suspicions. It was the closest investigators ever got to cracking the Hamburg cell.

Since the attacks, American investigators have scoured the world in an effort to break al-Qaeda and there have been notable successes. The arrest of Sheikh Ahmed Salim in Karachi in July 2002 provided a treasure trove of information on how al-Qaeda sympathisers were being smuggled out of the country. Salim, otherwise known as Swedan, already had a $25 million price tag on his head for his alleged role in the 1998 bombings of the US embassies in Nairobi, Kenya and Dar-es-Salaam in Tanzania. His one-time ownership of a Kenyan trucking firm led to him buying the Nissan and Toyota trucks used in the attacks. He flew out of Nairobi to Karachi five days before the trucks exploded, killing hundreds of innocent people.

Once in Karachi, he emerged as an important figure, directing and financing Islamist militants in Pakistan. ISI officers were led to his cell by satellite phone intercepts provided by the FBI. That led initially to the arrest in Karachi of a Saudi known only as Riyadh or Riaz, a more junior figure in the organisation. He in turn led the ISI to Salim, who was arrested in Kharadar, a slum area in the south of the city.

Salim told his interrogators that he had collected millions of dollars from local supporters, many connected to the militant Lashkar-e-Jhangvi organisation. His claims were partially backed up by the thousands of dollars seized at his house, along with fake passports and visa stamps.

Salim is known to have worked with the Lashkar-e-Jhangvi organisation to build a chemical laboratory in Karachi that was found to contain a number of toxins, including cyanide. More significantly, he revealed that al-Qaeda and the Taliban remnants had sent a number of carefully hidden shipments of gold by sea to the Gulf where it was off-loaded and flown on to Khartoum in the Sudan. He has also told interrogators that senior al-Qaeda officials were getting out of the country using the same route. The journey is not easy as US and Allied warships patrol the sea lanes, stopping cargo vessels and small fishing boats to check on their contents.

This was clearly illustrated on 11 December 2002 when two Spanish warships intercepted the North Korean freighter *So San* in the Arabian Sea. After initially ignoring warning shots, the captain allowed Spanish special forces to board the ship where they found 15 Scud missiles, 15 live warheads, 23 tanks of rocket propellant and 85 drums of unidentified chemicals hidden below bags of cement.

The ship had been tracked for nearly a month since leaving North Korea. When the Yemeni government quickly admitted that the cargo had been legally purchased and belonged to them, the US, with much grumbling, was forced to allow the vessel to continue on its way. Despite being portrayed as an embarrassing error in some quarters, the raid clearly illustrated that the US was closely monitoring shipping in the region and possibly also sent a message to Yemen that it would not countenance the missiles being sent on to Iraq. Yemen was one of the few Arab countries to support Iraq during the Gulf War in 1991 and was accused at the time of being a conduit for military supplies reaching its northern ally.

In July 2002 a French warship stopped a fast boat moving through the North Arabian Sea and arrested two al-Qaeda suspects. They were transferred to the US aircraft carrier, USS *George Washington*. A few days earlier a Canadian warship stopped a boat and detained another two men. Between

September 2001 and July 2002, agents from coalition warships boarded more than 180 ships and questioned operators of more than 15,000 vessels in the hunt for al-Qaeda members crossing from Pakistan to the Gulf.

Another significant arrest that has given US investigators an insight into the organisation of al-Qaeda in Pakistan was that of Abu Zubaydah on 28 March 2002. Although only 31, until his arrest in a gun battle in a two-storey house in the Faisal Town suburb of Faisalabad in western Pakistan, during which he was seriously injured, he was a senior member of the organisation. Born in Saudi Arabia, but brought up in Palestinian refugee camps in the Gaza Strip, he was a key figure in the plot by al-Qaeda cells in Jordan, Canada and the United States to carry out a series of devastating attacks in Jordan and the United States during the millennium celebrations.

According to Yoram Schweitzer, a researcher at the International Centre for Terrorism, 'Abu Zubaydah was the one who instructed Jamal Beghal, the ringleader of a European terror network whose members were detained in September 2001. The cell had planned several terror attacks in France and in Belgium. Beghal himself was arrested in Dubai on 28 July 2001.'[14]

As with Salim, the arrest was the result of information supplied by US intelligence experts. However, on this occasion, the raid was led by FBI officers who entered the building at 4 a.m. to find at least a dozen men, including Arabs, Afghans and Pakistanis, sleeping inside. While his comrades tried to hold off the FBI with kitchen knives, Zubaydah made an escape attempt, but was shot in the groin, the stomach and the thigh. Two other Arabs and two FBI agents were also wounded during the incident.

Abu Zubaydah was a big catch. Osama bin Laden appointed him to run the training camps in eastern Afghanistan when he was only 25 and he was an experienced fighter, with expertise in everything from assault rifles to heavy mortars and bomb-making techniques. Zubaydah was also directed to rebuild the organisation following the collapse of the Taliban regime in Afghanistan. Proficient in at least three languages, including English, he is known to have briefed the 'Shoe Bomber', Richard Reid, who tried to blow up a transatlantic airliner in December 2001.

He also has an intimate knowledge of al-Qaeda's structure in Western Europe and acted as a liaison between cell leaders and the main leadership in Afghanistan. He left Afghanistan as the US bombing started in October 2001 and moved to Faisalabad, where he found support amongst the membership of Lashkar-e-Toiba. As with other senior Al-Qaeda prisoners now in the custody of the Americans, there is no indication where he is presently being held.

In December 2002 the Pakistani ambassador to the United States said his country had arrested 422 suspected operatives since October 2001. 'We have been instrumental – the Pakistan intelligence agencies, the Pakistan Frontier Constabulary – in apprehending more than 400 suspected members of the al-Qaeda or other extremist groups.' At the same meeting he had to deny credible reports that Pakistan had insisted on its own intelligence service personnel accompanying raiding parties that the FBI sets up in Pakistan. He was also embarrassed by reports from Pakistan that courts were freeing al-Qaeda suspects arrested in joint raids for lack of evidence.

Since his arrest in September 2001, Ramzi Binalshibh has reportedly been providing US intelligence with vital information about al-Qaeda's potential for using nuclear, biological and chemical weapons. One source said that he has been 'very productive in understanding how close to nuke-bio-chem they were' and that he has also been providing helpful details about the organisation's command structure.

The same source said that he had expressed 'zero remorse' and that had he not been captured he would have continued doing what he had been doing before.[15]

Khalid's arrest in March 2003 was another severe blow to the organisation. According to reports, FBI agents took possession of his laptop computer, mobile phones, computer disks and notebooks. None of it, say the reports, was encrypted and the FBI were quick to announce that the material had given them leads to dozens of al-Qaeda operatives across the world. Khalid had recently been in touch with bin Laden himself and had handwritten letters from the al-Qaeda leader to his supporters. 'This is as good as it gets,' said one official.

Other significant arrests include those of Gulf operations chief Abd al-Rahim al-Nashiri, South-east Asia operations chief Umar al-Faruq, training camp commanders Ibn al-Shaikh al-Libi and Abd al-Hadi al-Iraqi and operational planner Abu Zubair al-Haili.

Several important senior members of the organisation have also been killed, including military chief Mohammed Atef, operational planner Mohammed Salah, financier Hamza al-Qatari and aide to Abu Zubaydah, Abu Jafar al-Jaziri.

An estimated 3,000 al-Qaeda trained operatives have been arrested, many of whom are now held at the American Camp X–Ray in Guantanamo Bay, Cuba. Most of these are people who have been at training camps in Afghanistan and are unlikely to be of significant interest to the intelligence agencies. According to one report, 'US authorities have yet to identify any senior al-Qaeda leaders among nearly 600 terror suspects from 43 countries in US military custody at Guantanamo Bay.'[16] Of five suspects released from the camp at the end of 2002, one turned out to be an Afghani man who claimed to be 105 years old and had no idea why he had been detained and transported halfway around the globe.

Other, more senior prisoners are being held in different locations, including US Navy ships and offshore bases. All are deemed to be 'illegal combatants' and face the prospect of years in custody with little chance of a trial. The legal status of the prisoners is murky, although there have been many appeals for them to be allowed access to legal representation. All have been turned down.

Many other senior figures remain at large, including bin Laden's deputy, Ayman al-Zawahiri, his security chief, Saif al-Adil, Midhat Mursi who ran al-Qaeda's research programme on poisons and weapons of mass destruction, Zakariya Essabar and Said Bahaji from the Hamburg group, Sulaiman Abu Ghaith, al-Qaeda's spokesman, and Abu Hafs al-Mauritani, operational and spiritual leader. As for Osama bin Laden himself, it is unclear at the time of writing whether or not he survived the bombing at Tora Bora in Afghanistan in early 2002. Experts are divided over whether or not various sound tapes are genuine.

There can be little doubt that the command structure of al-Qaeda has been severely damaged by aggressive military action and heightened vigilance now being shown by police and intelligence agencies around the world. But a brief review of actions by al-Qaeda since 11 September 2001 shows that it is still capable of mounting serious attacks and remains a substantial danger.

There were, on average, one or two attacks a month attributable to al-Qaeda throughout 2002, including the murder of Daniel Pearl, attacks on Christians in Pakistan, the attack on the Djerba synagogue, the suicide bombing against a bus carrying French naval engineers in Karachi, the bomb outside the US Consulate in Karachi, attacks on US military personnel in the Philippines, the bombing of the French oil tanker the *Limburg* off the Yemeni coast, bombings in Kenya against Israeli tourists, attacks on American soldiers in Kuwait and the Bali bomb.

Many other attacks were stopped only at the last minute, including plans to attack British warships in the Straits of Gibraltar and American ships off the Indonesian coast, US embassies in South-east Asia, the huge Ras Tanura oil terminal in Saudi Arabia and an attempt to poison the water supply in the US Embassy in Rome using cyanide. Traces of the deadly poison ricin were found in a London flat in January 2003, leading to the arrest of a group of Algerians. A few days later Special Branch detective Stephen Oake was killed in Manchester during the arrest of al-Qaeda suspects. Sixteen more arrests took place in Spain and five in Italy, with police claiming they had smashed al-Qaeda cells that were about to mount operations.

It is clear that al-Qaeda remains a potent force. While its regional structure may have been fragmented in the short term, it will attempt to regroup. At the same time, other organisations that were never part of bin Laden's International Islamic Front have begun to emulate its techniques. 'Al-Qaeda is altering its strategy of hitting "hard" targets – such as military installations and the twin towers – and is switching to "soft" targets like the Bali nightclub,' says terrorism expert Dr Rohan Gunaratna.[17] 'Expect to see suicide bombers in the West this year. A cost-conscious al-Qaeda may well adopt suicide as a principal terror tactic.'

Whether al-Qaeda continues to exist as an organisation or not, its methods have demonstrated to the world that a tiny organisation with limited resources can humiliate the greatest power on earth. That lesson has not been missed by the thousands of Islamist militants around the world. The destruction of al-Qaeda's bases and infrastructure in Afghanistan may only have served to spread the organisation's techniques. Without a fundamental reassessment of American foreign policy and its uncritical support for Israeli actions in the Occupied Territories, the war against terror will continue for many years to come.

NOTES

1. 'Joint Inquiry Staff Statement', Part 1, Eleanor Hill, Staff Director, Joint Inquiry Staff, 18 September 2002. See www.fas.org/irp/congress/2002_hr/091802hill.html
2. See www.number-10.gov.uk/output/page3554.asp
3. www.pbs.org/newshour/terrorism/international/binladen%5f10-7.html
4. 'Another US agency had clues before Sept 11, some officials say', *Mercury News*, 7 June 2002.
5. Hill, 'Joint Inquiry Staff Statement', Part 1, p. 10.
6. *Ibid.*, p. 10.
7. The resources needed to put just a single suspect under surveillance are illustrated by the following: 'The decision required as many as eight agents per shift to monitor the man's travels, from apartment to college, mosque to supermarket. Another half-dozen agents listened to his calls. Other agents filed wiretap reports or handled aerial surveillance. Two supervisory agents oversaw the case. In all, almost 40 agents were needed to tail one target.' Quoted in *Los Angeles Times*, 30 October 2002.
8. Hill, 'Joint Inquiry Staff Statement', Part 1, p. 21.
9. See www.time.com/time/covers/1101020603/memo.html
10. 'Final Report of the Congressional Joint Inquiry into 9/11', 10 December 2002. See www.fas.org/irp/congress/2002_rpt/findings.html
11. 'Prepared statement of a New York Special Agent before the Select Committee on Intelligence, United States Senate, and the Permanent Select Committee on Intelligence, House of Representatives', 20 September 2002. See www.fas.org/irp/congress/2002_hr/092002fbi.html
12. *Ibid.*, p. 4.
13. 'German investigators came close to busting cell in Sept 11 plot', *Wall Street Journal*, 17 January 2003.
14. Yoram Schweitzer, International Centre for Terrorism. See www.ict.org.il
15. 'Suspect helping US gauge al-Qaeda's arsenal', *USA Today*, 15 January 2003.
16. 'No al-Qaeda brass among detainees at Camp Delta', *Los Angeles Times*, 18 August 2002.
17. 'And now, a little local jihad', *The Sunday Times*, 26 January 2003.

Afterword

Shortly before *Masterminds of Terror* went to press, the authorities in Pakistan announced that Khalid Shaikh Mohammed had been arrested after a joint operation between the FBI and the Pakistani police.

In the early hours of Saturday, 1 March 2003, Khalid Shaikh Mohammed was arrested by a joint Pakistani–FBI team. According to the official version of events, he was captured, without a struggle, at a house in the middle-class Westridge area of Rawalpindi, just a few miles from the capital of Islamabad and traditionally a military town. The house is just five minutes from army headquarters in a guarded community that is home to top military officers. Behind the house is the army's central dog training school.

Khalid was arrested with Ahmed Abdul Qadoos, who lived at the house, and an Arab, named as Mustafa Ahmed al-Hawsawi, a man investigators say was a leading al-Qaeda financier and provided cash to Atta and the other hijackers through bank accounts in the United Arab Emirates. It was to al-Hawsawi that Atta returned unspent funds not used in the final stages of planning for the attacks on America.

Questions have been raised over the accuracy of the official version of events. The house where the arrest took place belongs to Ahmed Abdul Qadoos's father, Dr Abdul Qadoos, a microbiologist who is now the managing director of Hearts International, a cardiac hospital in Rawalpindi. Dr Qadoos spent 30 years working in Africa for the Food and Agriculture Organisation. His wife, Mrs Mahlaqa Khanum, is an activist in the women's wing of the Jamaat-e-Islami (JI), Pakistan's largest political party, with close

181

connections to the government and the ISI. JI is a leading member in a coalition of hard-line parties that won control of two of Pakistan's four provinces in Pakistan's November 2002 elections.

Neither the doctor nor his wife were at home when the arrests took place, as they were attending a wedding. But Mrs Mahlaqa Khanum strongly disputed the official version of events. She said her son was simple with a low IQ, a description supported by a neighbour, Colonel Shahida: 'Ahmed can't be a terrorist. He's a goof, simple in the head. Once he shot himself in the hand because he was cleaning a gun with the barrel against his palm. They are a purdah-observing household. We never saw anyone strange enter the house.'[1]

According to the family, Ahmed, his wife Aisha and their two children were asleep in a downstairs room when up to 25 armed police officers burst into the room just after midnight. They pushed Aisha and the children into a room and spent four hours ransacking the house, taking with them Mrs Mahlaqa Khanum's address book, family photographs, tapes of the Koran and a computer bought for the children.

Mrs Mahlaqa Khanum added that the arrest was a political ploy to discredit her and her party, a point strongly denied by the government. 'There was a single operation,' said Interior Ministry spokesman Iftikar Ahmed. 'Naturally they will deny it. Everybody says they are innocent, and you can draw your own conclusions.'[2]

Possibly of significance is the fact that the brother of Ahmed Abdul Qadoos was arrested on the same day. Major Adil Qadoos, from an army signals regiments, was arrested in Kohat in the North West Frontier Province and interrogated by intelligence officers. A family relative said the major was questioned about his dealings with his brother and Khalid.

Within hours of the arrests, the news had travelled around the world. The White House welcomed Khalid's capture. 'The United States commends Pakistani and US authorities on the completion of a successful joint operation which resulted in the detention of several al-Qaeda operatives, including Khalid Shaikh Mohammed,' said a statement, adding that he was 'one of Osama bin Laden's most senior and significant lieutenants, a key al-Qaeda planner and the mastermind of the 11 September attacks. He is known to have been centrally involved in plotting by al-Qaeda terrorists since 11 September 2001 – including plots to launch attacks within the United States.'[3]

US Homeland Security Secretary Tom Ridge was delighted: 'The truth be told, I was ecstatic when we got the son of a gun,' he said. 'We cannot overestimate his importance to the al-Qaeda terrorist organisation. But we shouldn't underestimate the continuing abilities that he has helped develop around the world.' Ridge added that Khalid had been trying to organise an attack on a target in America and it was this which contributed to the government's decision in February 2003 to ratchet up the terrorist threat alert level from yellow to orange.

'There was one plot line that we were able to connect with him that related to a potential terrorist attack during the time that this whole thing was being discussed,' said Ridge.[4] There was speculation that the attack involved fuel trucks, gas stations and bridges.

US president George Bush described Khalid as 'al-Qaeda's senior general when it comes to plotting attacks on America', and vowed to pursue the organisation until it was 'completely dismantled'.

Al-Qaeda's supporters tried to make the best of the bad news. 'There is not just one person there,' said one Afghan rebel interviewed by Associated Press. 'For every Khalid Shaikh there are ten others. There are lots of people who can do his work.'[5]

Khalid had been tracked for several weeks before his arrest. He appears to have moved back towards Quetta in Baluchistan following the September 2002 arrest in Karachi of his co-planner Ramzi Binalshibh. Khalid himself only just evaded capture on that occasion, although his wife and two children were taken into 'protective custody' by the Pakistanis. In Quetta, close to his ancestral family home, he could rely on a wide network of supporters to hide him while agents and police spies – many of them with an eye on the $25-million bounty on his head – scoured the country looking for him.

The first breakthrough came on 14 February 2003 when Pakistani police raided a house in Quetta's Wahdat Colony. Days earlier they had tracked a group seen travelling across the nearby border with Iran, which appeared to contain two Arabs. Instead of netting Khalid they were surprised to find they had captured Mohammed Abdel Rahman, one of two sons of Sheikh Omar Abdel Rahman, the blind Egyptian cleric who was convicted in 1995, along with ten of his followers, of conspiring to blow up the United Nations headquarters and other New York landmarks. Khalid's nephew, Ramzi Yousef, had connections with the blind cleric and his two sons had both come to join bin Laden in Afghanistan. It was yet another example of Khalid relying on his old contacts.

Mohammed Abdel Rahman admitted to his interrogators that Khalid had recently been staying in the house and the authorities were quickly able to pick up on a fresh trail. Cellphone messages and information gleaned from Internet cafés in Quetta used by Khalid showed that their main quarry was once again on the move. They tracked him to Rawalpindi the day before the arrest and made sure he was arrested with the minimum of fuss.

'They got information from the man they picked up in Quetta and from phone calls until they tracked him down to Rawalpindi,' a top police official in Quetta said. A Pakistani official with knowledge of the case said American communications experts helped the Pakistanis trace an email Rahman sent to Qadoos in Rawalpindi.

Khalid and al-Hawsawi were both interrogated at the ISI headquarters in Islamabad by a joint ISI–CIA team before the two men were quickly shipped out of the country, probably to Bagram Airbase in Afghanistan, where their interrogation continued. Khalid revealed that he had met bin Laden within the previous two months, confirming intelligence reports that the al-Qaeda leader was concentrating his forces in the tribal areas in south Waziristan and that he had formed an alliance with Gulbuddin Hekmatyar, one of Afghanistan's most notorious warlords. Their intention was to launch a spring offensive against the coalition forces in Afghanistan just as American troops moved in to Iraq to topple Saddam Hussein.

He said that bin Laden was in good health, having met him after a journey that involved a complicated network of phone calls, runners and intermediaries. Residents of the border town of Chaman in Baluchistan said that, within days of Khalid's arrest, US aircraft dropped millions of Pushto-language leaflets reminding locals of the $25-million reward for bin Laden's capture. Khalid's meeting with him took place somewhere in the remote provinces of Baluchistan or amidst the rugged peaks that run along the border. The al-Qaeda leader was moving with a small group of guards and never used satellite phones that could be used to track his whereabouts.

Reports say Khalid has also revealed that Ayman al-Zawahiri, bin Laden's deputy and the intellectual brains behind the organisation, had recently returned to Afghanistan from the Middle East. He had, said Khalid, been staying in the border area near Quetta, between Chaman and Spinboldak. He, too, was subject to a leaflet-dropping campaign in the area. The leaflets, showing al-Zawahiri's photo behind bars and carrying the headline 'Killer Being Hunted' were dropped over the border area in the days following Khalid's capture.

Khalid's arrest was undoubtedly a great blow to al-Qaeda, but soon speculation was growing that several of his close relatives were poised to take over his role. Once again, it seemed that the Baluchi clan around Khalid was determined to play the leading role in al-Qaeda's military operations. US officials announced two days after Khalid's arrest that they were concerned that two of his nephews – brothers of the imprisoned Ramzi Yousef – were the most likely candidates. They named them as Abdel Munim Yousef and Abdel Karim Yousef, who attended North Carolina Agricultural and Technical University with Khalid during the 1980s. Both men are in their 40s. Another cousin, Ali Abdel Aziz, 25, was also named as a leading figure in Khalid's network. The two nephews have worked closely with him in the past in handling al-Qaeda's communications, travel and financial transfers.

Khalid's eventual fate, as we write these lines, is unclear. Whether or not he will eventually stand trial for his role in planning the attacks on America has yet to be decided. He holds many of al-Qaeda's most intimate secrets and his American interrogators will be desperate to learn all they can about plans he made in the months before his capture for further terrorist attacks. Only once this process has been completed will thoughts turn to what to do with him.

NOTES

1. Christina Lamb, 'Was Khalid arrested where the FBI said he was?', *The Sunday Times*, 9 March 2003.
2. 'Interrogations led to al-Qaeda arrest', *Pakistan Today*, 3 March 2003.
3. 'Bush praises al-Qaeda arrests', *The Age*, 3 March 2003.
4. David Johnston, 'Raid on Feb 13 smoothed way in Qaeda arrest', *New York Times*, 4 March 2003.
5. Kathy Gannon, 'Bin Laden allies: al-Qaeda will survive arrest of Khalid Shaikh Mohammed', Associated Press, 3 March 2003.

APPENDIX I

In November 2002, Al-Qaeda issued a statement in response to a debate taking place between American and Saudi Arabian academics about the consequences of the attacks on America. It is important in that it is the first time that bin Laden's organisation has attempted to take part in a dialogue with anybody to justify its actions and for that reason, we have decided to publish it in full.

The background is as follows. In February 2002 a group of American academics signed a paper entitled 'What We're Fighting For: A Letter from America'. The reasons behind the document were spelled out very clearly:

> The leader of al-Qaeda described the 'blessed strikes' of 11 September as blows against America, the 'head of world infidelity'. Clearly, then, our attackers despise not just our government, but also our overall society, our entire way of living. Fundamentally their grievance concerns not only what our leaders do, but also *who we are.*

The authors included some of America's most eminent academics, including Francis Fukuyama, William Galston, Daniel Patrick Moynihan, Robert D. Putnam, and about 60 others – many of them professors of law, history, theology, public policy and political science.

The signatories affirmed five fundamental truths:

1) All people are born free and equal in dignity and rights.

2) The basic subject of society is the human person and the legitimate role of government is to protect and help to foster the conditions for human flourishing.

3) Human beings naturally desire to seek the truth about life's purpose and ultimate ends.

4) Freedom of conscience and religious freedom are inviolable rights of the human person.

5) Killing in the name of God is contrary to faith in God and is the greatest betrayal of the universality of religious faith.

They stated that they were unhappy with many aspects of modern American life – consumerism, the notion of freedom as no rules, the weakening of marriage and family life, and so on – but that they stood in defence of these five truths. The truths are not culturally specific, but relate to all societies and are related to the thinking behind the United Nations Universal Declaration of Human Rights.

They take issue with the 11 September hijackers who had declared they were engaged in holy war. 'None of us believe that God ever instructs some of us to kill or conquer others of us.' The experience of the American Civil War, in which both sides invoked God's aid against the other, had illustrated the futility of this approach.

This raises the question of the relationship between religion and the state. Instead of theocracy or ideological secularism, they argue that the United States should be a society where faith and freedom can go together. The state itself is secular, but figures show that the people of the United States are by far the most religious in the Western World. 'Spiritually, our separation of church and state permits religion to *be* religion, by detaching it from the coercive power of government. In short, we seek to separate church and state for the protection and proper vitality of both.'

On the question of war, they argue that there are times when a just war can be fought and that the conflict against the aggressors of 11 September is one of those times. 'This extremist movement claims to speak for Islam, but betrays fundamental Islamic principles. Islam sets its face *against* moral atrocities.' The signatories are anxious to make clear that they are not opposed to Islam in general, but to those who have hijacked it and distorted its teachings to their own benefit.

'Organised killers with global reach now threaten all of us. In the name of universal human morality, and fully conscious of the restrictions and requirements of a just war, we support our government's and our society's decision to use force of arms against them.'

The powerful document was met with an equally powerful reply, entitled 'How We Can Coexist', from a large group of religious scholars and academics in Saudi Arabia. Its 200 signatories included authors, doctors, professors and judges from across the Kingdom.

They declare they want to discuss the issues raised by 'What We're Fighting For', but that a dialogue has to take place. There are points of agreement, but also some differences. They state that:

1) Human beings are sacred and inviolable.
2) It is forbidden to kill a human unjustly.
3) It is forbidden to impose a religious faith on anyone.
4) Human relationships must be established on the highest moral standards.
5) All the resources of the Earth were created for humanity.
6) Responsibility for a crime rests solely upon the perpetrator.
7) Justice for all people is an inalienable right.
8) Dialogue and invitation must be done in the best possible manner.

These principles, from the teachings of Mohammed, are what they stand for. Some of these aligned with the American principles and are a foundation for a productive discussion. Other points appear strongly to contradict the American document.

> The West must realise that by blocking the specific options and moderate aspirations of the Muslim world and by creating conflicts, they will bring about perspectives in the Muslim world that will be hard to overcome in the future and will create problems for generations to come all over the world.

Without seeking to justify the actions of the hijackers, they say, 'it is necessary to recognise that some sort of causative relationship exists between American policy and what happened.' They give a reasoned and balanced explanation for the adoption of Islamic principles to all aspects of society, including law and government. They stress that while there are radical Islamic organisations, most are 'essentially moderate'. They are opposed to terrorism, but strongly condemn Israeli actions against the Palestinians.

This response provoked another reply from the American academics, entitled 'Can We Coexist?', published on 23 October 2002. The writers acknowledged that the Saudis had come under criticism in their own country from some quarters for even taking part in the debate. They noted the points of agreement, but pointed to remaining differences.

'Our most important disagreement with you,' they say, 'is that nowhere in your letter do you discuss or even acknowledge the role of your society in creating, protecting and spreading the jihadist violence that today threatens the world, including the Muslim world.' They reject what they see as a theme within the Saudi document, namely that America brought the attacks upon itself.

This was the context in which the al-Qaeda letter was written. It was issued to coincide with the release of an audiotape of bin Laden in November 2002. As can be seen below, it is an uncompromising document that attacks all aspects of American society and values. It is, effectively, the radical Islamic critique of the Saudi document and possibly shows the real extent of the gap between the West and the Islamic worlds.

(Note the three documents, 'What We're Fighting For: A Letter From America', 'How We Can Coexist' and 'Can We Coexist? A Response From Americans to Colleagues in Saudi Arabia', can all be found on the website www.americanvalues.org)

IN THE NAME OF ALLAH, THE COMPASSIONATE, THE MERCIFUL

'Sanction is given unto those who fight because they have been wronged; and Allah is indeed Able to give them victory.' *The Glorious Qur'an*, Surah 22, Verse 39.

Statements have been published by some American writers with the title 'What We're Fighting For'. The appearance of such an article provoked a number of responses and reactions, some of which were based on rightful notions, and some that were not. Our aim here is to make an effort to give the rightful excuses and warnings, trusting that what we are writing will be blessed by God.

We intended, with God's help, to make this statement as an answer to two questions we address to the Americans, namely 'Why do we fight and oppose you?' and second, 'Why are we calling upon you and what do we want from you?'

The answer to the first question about why we fight and oppose you is simple. We are fighting and opposing you because you have attacked us, and are still doing so.

You attacked us in Palestine:

(1) Palestine, which has been under a military occupation for more than 80 years, was handed over by the British, with your consent and support, to the Jews who have occupied it for more than 50 years. Palestine has had more than its share of injustice, crimes, killing, destruction and hostility. And if the 'creation' of Israel and its continuity to this day is a crime, then you are the chief of criminals in this crime.

Clarification of the American support to Israel is a matter that does not need proof.

Israel is a crime that needs to be punished and whoever's hands have been involved in this crime should pay the price, and very dearly.

(2) What is funny as well as sad is the fact that you do not give up on repeating the slander that says that Palestine is the historical right of the Jews, as promised in the Torah, and whoever questions this right is not real.

This slander is the most wrongful and common slander in history as the people of Palestine are real Arabs, as for the Muslims, they are heirs of Moses (peace be upon him), and also heirs of the real Torah.

Muslims believe in all the prophets, namely Abraham, Moses, Jesus and Mohammed, Peace be on Them all, and if there is a promise in the Torah that Moses' followers have the right to Palestine, then we think that the Muslims should have that right. Therefore, the historical claim for the right to Palestine cannot be overlooked by the Islamic nation.

(3) The Palestinian blood that is being spilt in Palestine should not be overlooked and you should be certain that the people of Palestine will not cry alone, their women will not be widowed alone, and their children will not be orphaned alone. You, who attacked in Somalia, and backed the Russian attacks on us in Chechnya, the Indian attacks in Kashmir, the Jews' attacks in Lebanon, under your monitoring, follow-up, instructions and direction, our countries' regimes (your agents) are attacking us every day:

These regimes that are preventing, by force, our nations from taking control of our countries.

These regimes that are giving us hell and putting us in one big prison of fear.

These regimes that are stealing the riches of our land and granting them to you at a very cheap prices.

And these regimes that have surrendered to the Jews, given over to them most of Palestine, and recognised their existence over the corpses of the real owners of the land.

The removal of these regimes is a legal task and an essential step to free our nation, retrieve our rights and take back Palestine. Our fight with these regimes runs parallel with our fight with you.

And you, who are stealing our riches and our petrol at the cheapest costs under military threat, which actions are considered the largest robbery in the history of mankind.

And you, who are occupying our countries with your forces and spreading your military bases, treading on our holy lands and invading our holy places for the protection of the Jews and ensuring continuous robbery of our riches.

And you, who are blocking the Muslims of Iraq, where children are dying every day. How do you compare your ignorance to the death of 1.5 million Iraqi babies who died under your 'sanctions' to the fuss that rocked the world with the death of only 3,000 of your people?

And you, who are supporting Israel's assumption that Jerusalem is its eternal capital, and transferred your embassy to it, and under your support and protection Israel is planning to destroy 'al-Aqsa' Mosque, and under the protection of your weapons Sharon entered the Aqsa Mosque and stained its ground.

If all these tragedies and mishaps form part of your attacks on us, then it must be legal and common sense that the people who are 'attacked' should have the right to fight back. Therefore, what you should expect from us would not be less than Jihad, fighting back and punishment. Is it common sense that America should continue to attack us for more than 50 years and should be left to live in peace?

You might turn back to us and negotiate by saying that all that has been mentioned here does not excuse attacks on civilians for crimes they had not committed and wrongdoings they had not participated in.

But this statement contradicts with your continuous declaration that your country is a free country and you are a free nation. Therefore, the Americans have the right to choose their government freely and agree to its policies. Therefore, again, the Americans have chosen and agreed to America's support for Israel in its occupation of Palestine and its continuous attacks, torture and assault of the Palestinians.

The American people can, also, reject the policies of their government and overturn the same if they wished. The American people pay the taxes that finance the fighter planes that bombed Afghanistan, the tanks that demolish our houses over our heads in Palestine, the armies that are occupying us in the Arab world and the forces that are killing our children in Iraq.

They are the same taxes that finance Israel to continue its attacks on our people in Palestine and expand on our land.

The conclusion is that the American people are the financiers of the attacks that are taking place against us, they are watching, through their Senators whom they elected, the spending of those taxes.

The American people, men and women, are the ones serving in the forces that are attacking us.

Therefore, the American people cannot be innocent of all the crimes that are committed by the Americans and Jews against us.

Allah has allowed punishment in such cases. We have the right to attack our attackers, we have the right to destroy villages and cities of whoever destroyed our villages and cities, we have the right to destroy the economy of those who have robbed our wealth, we have the right to kill civilians of the country which has killed ours.

The American policy and the press are refusing, up till now, to answer the question: 'Why did they hit us in Washington and New York?'

If Sharon is a man of peace in the eyes of Bush, then we are also men of peace!

America does not understand the language of principles and morals, and we are communicating with America in the language that it understands.

As for the second question which we would like to answer: Why we are calling upon you and what we want from you:

The first reason we are calling upon you is to join Islam, a religion of unity and innocence, a religion of complete love to Almighty Allah to whom everything is surrendered. A religion that does not discriminate against anybody.

To this religion we call upon you so that you can realise its objectives and understand that Allah's word is above all and that every human being is looked upon in the same manner irrespective of his language or origin.

A religion whose holy book – the Koran – is kept unchanged, whereas changes have been made to other holy books and messages. The Koran is an eternal miracle that, up to this hour, no one has been able to produce a similar book or even part of it.

The second matter is that we would call upon you to stop the oppression and lies that are spread amongst you. We call upon you to live in respect and look to principles and purity and to abandon adultery, homosexuality, alcohol, gambling, prostitution and interest payments.

We call upon you to free yourselves from what you have involved yourselves in and to free yourselves from the deceptions that politicians promote among you that you are a great nation, so that they can hide from you the bad state that you have reached.

We regret having to declare frankly to you that you are the worst nation in the history of mankind.

You are a nation that is not bound by Allah's doctrine in its reign and rules. You set out your own rules according to your wishes, you distance religion from your rules and regulations, thus going against common sense and logic of the mind. You run away from the shameful question that haunts you: How can Almighty Allah create this world for you with all its riches but deprive you of the religion that can regulate your lives?

You are a nation that legalises 'interest' – which has been banned by other religions – and makes it a base for your economy, investments and dealings. It is through this 'interest' system, in all its many forms, that the Jews have controlled your economy, and by this they have also controlled your media, your lives and they have put you in their service. They have made of you what Benjamin Franklin warned you about.

You are a nation that has allowed the production of alcohol and its trade and consumption. You are the biggest consumer and trader of alcohol in the world. You allow drugs and only ban their trade, whereas you are their biggest consumer and trader.

You are a nation that allows adultery, which you consider to be a pillar of personal freedom. In this respect, who can forget your President Bill Clinton and his scandals which he exercised through his official position, and who was only questioned for perjury? History will mention your wrongdoings in time.

You are a nation that allows gambling as a trade in all its forms. There are big establishments that carry out this work and invest in its activities and criminals make riches out of it.

You are a nation that uses women as a method of enjoyment and customer promotion for dealings and marketing of products and to provide services to passengers and clients. You consider this as a successful method in trade and a way to make profits, and then you turn and declare that you are supporters of freedom for women.

You are a nation that makes use of prostitution in all its forms and uses it in giant industries and trade under the excuse of art, entertainment, tourism and liberalism and other deceptions to which you are being misled.

It is for these reasons and the disgusting things that you are involved in, that you have been marked out as a nation that spreads diseases unknown to human kind. You can be proud of yourselves for spreading HIV/Aids.

You are the biggest destroyer of nature with your polluting gases from your factories, in spite of which you brag about signing the Kyoto Agreement for the protection of profits for your greedy companies and factories. [Author's note: The USA pulled out of the Kyoto Agreement.]

Your policies are well known as that of wealthy individuals controlling the world with their money and financing election campaigns, behind which the Jews hide to manage your policies, media and economy.

You are well known in the history of mankind for using your force to destroy other nations, not fighting for principles, but securing advantages and profits. You dropped a nuclear bomb on Japan after the Japanese were ready to end the war. So what kind of people are you for what you have done to the world, you who claim that you are supporters of freedom?

We should not forget to mention a very important trait in you, which is the fact that you claim to be supporting a cause whereas you have double standards.

The freedom and democracy which you always claim to support is legitimate only for you and the white man. As for the rest of the peoples of the world, on whom you impose corrupt and corrupting governments and that you call America's friends, you prevent them from exercising democracy. When the Islamic forces in Algeria tried to follow the democratic path to reach power, you released your agents in the Algerian Army to use their tanks, guns, gaols and torture to give them a lesson from your American book of democracy.

As to what you call removing weapons of mass destruction in order to secure world peace, it is meant to remove them from those you do not permit to own them. As for those you favour, like Israel, they are permitted to stockpile those weapons in defence of their security. For others who wish to own such weapons, or are suspected of having the ability to manufacture them, but are not your friends, you consider this an international crime that necessitates the destruction of their country.

You punish any nation that does not comply with international laws, but for Israel that has been neglecting the Security Council resolutions for the past 50 years, you offer backing and encouragement.

You are after those who are named as war criminals, but you overlook your friends, the real war criminals. History will never forget the war crimes that you committed against the Muslims and other nations of mankind, such as your killings in Japan, Somalia, Afghanistan, Lebanon and Iraq, which will scar your reputation always. The least we can remind you of are your recent crimes in Afghanistan, where villages were destroyed over the heads of human beings, mosques were bombed over the heads of worshippers, as well as your going back on your word to thousands of mujahideen on their way out of Kunduz. You killed more than a thousand prisoners in the back of trucks through lack of oxygen and thirst. You bombed Qala Jhangi prison with the excuse of suppressing the rebellion there. Only Allah knows who else you killed and tortured through your agents all over the world. Your fighter planes are still flying the Afghani skies looking for suspects.

Human rights regulations to which you have appointed yourselves as judges and on which your Foreign Ministry issues annual reports, were all neglected when you were hit by the mujahideen. And you have adopted ways of corrupt government that you have damned in others.

What is happening in Guantanamo Bay is an historical scandal for America and its values. You are hypocrites, so what's the use of signing any peace agreement if you do not stick to it?

The third thing we invite you to do is to take an honest stand with yourselves – which we believe you will not do – to discover that you are a nation with no values, principles or morals, as these are what you ask other nations to have.

The fourth thing we invite you to do is to stop your support for Israel, your backing to the Indians against the Muslims in Kashmir, your support to the Russians against Muslims in Chechnya, and your backing for the Manila Government against the Muslims in the southern Philippines.

The fifth thing we invite you to do is to pack your bags and leave our countries. We wish you well, so don't push us to send you back home in coffins.

The sixth thing we invite you to do is to stop backing corrupt regimes in our countries, stop interfering with our policies and education curricula and leave us alone, otherwise expect us in Washington and New York.

The seventh thing is that you should deal with us on the basis of free mutual interest rather than the policy of oppression, robbery, occupation and the support of the Jews, which will bring nothing for you except for further catastrophes.

So, if you don't respond to what we invite you to do, be prepared to fight the Islamic nation. The nation that only fears Allah and to which the Koran says:

> What! Fear ye them? Now Allah hath more right that ye should fear Him, if ye are believers. Fight them! Allah will chastise them at your hands, and He will lay them low and give you victory over them, and He will heal the breasts of folk who are believers. And He will remove the anger of their hearts. Allah relenteth toward whom He will. Allah is Knower, Wise. *The Glorious Qur'an*, Surah 9, Verses 13–15

The nation that cares about death more than you care about life:

> Think not of those, who are slain in the way of Allah, as dead. Nay, they are living. With their lord they have provision. Jubilant (are they) because of that which Allah hath bestowed upon them of His bounty, rejoicing for the sake of those who have not joined them but are left behind: that there shall no fear come upon them neither shall they grieve. They rejoice because of favour from Allah and kindness, and that Allah wasteth not the wage of the believers. *The Glorious Qur'an*, Surah 3, Verses 169–171

If the Americans do not respond to our advice, they will be cursed by Bush's sad tidings inviting them to a Crusade in which they will be defeated at the hands of the mujahideen, with the permission of Allah, as did their predecessors, the Crusaders at the hands of our predecessors, the mujahideen.

If the Americans do not respond, then they will face the same fate as the Soviets who ran away from Afghanistan to face military defeat, political fragmentation, ideological collapse and economic bankruptcy.

This is our message to the Americans in reply to theirs. Have they now realised why we resist and why, with the permission of Allah, we will prevail?

APPENDIX 2

The following text is a translation extracted from a 112-page document produced by al-Qaeda in an attempt to justify the 11 September attacks. The document, handed to Yosri Fouda by Ramzi Binalshibh in Karachi in April 2002, and which Fouda believes was written or edited by Binalshibh, does not claim responsibility for the attacks, as, at the time it was written, bin Laden was still hopeful that he could avert an American backlash. Nevertheless, it not only praises the attacks but also spreads on the opening page pictures of the World Trade Center as it collapsed on a day the author describes as 'Holy Tuesday'.

Much of the rhetoric contained in this document is based on the Koran and the *sunnah* (the deeds and sayings of the Prophet Mohammed). It has to be underlined, however, that all mainstream Muslim scholars and imams – both Sunni and Shia – whom we have consulted, disagree with the author's reasoning. In particular, they criticise the 'deliberate and misguided taking out of context' of both the Koran and the sunnah.

Rhetorical and extremely repetitive, the second edition of this document contains 42 articles preceded by a long dedication to Osama bin Laden's mentor and idol, Sheikh Abdullah Bin Yousef Azzam. It begins with an introduction to the second edition, signed by the author who defiantly calls himself Saladin Al-Ayyubi, defeater of the Crusaders:

Please translate into English, publish and lodge with the library of the American Congress.

(By):
Defeater of the Crusaders: Saladin Al-Ayyubi

Second edition, revised and corrected
Rajab/1422 AH (2nd half of September 2001)

Praise be to Allah, and peace be upon the messenger of Allah and all his house and companions. The rush to produce the first edition of (this) book in eight days had a negative effect on its quality as it contained some errors and deficiencies in the text. I therefore thought it should be published again in a more precise and corrected edition, bearing in mind that it would be a human effort which could still be incomplete in quality as only Almighty Allah is Perfect.

In this second edition, I have added some issues the most important of which are:

1) I have written a dedication to he who has indebted me, may Allah have mercy on his soul.

2) I have added an article by Dr Mohammed Abbas to the introduction in which he lists some of America's crimes.

3) I have taken particular care of the summary of the book and added the cases in which it is permissible to kill the spared of the infidels.

4) I have added some of the international material losses (which occurred) as a result of the operations.

5) I have added more text by the *ulema* [religious scholars] on (the verdict on) the backing (of the infidels).

6) I have answered in the chapter of 'the meaning of the backing of the infidels' (with) the inadmissibility of Hatib's *hadith*, or saying that the backing of the infidels does not make one an infidel.

7) I have also added in the chapter of 'Oh! Horses of Allah . . . ' some articles by leaders of the crusaders in which they call for a war against Islam and the Islamic resurrection.

8) I have then written an invitation to review the path in the chapter of 'the duty of jihad on Muslims today'.

9) And I have relayed another letter from the amir of the faithful, Mullah Mohammed Omar, may Allah protect him, in which he seeks the support of Muslims and ulema everywhere on earth.

10) I have also taken care of the structure of the book, made clearer some phrases and corrected linguistic errors.

I ask Allah to accept this work of ours and to make it an argument for us and not against us. He is Able.

These are highlights and extracts that we believe are representative of the whole document:

Prior to reaching a conclusion on which to base the issue of killing women and children of the infidels in America, one important point needs to be clarified and that is: is America a country of war or is it a country of peace? . . . The common answer is that America is not a country of peace and has never been so. If we were to negotiate this matter with anybody whose opinion is otherwise, and agreed that it is a country of peace, then we would say that it turned into a country of war when it broke the peace and helped the Jewish people more than 50 years ago to occupy Palestine and displace its people. It broke the peace the day it bombed Iraq and put it under siege, the day it bombed Sudan and put it under siege, the day it bombed Afghanistan and put it under siege, and the day it assaulted Muslims . . .

It is agreed upon that it [America] is a country of war, and a country of war is for Muslims to harm in every way. The blood of its people, their wealth and their women are legitimate targets for Muslims, in the same manner that the Prophet, peace be upon him, did with his foes. He abducted their subjects as he did with Bani Oqail, intercepted their caravans as he did with Qureysh, assassinated their leaders as he did with Ka'ab'bn'l'Ashraf and Salamata'bn Abi'l'Haqeeq, set their land ablaze as he did with Bani'n'Nadheer, and destroyed their fortresses as he did in Al-Ta'if, etc. . . .

As for the talk about the blessed Tuesday operations in America, we want to say to he who seeks to condemn them that it has not been evidently proven yet that the Muslims were responsible for them. If the country of the Cross blames Muslims, then we would say that the investigations are illegitimate and do not correspond to any rules. We would also say that the investigations are void because the opponent is also acting as judge. We therefore want to ask them not to jump into conclusions in judging people . . .

If the operations which took place in America were the doing of Muslims, then they are (religiously) legitimate, for these operations were against an enemy state whose people are all enemies . . .

It is permitted for Muslims to kill the spared of the infidels under a principle of reciprocity, because if those infidels are targeting Muslim women, children and the elderly, then Muslims can do the same . . .

(It is believed that) you can burn and drown the enemy's country even if there were Muslims there at risk of perishing as a result, for sparing a country from war would (necessarily) lead to the abandoning of jihad . . .

The critics have claimed that these operations would result in the termination of jihad in the world (including) Chechnya and Palestine. We, in turn, would like to comment (by saying) that firstly this will never be because we have seen from the Koran and sunnah that jihad will continue till doomsday. Secondly, the infidels and their subordinates have already done their best (attempting to stop jihad) and they have little more to add. Thirdly, the European Union had decided eight months ago to suffocate jihad movements financially and humanly, and had begun to carry out its plan (even) before the operations took place . . .

Charitable activities (of Islamic organisations) have been persecuted. Arab interior ministers met in Algeria in 1414AH (1994), and took a decision to besiege these charity and relief organisations. Arab leaders confirmed the decision in Tunisia. So, the targeting and besieging of these organisations had already been practised for a long time (before the operations) . . .

They [the critics] also claimed that it was because of these operations [11 September attacks] that Muslim peoples have been targeted and persecuted, and that the Afghani people have been susceptible to invasion . . . (But) it is you who have let the Afghans down. Why come now and pretend that you are crying for them? You have never fought against those who fought against them. You have never tried to lift the siege imposed on them. You have never tried to help them out of their catastrophe. Nay, they were never safe from your harsh criticism and your accusations to them that they are infidels . . .

You have never known what reality is in the Islamic Emirate [Taliban's Afghanistan] so that you may judge whether these operations were for the benefit of Islam or otherwise. The Islamic Emirate exists within three options, the best of which is sour.

The first option is to give in to international pressure, do what they dictate, be ruled by tyranny and abandon Islam. The second option is to insist on its stand and stick to its principles and thus eventually die slowly after a number of years. And the third option is to defend itself, fight back, try to lure its enemy to its land so that it can defeat him as it did with those who came before . . .

America however had already drawn up a plan for the invasion of Afghanistan through a comprehensive attack in which several countries would take part before the operations [11 September attacks]. Therefore, if news of such a plan had reached the Islamic Emirate and it had reacted and executed those operations, then all we can say is 'well done' . . .

On the other hand, there have been advantages gained from those operations which have not been observed or mentioned. One of the advantages is that even though America has taken immediate and destructive revenge on Afghanistan, it will be looking into Muslim affairs with more reason, especially in the Palestine case. Also, these operations have landed America in the worst economic crisis ever known in history. America's losses have reached a trillion. It lost nearly 2,000 economic experts. Its stock exchange has fallen tremendously. The dollar has lost a lot of its value. Airline companies have been affected; they have had to fire 68,000 employees and very soon the figure will reach 100,000. The American globalisation order that was going to corrupt the world is gone never to come back, as well as many other financial losses . . .

Now the Crusades have all but become clear. The Crusade has gathered its party and prepared its gear. The American President, Bush, has declared that this war is a long Crusade that will require patience. He also revealed that his campaign will involve 60 targets, 27 of which – according to him – are in the Muslim world. Therefore, every Muslim has to be on the alert and take responsiblity in standing against the campaign of the Crusaders with everything he owns: his soul, his money, his children and his time. It is a decisive war which cannot afford the absence of any Muslim . . .

Anyone who happened to be following the events cannot but say that what happened in America was a punishment from Allah for all the injustice and oppression that America has inflicted upon nations all over the world and especially to Muslims. If one felt sorrow for the nearly 20,000 people who were injured as a result of the operations, then one should think about the people of Iraq who lost, as a result of sanctions, nearly two million Muslims. One should think about the Palestinians who lost half their people during Israeli attacks over more than half a century. One should also think of Afghanistan where 7,000 Muslims were killed. All this in addition to the Muslims in the Philippines, Indonesia, Kosovo, Somalia, Libya, Sudan and many other Muslim nations whose blood is on America's hands . . .

Because of Saddam and his Party, America has punished a whole nation. It bombed Iraq, imposed sanctions on it and, as a result, killed millions of Muslims. Because of Osama bin Laden, Afghanistan was bombed and tens of thousands of Muslims died. Because of an imaginary factory in Sudan, the country was attacked and a factory for medicines was bombed and all Muslims in it died. And so on . . . and on . . . and on . . .

We, in turn, would like to say that due to the fact that the American administration punishes the world because of individuals, we will apply the same rule and punish the American people because of its administration . . .

What would anger America if we punished its people? Is it not their own rule? Does not America decide on who to attack with an excuse of fighting a terrorist or a supporter of terrorism where it does not kill the actual doer but the innocent?

. . . The Islamic Emirate was aware that America was putting together a military plan to invade its land and hit it by air. It planned to depose the Emirate and form a government led by the former king Zahir Shah who was in exile in Rome two months prior to the September events. The Pakistani Islamic paper *Zarb Mu'min* published an article by Pakistan's former foreign secretary, Niaz A. Naik, in which he pointed out that high ranking officials in the American administration informed him around the middle of July 2001 that America would take military action against Afghanistan in the middle of October 2001. The Pakistani minister also said that American officials informed him of the plan during a conference held under the patronage of the United Nations in Berlin. He added that the American officials stated that if bin Laden was not handed over immediately, the United States would take military action to capture him, or even kill him, together with Mullah Omar, Head of the Taliban movement . . .

The Pakistani former official explained that America would be proceeding with its operations from bases in Tajikistan where there were a number of American consultants. He also said that Uzbekistan would participate in the operations and that 17,000 Russian soldiers were put on standby as the operations were planned to start with the snow season in Afghanistan, which is around the middle of October. He expressed his doubts that America would go back on its plans even if the handing over of bin Laden took place . . .

The BBC transmitted this report explaining that the United States was planning for these military operations against Osama bin Laden and the Taliban movement even before the attack . . .

If the above news had reached the Islamic Emirate, then its initiative to attack – if it was actually true – is a great military action. Based on the above information, it carried out the assassination of Ahmed Shah Massoud and thus confused the plans of the opposition and perplexed its thoughts. If it was true that it [the Islamic Emirate] did carry out the attacks on America, then this is the political and military wisdom required, as it would have been foolish to sit and wait until the Americans and their subordinates finish it. Furthermore, the attacks that took place in America have split the American-led alliance against the Emirate . . .

The fall of 6,333 casualties and double this figure injured (as a result of the 11 September attacks) does not heal the breasts of Muslims or bring about their revenge from America. We therefore need a thousand operations like these . . .

America's pride has been thrown in the dirt and it has come to realise what it is worth. One day before the operations, some newspapers wrote that the CIA was planning to recruit cats as spies, and that it has spy planes the size of a bee. What bullshit this has all turned out to be. America, with all its armies and fleets is incapable of defending its own ministry of defence or its own White House. These operations have laid bare the truth behind America's claims of security . . .

We should not forget to advise our Muslim brothers who live amongst the infidels not to forget that they are first in line to be loyal and not to be tempted by the lives they live in those countries . . .

Allah has disclosed the beliefs of the crusaders and brought out into the light what their hearts held towards the Muslims. The American President, Bush, ran out of patience and could not keep his belief secret. He stated in a press conference on Sunday, 16 September 2001 that 'this Crusade, this war on terrorism, is going to take a long time'. He tried later to cover up the real meaning of that statement by visiting the Islamic Center in America . . .

One of America's most senior politicians remarked during the famous 'Nightline' show on ABC channel, by saying that 'it was a mistake that the President made by using that particular phrase, for several reasons. First, the Crusaders were actually defeated in those wars by Saladin al-Ayyubi, and it is not the right time to recall a defeat when we are in need of victory. Second, the word 'Crusade' would provoke our allies of Muslims whom we need in our fight against terrorism . . .

We are all hoping that these attacks are only the beginning of the end of America. We pray to Allah that we shall see the destruction and fall of America sooner rather than later. We ask Him to chastise their state, make the earth quake under their feet, defeat them and make them a cold spoil for Muslims.

INDEX

INDEX

INDEX